BEYOND BASIC
DOG TRAINING

OTCH Meadowpond Fem De Fortune, WC. Charo is a three-time Gaines Superdog winner. She is a member of the Golden Retriever Obedience Hall of Fame and retired with six perfect scores of 200. Charo is owned, trained, and loved by Diane Bauman.

BEYOND BASIC DOG TRAINING

Third Edition

DIANE L. BAUMAN

HOWELL
BOOK
HOUSE

Howell Book House
Published by Wiley Publishing, Inc., Indianapolis, Indiana

For general information on our other products and services or to obtain technical support please contact our Customer Care Department within the U.S. at 800-762-2974, outside the U.S. at 317-572-3993 or fax 317-572-4002.

Wiley also publishes its books in a variety of electronic formats. Some content that appears in print may not be available in electronic books.

Library of Congress Cataloging-in-Publication Data:
Bauman, Diane L.
  Beyond basic dog training / Diane L. Bauman.–3rd ed.
    p. cm.
  ISBN 0-7645-4164-1 (alk. paper)
  1. Dogs–Training. I. Title.
  SF431.B37 2003
  636.7'0887–dc21
                                    2003009303

Manufactured in the United States of America

10 9 8 7 6 5 4 3

FOR MY FATHER
whose last words to me before he died were,
"Write the book—it's important."

Diane Bauman and Keeshond AM/CAN OTCH Vandy's Faun, TD; Pekingese OTCH Giget to the Rescue, UDX, NA; and Papillon MACH Mysin Alacazzam, UD, TD.

Contents

Foreword

Y ou are about to embark on an adventure in dog obedience as only Diane Bauman can take you. Her remarkable ability to view training from the dog's perspective has enabled her to create a style so pervasive that it will enchant even the most seasoned of trainers.

Clear understanding has led Diane to the development of training methods that afford dog and handler a relationship of powerful communication.

It is a refreshing realization that our canine companions have a higher level of intelligence than is traditionally granted.

Many dogs labeled unmanageable, dangerous or just unwanted have been rescued by Diane. Once adopted and trained by her, they developed a new outlook on life and were later carefully placed in new homes to become happy companions or obedience competitors.

The author's brilliance as a trainer, together with her extraordinary talent as a teacher, makes it a privilege to be her student.

I'm sure I speak for many when I thank Diane for so generously revealing her secrets and ideas that have developed over many years of experience and intuitive thought.

Clearly much time, devotion and effort have gone into making this book a pleasure to read. *Beyond Basic Dog Training* will be an invaluable source of reference to read and re-read with each and every chapter essential. My favorite part of this book is the conclusion, where my heart skipped a few beats. I believe that this is where Diane has captured the true meaning of "dog training."

–Laurie Rubenfeld

Acknowledgments

The pages that follow hold my thoughts about training dogs. These thoughts combine ideas developed from books, seminars, other trainers, dogs themselves and original thought. I have been very fortunate to have known some very knowledgeable and generous people. For their continued support and appreciation of my endeavors, I thank some who have made this book possible: Nancy Overton, Bill and Mary Chaillot, Margaret Fitch, Dr. H. L. Yandell, Larry Schillenkamp, Jack Godsil, Bob Self, Marly Whiting, Alfred Einhorn, Sheila Eckstein, Ruth Rosbach-Chandler, Jeff Bauman, my parents, students and every dog's leash that has ever passed through my hands.

Of all those who helped shape my training methods, Ruth Rosbach-Chandler (my partner) has had the greatest influence. Her intuitive understanding of people and dogs and her undying sense of humor helped this book take shape. Thank you, Ruth, for all you have given me in so many ways.

Introduction

This book was written with the best interests of dogs in mind. I believe it is time to go beyond *training* dogs and start *teaching* them how to please us. Assuming that dogs are capable of reasoning and simple problem solving, I feel dogs need not be trained as if they were merely simple stimulus-response mice.

The teaching methods presented in this book encourage and cultivate dogs' cognitive abilities. I believe dogs learn by trial and error, and I encourage dogs by removing corrections for incorrect responses. As a result, the dogs do not fear failure and are taught to exercise options in a quest for the desired behavior. The concept that "wrong is wonderful" when teaching dogs is new to the world of competitive dog trainers.

My novel teaching approach has produced many top obedience performers in many breeds. They exhibit confident, alert, accurate, enthusiastic style in the obedience ring. Their minds have been stimulated while their egos have been left intact. They are happy to be doing what they understand.

1

Training the Thinking Dog

Dog training, like religion, embraces different beliefs based on different premises resulting in different training methods. When you consider that obedience fans go to trials on Sundays and often resort to prayer, the analogy is further strengthened! Many trainers tell students to verbally scold and others advocate "no verbal harshness." Some say to yell "no" and others believe this is unnecessary. There are those who tell you to starve your dog, feed your dog, snap your dog, love your dog, and some who will even suggest you get a new dog. If you read enough books and attend enough seminars, you'll go crazy searching for the "right" way to train dogs! A training method is only successful for you if you fully understand it and feel comfortable with it.

One thing I have learned over the years of training my own dogs and instructing others is that dogs will learn in spite of what is done to them! This is both encouraging and misleading. Encouraging because it means that if you hack away long enough, your dog will eventually learn (providing he lives long enough) but misleading because many ridiculous methods of training dogs have developed and the dogs eventually respond even though the methods make no sense. If you scratch your head just before your dog does a fast sit, does this mean that scratching your head should become a method used to teach fast sits?

To complicate matters further, good dog trainers are always changing their methods! They remain open to new ideas and search for more effective techniques. Trainers who resist change and lose creativity in their training become stagnant and limited. They often resent and resist new ideas; it is easier to resist than to change.

The only thing trainers agree on is that there is no one way to teach something. I have heard it said that if the method works, it's a good method. There was a time I agreed with this philosophy, but after watching dogs trained different ways,

1

I now feel that how you teach something can be as important as the fact that the dog learns it. The end does not always justify the means.

A child is told by a parent that he must get good grades or severe consequences will follow. If the child is not naturally intelligent, he might work himself into exhaustion or a nervous breakdown or might even resort to cheating to get the grades. At the end of the year, he has received the grades but has lost his integrity, mental stability and health in doing so.

The dog who slowly slinks out to retrieve a dumbbell is a dog who has not been trained with the best possible methods. The dog who heels with his head down, lagging three feet (or more, sometimes) behind his owner, was not born this way; this poor heeling was caused by poor training. While the dog may be heeling, the method used was perhaps not the best approach.

There are people who look at the depressed, lagging, slinky dog and immediately analyze, "Aha, this dog has been beaten—isn't it awful that people could do such a thing!" I have seen many dogs perform in a pitiful manner and know of very few books or training schools that advocate beating a dog to teach him to heel. I also know of very few concerned dog owners who would beat their dogs even if told to do so. So why the pitiful lagging? While the dog has not been abused physically, poor training has abused him mentally. The trainer did not clearly *explain* to the dog what was expected, but he did correct him for what he had not yet learned. The method lacked clarity, fairness and motivation.

While heeling will be covered in detail later, let me whet your appetite. If you are trying to teach a dog what "heel" position is, why would you give him enough leash to get out of "heel" position? Now you have to correct him for what he has not yet learned. How can we correct a dog for being wrong before we teach him what right is? And finally, how can you expect a dog to heel perfectly if you, the handler, can't walk a straight line or stick your feet out to trip the dog on about turns?

In the pages that follow I have outlined training methods that make sense to me and my dogs. It is not the purpose of this book to teach you to train your dog, for I truly believe that you cannot train a dog to his full potential from a book. The objective is to get you, the owner, handler, trainer of your little "furry friend" to *think* about what you are doing and why you are doing it, for it is only a thinking handler who can train the thinking dog!

GODSIL

Diane Bauman and Pomeranian Noah's Abra Ka Dabra, CD, shown winning the Novice division of the 1985 Gaines Eastern Regional. Abra was rescued from Noah's Ark Animal Shelter at the age of three. At the age of four she was awarded the top Novice Dog in the Eastern Region. Abra completed her OTCH one and a half years later.

2
Wrong Is Wonderful

$\mathbf{A}$ "thinking dog" is a confident, happy working animal who understands fully what he is expected to do on any given command, enjoys meeting new challenges, is rarely bored with obedience and can be fine-tuned to the utmost accuracy. He has been guided and trained in such a way that he is not afraid to be wrong. Yes, folks, contrary to much of what you have been told or have read, I want to see my dogs making mistakes during training sessions. There are trainers who believe the dog is nothing more than a stimulus-response animal who does not have the ability to reason; others maintain that the dog has reasoning capabilities beyond that of a simple animal.

The training that evolves from the first premise is what I refer to as pattern training. Sequences of commands are repeated over and over again until the dog performs them on one command. A pattern trainer would teach a Broad Jump, for example, by setting up a situation where the dog couldn't be wrong and by having the dog repeat the jump many times. Does pattern training get good results? You bet it does! It produces non-thinking, fast-responding, good-working dogs. The drawback, however, of a pattern-trained dog is that if the pattern is broken by a distraction or by a new situation, the dog is at a loss to perform the task. For example, the pattern-trained dog is taught to retrieve a dumbbell quickly—get out there, grab it and get back. He has done this so many times that he hardly has to think about what he's doing. He would probably even retrieve on any command if it followed the sequence of stay, throw dumbbell, send. One day the dumbbell goes under the ring gate. The pattern-trained dog runs out for his dumbbell and is faced with a problem. Since he cannot complete the patterned response and has not been taught while practicing the exercise to reason, he runs out, indicates the dumbbell, but comes back without it. Another example of pattern training is the dog who is taught the High Jump by jumping it over and over again as his owner runs alongside with him. Then, when owner and dog are in an obedience trial performing Off-lead Heeling and the judge calls a Fast alongside the High

Jump, the dog goes over the jump. Even though no command was given, the dog remembered the High Jump pattern. Pattern-trained dogs have more problems with the Drop-on-Recall exercise and in distinguishing between a Retrieve Over High Jump and a Retrieve on Flat than do dogs taught to think.

The Drop-on-Recall exercise is perhaps the most difficult exercise to pattern train because the pattern changes. Sometimes the pattern is to drop and sometimes the pattern omits the drop. For a pattern trained dog, this exercise can be a nightmare for both dog and handler. Dogs trained not to think will often be seen doing very fast, impressive drops but also frequently anticipating drops. Every dog who has ever learned a Drop on Recall is going to anticipate at some point in training. How you work through the anticipation (either to pattern past it, often with repeated recalls on a long line, or to teach the dog to understand the exercise by reasoning it out) determines whether the dog will *continue* to anticipate a drop. Pattern trainers talk about "only dropping the dog in the ring" to avoid anticipation. Trainers of thinking dogs frequently drop their dogs in practice with no ill effects because the dogs understand the exercise and are confidently waiting for the signal or command to drop.

An alternative to pattern training is practiced by trainers who believe dogs are capable of reasoning and who want dogs to think before reacting. Most guide-dog trainers also approach training in this manner. A guide dog is forever being faced with new situations—he must be able to reason and to solve simple problems. Trainers who teach dogs to think believe that dogs learn by trial and error and that when a dog is wrong, that is wonderful because when he exhausts all the wrong possibilities, he will then be right. Wrong is never "bad," it is just wrong. Future guide dogs are repeatedly allowed to make their own mistakes. In fact, the trainers set up situations that will cause mistakes, without the intention of correcting the dog! In guide work, a slow-moving car is planted and the dog is allowed to walk a trainer into the car. The trainer then bangs on the car to make noise, but *no correction* is given to the dog. This is how the dog learns what happens and later avoids moving vehicles. The dog is not reprimanded for being wrong. If you reprimand a dog when he is wrong, he then becomes afraid to be wrong ("fear of failure"). A dog who is afraid to make a mistake becomes so panicked that learning is impaired. For example, when learning Directed Jumping, if the dog takes the wrong jump and is yelled at, he will often resort to not jumping at all. If, on the other hand, the dog is permitted to come over the wrong jump but receives no praise as the owner continues to stand there with his arm pointing to the right jump, the dog will realize that something is wrong yet not be afraid to try again. I have seen many dogs go back out without any command and fix their own mistake, but these were dogs who had been taught from the beginning that it is okay to be wrong and to try another approach.

A thinking dog is taught to listen. A dumbbell is thrown, and the handler commands "Heel" instead of "Take it." A thinking dog does what he is told and does not do what the sight picture might indicate. Thinking dogs derive a lot of pleasure from solving problems on their own. They are more confident, consistent workers and rarely get bored with obedience.

If you'd like to know what type of training you've been doing, try this experiment. Tell your dog to stay, walk out 15 feet and show the dog that you are placing a dumbbell on the ground. Then walk another 15 feet and turn to face your dog as though it were a Recall exercise. Command your dog to take it (no pointing permitted). Do not be surprised if he comes straight to you on a Recall because he was not thinking and was responding to a patterned situation. If he makes this mistake, *don't correct him!* Help explain to him by saying nothing and by walking slowly back while pointing to the dumbbell. When he finally picks up the dumbbell, praise profusely and try again. You may shorten the distances if he repeatedly does it wrong.

People who teach dogs to think never get upset when the dog is repeatedly wrong. They know that when the "light goes on" and the dog understands, he will no longer make the mistake. In fact, when training a thinking dog, the trainer sets up situations to tempt the dog to be wrong. This is referred to as proofing, and is discussed in detail later in this book. Pattern trainers, on the other hand, get very upset when a dog is wrong because they fear patterning an undesired response. Pattern trainers rush to correct mistakes, often frightening the dog, in an effort to avoid a bad pattern of behavior. Trainers of thinking dogs, on the other hand, take their time when correcting because they want the dog to see what happens when he is "good, but wrong." Thinking dogs are never seen running from their owners after a mistake because they are *not afraid to be wrong*.

Every time a dog breaks a Sit Stay and is gently put back into position, he has learned something. If he coincidentally remains sitting, or does so because you prevent a mistake, he never really understands the exercise. Most good trainers want dogs to be wrong on Sit Stays during early training, but this approach is abandoned in advanced work.

Not all dogs can be taught to reason as easily as others. For some breeds, perhaps, pattern training is the better approach. Some breeds, like Border Collies, pattern extremely fast, and the trainer must work hard to keep changing the exercises to discourage patterning. Border Collies are often thought to be very smart dogs. Are we really talking about intelligence, or the ability to pick up and repeat patterns with very few repetitions? While a pattern-trained dog is capable of a superb performance on any given day, thinking dogs are much more consistent, reliable workers. It takes longer to train a thinking dog. Is it worth it?

3
Good News
and Bad News

I have good news for you and I have bad news. The good news is that this book has a lot to offer a person currently training dogs. The bad news is that it will not teach you to train your dog. This is not to say that you should give up reading books on training, but understand that it is impossible for the author of a book to offer every possible response to a dog's action, primarily because he can't see the dog react. A book can tell you what to do, what to say, what hand to use and what order to do this in. A book cannot ensure that you will say things in the right tone, with the right volume, do things with the right timing and, most importantly, refrain from doing something because the dog is reacting poorly to it. A book will not teach you to read a dog, that is to say, judge from the dog's body language what he is thinking.

Trainers have tried to explain obedience in very simple terms. If the dog is right, he is praised and/or rewarded. If he is wrong, he is corrected. It would be easy if training really were this simple, but it is not.

What about the dog who is confused or afraid? Is he to be corrected the same as the dog who knows what you want and was distracted or feels he has a choice? What if the methods offered by the book don't cause the result the book predicted? A book can never tell you what to do for every response.

The purpose of this book is to encourage you to evaluate your current training methods and to consider alternative approaches by understanding the reasons why these approaches have been chosen.

The methods described in this book have been chosen based on the fact that they work on many different breeds when employed by inexperienced as well as experienced trainers. My own dogs and students' dogs indicate that these techniques produce an extremely reliable, accurate, secure, enthusiastic working dog. Our dogs exhibit animation because they are comfortable with their understanding of what is expected of them. This animation should not be confused with dogs who work with incredible speed that is a result of panic. A dog who never knows when or if he is going to be corrected can appear to be very flashy when in fact he is really nervous. While nervous dogs are often impressive in the ring, their performance is far less consistent compared to that of a calm, thinking animal.

The training methods explained in this book will change slightly as I continue to train. The day a person stops learning from his dogs and his students is the day he loses interest in the sport of obedience. The chapters that teach specific exercises of this book are included with the hope that you will compare these methods to the ones you currently use, notice the differences and question why you are doing things the way you are. It is not the intention of this book to totally convert anyone to these training methods, only to stimulate *thoughtful* training.

4
Honesty–The Best Policy

One of the basic premises of this training method requires that you always be honest with your dog. When he is right, let him know he is right. When he is wrong, let him know that he is wrong (and that it is okay to be wrong). I have seen handlers who will praise a dog for sitting crooked because it was better than the sit before. Dogs cannot comprehend "better." A dog only understands right or wrong, yes or no. When you praise a dog for being better but not right, you confuse him.

I'm sure you've seen the person who calls his dog to come on a Recall and the dog stands up and doesn't move. The owner yells, "Good boy, hurry!" Well, he is not good for only standing when you said, "Come," and how do you hurry a stand, anyway?

Perhaps the greatest damage is done while heeling. A dog lags and his owner, in an attempt to encourage, says, "That's it, come on, good boy, let's go." Since it all sounds like praise to the dog, the dog assumes he is correct and lags worse. This frustrates the owner, who gets angry, which the dog doesn't understand. Finally, the owner yells obscenities at the dog, and the poor dog feels so rejected he no longer wants to even try. The end result is the hang-dog look we often see in a ring.

What about the handler who calls his dog to come on a Recall, and the dog comes in briskly and sits front. The handler then says, "Good boy! Get it straight!" While the handler might have intended the praise to be for the Recall, it came after the sit. To the dog, if the sit was praised, why is he being told to "get it straight"? You cannot praise a "sit" that you then decide to fix!

Reserve the words "good" or "terrific" for the correct action. The dog has learned from early training that certain words (different for each dog) mean he has succeeded. Be careful to save these words for only the correct behavior. If you feel the need to encourage an attempt by the dog, try cheering, "Yeeeah!" or words like "Attaboy, you can do it!" Praise a perfectly completed exercise or part of an exercise; encourage an attempt. When a dog lags, tell him in no uncertain terms, "Get up here! Let's go!" Your tone should be calmly demanding and in no way confused with approval. I'm sure you do not approve of lagging, so be honest with him.

Lying to your dog never pays! You cannot praise a dog into doing what you want; you must teach him. You cannot "happy him up"; he will be happy when he is secure with his understanding of what is expected of him. Bribing him with tidbits is only a temporary remedy. Eventually he must perform because you tell him to, and he understands what is expected of him. Food training is becoming more and more popular among competitive trainers. I guess you could say it's the current trend. There is certainly a time and a place for food rewards in training, but be careful not to rely on food as an answer to all problems. As soon as treats come on the obedience scene, the dog's thoughts are on food and are no longer focused on the exercise. Perhaps my biggest difficulty with using food in training is that when used as a bribe, it is not honest. The dog responds to the "drop" signal and in practice receives a tidbit. He then does the same thing in the ring and is not rewarded. Unfair! I am never going to be able to reward my dog with food in a ring. Since praise is permitted in the ring, I prefer to train with praise. A combination of food rewards *and praise,* used in moderation, can be very effective in early training, but you will be better off if you eventually wean the dog off the food. (Note: For specific problems where the dog is overly anxious, food rewards do seem to help the dog over his anxiety attack but should be discontinued when the anxiety dissipates. See Chapter 21, Using Food in Obedience Training.) In keeping with the concept of being honest with your dog, it would not be fair to correct a dog before he made a mistake. While there are trainers who advocate automatic corrections, I feel this works to destroy an honest working relationship with your dog. For a dog to work confidently, he should feel that he will not be unfairly or automatically corrected. There is no doubt that automatic corrections solve training problems, but at what cost? Why upset your partner if it's not necessary? There are other fair ways to solve the same problems.

5

Slow Down
and Shut Up!

The approach to training dogs in this book is accurately described in a phrase initiated by one of my students, "Slow down and shut up!" When people learn to touch-type, an activity that becomes automatic, they start off by thinking hard and pushing the keys slowly. With time and repetition, they get faster and faster. In fact, if you observe people closely any time they are deeply involved in thought, their motor activity slows down. This information is critical when we talk in terms of training a thinking dog. If you want your dog to think and understand what he is doing, you cannot pressure him for speed in the beginning of the learning process. Teach the dog slowly and let him perform at whatever speed he is comfortable with. After he is reacting confidently to a command, and exhibits understanding, it is safe to encourage speed.

A perfect example of a dog slowing down to think is found when teaching the Drop-on-Recall exercise. As soon as you begin dropping a dog on a Recall, the Recall is going to slow down because the dog is thinking about when to drop. The more you have pressured him to drop with speed (prompted by a "flashed signal"), the more fear he has of being wrong, and the slower he will come in on a Recall. If you get no Recall at all, consider that you may have pressured the dog beyond the point of good training. The trainer who can't bear to see a dog coming in slowly and tries to speed him up with verbal encouragement or lead corrections (long line) is gambling with both upsetting the dog and preventing the dog from thinking through the exercise. What is so awful about a dog who is coming in slowly (or crouched) because he is thinking about dropping and doesn't want to miss the command or signal? All of my dogs have at one time in practice come in very slowly on the Recall because they were concerned with the drop, but after they learn when to drop and when not to, and when they are not afraid of missing a signal (because the signal is clearly given and not flashed), they all pick up their speed on Recall to what it was before the drop was introduced.

There are exercises you can incorporate into the teaching of the Drop on Recall that help to get the dog up off the drop quickly and things you can do to speed up your basic Recalls. These techniques will be discussed in detail in later chapters (see Chapter 17, Special Small Dog and Big Dog Techniques, and Chapter 35, Teaching the Drop on Recall).

Your voice can be a valuable training tool, but too much talking can cause problems. I advocate teaching every exercise by giving a command *one time* and then enforcing it. A familiar phrase to our beginning students is "Sit, sit is a no, no." Sometimes I will turn to someone who has just repeated "sit" three times and question, "How many dogs did you say you were training?" As soon as you repeat a command, you have effectively told the dog that the first command didn't count. In addition to the fact that AKC trials only permit one command, to repeat yourself confuses a dog. The dog really doesn't know which "sit" is the *real* "sit"! Trainers who advocate repeating commands talk about letting the command "sink in." I'm still trying to decide what they think the dog's brain is made of, sand?

Repeating something has never made it easier to understand. Saying it louder has never helped to clarify its meaning, and certainly correcting confusion only makes it worse. Dogs have excellent hearing; it's their listening that isn't always so good! If I were to start commanding you to "scubernog," and when you didn't respond I snapped your wrist with a choke chain, and each time you didn't respond I commanded "scubernog" louder and snapped harder, how would you feel? Would you now understand the meaning of "scubernog"? When you arbitrarily command a dog to heel and then correct him for being out of position, are you not doing the same thing? When you repeat the command "heel" loudly and forcefully while the dog is moving (and thinking he is heeling), does this help define the meaning of "heel"? If you repeat "heel" 2,000 times, does this teach him how to heel? *No!* For more effective techniques, see Chapter 24, Teaching the Dog to Heel.

The philosophy of giving only one command is very effective when teaching the Sit Stay. Tell the dog to sit, he does, and then you command "Stay" and leave him. If the dog breaks the "stay" and gets up, reposition and praise him, but no extra "sit" or "stay" commands are necessary. My feeling is that if I keep reminding the dog to sit and stay, why should he bother to remember it? By the time the dog is in Open, he must remember what he's doing for three and five minutes. All too often, dogs break "stays" because they forget what they are doing. By placing the dog in the "sit" and praising him for being there and then leaving without a second command, the burden of thought is now placed on the dog. He must *think* about what he is doing and work to remember it if he is to avoid correction. No one is going to be there to keep telling him to sit and stay. Some of you may be doubting your dog's ability to learn without the repetition of commands. Give dogs more credit for intelligence and you may be surprised to find they won't let you down. Of course, if you never challenge their thinking abilities, you'll never know their potential.

Perhaps the most important time to remain quiet is when the dog is moving away from you, as in the Retrieve or Go-Out exercises. I have seen dogs leave their owners' sides at a nice speed, only to hear the owner command, "Hurry!" and the dog stops and turns back as if to say, "What did you say?" The clearest example of this was a student of mine who was teaching Go Outs to her dog, who had a tendency to stop short. One day she sent the dog out and just before the dog reached the point where she usually stopped, the owner shrieked, "Ginger, don't stop there!" Ginger turned on her name and sat facing her owner with her tail wagging a mile a minute. She was so pleased that she had finally taught her owner where to stop her!

Another time to be quiet is whenever the dog is thinking. I am sure that at some time you were trying to concentrate while some well-meaning person insisted on talking to you. Dogs find chatter distracting. In a case where a dog has to work to get a dumbbell out from under a gate, be quiet and let him do it by himself. When he succeeds, then you can become hysterical with joy and praise. If a dog starts for a jump in the Directed Jumping exercise and then stops because he's not sure (early training stages), use your arm, your body, your facial expression, any kind of pantomime–but, if at all possible, avoid double commanding. Letting a dog work out his problems is much more advantageous than doing all the work for him or repeating commands. Have you ever noticed that when a dog figures out how to get into the garbage, he knows it forever! He doesn't need to practice it over and over! Dogs learn best what *they* discover. Dogs get a great deal of satisfaction when they have figured something out. When the trainer is simply repeating a command over and over again, dogs tend to get bored or frightened and tune out or give up.

6

A "Pity Party" for Rover, or Little People in Fur Coats

Dogs learn to be manipulative at an early age. They quickly realize that a pitiful, hangdog look or sad whimpering results in a tidbit of food from the table. If this behavior is allowed to continue, your dog will have you convinced that he is unable to do anything you ask. The "pitiful dog" act, which is learned by the dog through trial and error, is often seen in obedience.

Handlers who love their dogs are easily made to feel guilty about commanding the dog to perform. Usually when you find a depressed-looking dog, there is a guilty handler nearby!

You really have no reason to ever feel guilty about asking your dog to obey. You love him, feed him, house him, provide for his health, education, and take him on vacations. As Jack Godsil used to say, "You find me a job where I get room, board, education, entertainment, medical care, grooming, vacations, and I only have to work 20 minutes a day and occasional weekends, and I'll take it!" Our dogs live a wonderful life. I do not believe that three minutes of attentive heeling in a ring is too much to ask.

Most dogs will put forth as little effort as necessary to perform a task. Good jumpers will clear a 24-inch jump by one inch as well as clear a 36-inch jump by one inch. If you want your dog to reach his full potential in obedience, you will have to learn to "sweetly demand." You can be a very demanding trainer without ever raising your voice by being consistent, fair, honest and liberal with praise. If, on the other hand, you are waiting for the dog to give of himself, simply to please you, you are waiting for a very special dog you may never meet.

At the risk of shattering dreams, I must state that I do not believe dogs obey because they wish to please man or because they love you. They may love you, but this has no bearing on how they perform obedience. A dog obeys because it

14

is *to his advantage* to do so, either because you will lavish praise on him, and thus feed his ego, offer him treats, or because by obeying he avoids a correction.

How do I know this to be true? If you are housebreaking a puppy and every time he has an accident you turn to him and say, "Sweetheart, you're breaking my heart. I love you. How could you do this to me?" would the dog become house-broken? If, on the other hand, every time you catch the dog having an accident you lift him up and put him outside, will he not learn? If someone picked you up in the middle of going to the bathroom, would you not think twice about going in that spot again?

If you are to become an effective trainer, it is important that you make an effort to view life through the eyes of a dog.

Attributing human characteristics to our canines, while cute, hinders our ability to train. While I may live with "little people in fur coats," when I train, I train dogs.

Shed your guilt and learn to *demand,* sweetly.

7
Demand Sweetly

Have you ever noticed that you can follow instructions exactly, perform every step with perfect timing and coordination and still you can't get your dog to respond the way your instructor can? In addition to learning *what* to do and *when* to do it, there is something I call "attitude" that is a key ingredient if anything you learn is to be effective. Attitude is something that develops in time and with experience.

By the time you train your second dog, you have no doubt that you can teach a dog to sit and stay. You approach the teaching of these exercises with a calm confidence that the dog senses. If the dog resists, you do not become flustered because there is no doubt in your mind that you can teach the dog to sit. You are patient, insistent and sweetly demanding because your confidence allows you to be.

On the other hand, the first time you attempted to teach a dog to sit, you were not so sure you could do it. If the dog resisted, you became flustered, insecure, often embarrassed. The dog, sensing your insecurity and uneasiness, became more resistant.

In both cases you applied the same methods, with perfect timing, coordination and voice control, and you got two different responses because of *your* attitude. You can't force yourself to become confident, but you can gain confidence by training with someone whom you trust totally to lead you through the woods to the UD (Utility Dog) degree at the end of the path.

I always assure my students that it only gets easier, and each subsequent dog they train gets better. Knowing in your heart that you *can* do it makes all the difference in the world. Whenever possible, appear secure, confident and in control to your dog. You are always better off doing the wrong thing affirmatively than doing the right thing tentatively.

If your instructor makes *you* feel insecure, find a new instructor because "the blind leading the blind" doesn't get you very far.

Difficult dogs teach you more than dogs who are eager to please. Once you have successfully trained a "strong-willed" dog, you have become a more effective trainer.

8
Where to Go to Train

It has been said that a school is only as good as the teacher your child has. Whether you choose to take private or group classes or train with a school or a club, the most important element is the knowledge, experience and ability to teach of the person you are learning from. Unfortunately, there is no formal education or licensing required for someone to advertise as a "dog trainer." As a result, many people teaching obedience today are barely qualified.

If you are interested in showing your dog in obedience trials, learn from someone who is actively competing and doing well. Choose someone whose style of handling his dog you admire. If you are by nature a soft-spoken person, you will never feel comfortable taking lessons from someone who issues commands like a marine drill instructor. No, you do not have to sound authoritative or angry to get a response from a dog. Any command is only as effective as its enforcement. Threatening commands have never worked any better than sweet, enforced commands. Try to find an instructor who has had some experience with your breed or similar size of breed. Make sure your instructor has trained at least through a UD (Utility Dog) degree, even though you are starting with Beginners, for a good foundation is essential to advanced training. Beginners is really Beginning Utility and should be taught as such. If your instructor has never trained a UD dog, he may not be aware of the things you learn in Beginners that will affect future training. For example, if you are taught to give a "stay" command with your right hand in Beginners, when you get to Utility are you going to give a "stand" command also with your right hand? And, if you use your left hand for the "stand," what hand will give the "heel" command? To give clear, logical signals, the "stay" command should always be given with your left hand from Beginners through Utility, but if an instructor has never been in Utility, he would not be aware of this.

There should be a reason for everything you do with your dog, and your instructor should welcome your questions and be able to explain why he or she is using a particular method. By the way, just because it works is not a good enough reason. Good instructors have numerous methods to teach the same exercise. An instructor who repeatedly tells you to "go home and work on it" or "you need to do it for another two weeks before you get any results" is perhaps not versatile enough for your dog.

Before you can train a dog for competition, you must have a mental picture of what you are working toward. My first Open dog did the Drop-on-Recall exercise the way he had been taught. He came at a trot, lay down, waited for another command to come and trotted briskly to me. For a year I was quite pleased with his Drop on Recall. One day I went to an obedience seminar and saw a dog perform a Drop on Recall with such speed and style that I was amazed. The dog dropped so fast and remained so attentive to his owner that it didn't even resemble the same exercise I was teaching. From then on my mental picture of the Drop-on-Recall exercise was different, and not only was I able to improve the performance of my first dog, but every dog following has been trained to the new mental picture. It is an advantage to be able to take lessons from someone who can help provide you with good mental pictures or, at the very least, has the picture of the perfect exercise clearly in mind. For the sake of the mental picture, it is advantageous to attend major competitions to watch the most highly trained dogs and handlers in the country perform.

If you live in an area where there is no one teaching classes who meets the description I have outlined, you can do it on your own. Dog training is logical—it should make sense. Trust your instincts and evaluate your results. The old cliché "necessity is the mother of invention" has produced some excellent training methods. Thinking handlers who work alone often achieve more than non-questioning students who are spoon-fed by the unqualified. One of the most thinking handlers I have ever met came from a small mining town in the mountains of Colorado and only had one other person to train with. She didn't know all the answers, but she was asking all the right questions. Have you ever noticed that someone who is really proficient at a skill makes it appear simple? The same is true of dog trainers. A good instructor knows his material so well that all his attention goes toward making the student and dog team feel at ease. There is a very definite place for humor in teaching obedience, and a qualified instructor is relaxed and comfortable enough to see the humorous side of training dogs. Laughter eases the stress of learning.

9
Thereby Hangs a Tale

Learning is stressful! (Of course, it has been said that teaching is worse!) Any time you have been placed in a learning situation, you have felt tension that comes from concentration and an inner need to succeed. Chances are when you were studying for an exam, you had a serious, pensive, almost pained expression on your face. Your body was often stiffened, and you may have even appeared withdrawn. Learning is hard work and is not always fun. Having learned, however, is rewarding and satisfying.

No matter how you try to sugarcoat obedience training, learning for a dog is stressful. It is important that you, as a trainer, understand that at some time, every dog is going to go through periods of tension and stress as he learns new exercises. It is not at all uncommon for dogs to avoid the collar and leash or to run to their crates at some stressful point in their training. Of course, if the dog is still showing avoidance after he is fully trained, I would reevaluate your training methods.

Everyone wants his or her dogs to perform obedience happily, but you cannot become obsessed with the position of the dog's tail. It is not normal for a dog to have his ears perked and his tail high when he is concentrating or feeling stressed by a new learning situation. Herding dogs who are working livestock carry their tails low and almost tucked underneath. Should you be expected to study hard for an exam with a constant smile on your face?

There are procedures you can follow to help keep the stress of learning to a minimum. Frequent brief sessions that incorporate lots of play and praise will ease the tension. Do not become overly concerned if your dog's tail temporarily goes down while he works at thinking out a problem. If you are fair and honest in your training, his carefree, happy-go-lucky attitude will return once he understands and is confident with the new exercises. Stress cannot be avoided, but a trainer should always be aware of how much stress the dog is exhibiting and stop training before it reaches a point where the dog cannot think.

Early signs of stress include a "tongue flick," ears plastered to the dog's head, salivating, licking lips, panting, even a groveling, creeping posture. A common stress signal is the dog who submissively raises one foot in the air as if to say, "I can't possibly do this, it's too difficult!" Individual dogs have been known to cough, yawn, wheeze, shake, sneeze or even scratch when feeling stressed. It is important that you learn the signs of stress for your dog.

Dogs deal with stress in different ways. Extreme anxiety can be paralyzing as in the case of a dog who is so anxious about jumping that he will not pass the "jumps" to do a Go Out. The dog knows that if he does the Go Out, the jumping follows. Another example is the dog who is so anxious about the Drop on Recall that he will not even come when called.

Dogs, not unlike people, develop defense mechanisms to handle anxiety. Avoidance and substitution, both anxiety-reducing defense systems, are frequently evident in training. A dog who finds retrieving stressful may avoid making eye contact with where the dumbbell lands, as if to say, "If I don't see it, it isn't there, so I don't have to retrieve it." Similar avoidance is noticeable when first teaching hand signals. The dog who intentionally turns his head away as soon as you leave him on the stand may be avoiding the stress of learning signals. The good trainer will be able to make the distinction in this case between avoidance and distraction.

Were you ever in a class situation when the teacher asked a question that you did not know the answer to, so you dropped a pencil and pretended to be busy so you wouldn't be called on? Dogs who are confused may appear distracted! Watch them closely to discern the difference.

A substitution process is demonstrated by the dog who is perhaps anxious about doing articles and when sent to the article pile does a Go Out instead—confusion or avoidance of anxiety? By allowing the dog to make the mistake of passing the article pile and going to the Go-Out point, and by observing the dog's body language, the thinking trainer will know why the dog is not doing articles.

Since we know that dogs are stressed while learning, it makes sense to teach the dog all of the obedience exercises in Novice, Open and Utility before beginning the dog's show career. Once his show career starts, you want to avoid the pressures of learning new things. The beauty of a training method that allows a dog to think is that since the dog understands what he is doing and is not pattern trained, he will not confuse the various exercises. I have taken my dogs to matches and shown (for exhibition) in Novice, Open and Utility, in all different orders, in one day without a single non-qualifying (NQ) score. Imagine your security as a handler in the Novice ring knowing your dog can do Open and Utility! Imagine how polished your dog will look compared to the other dogs who barely know Novice and are in the midst of learning Open!

10
Why Not "No!"

Yes, you can train a dog successfully without the word "no." With my dogs, and in my classes, I have elected to totally remove the command "no" from our methods of training dogs. The reason for this is simply that most pet owners cannot say "No!" without sounding angry. There is no place for anger in training dogs. Anger is an emotion dogs cannot understand and they either fear it or learn to ignore it. By the time most students come into class, they have already used "no" to mean stop barking, don't bite, don't steal socks, don't jump, don't go to the bathroom in the house, and since they have rarely enforced the command, the dogs have learned to tune it out. I have seen dogs look at their owners who are screaming "No!" as if to say, "My owner is having a temper tantrum. She will get over it shortly."

I have substituted the sound "Anh" (which sounds like you have a stomach ache). I have yet to find a person who can say "Anh" angrily, and the dogs soon learn that it simply means "stop what you are doing." "Anh" is to be used only when a dog is off leash and too far away from you to physically stop the undesired behavior. Along with "Anh," the students are taught how to enforce the command by physically stopping the action. For household obedience problems like mouthing or stealing garbage, I prefer to stop the action physically and then praise the dog verbally. The emphasis is on the positive, not the negative. After all, we want the dog to focus on what is right. We accomplish this by not emphasizing the negative (simply stopping the bad behavior) and then praising profusely the positive. Suppose I sent you to the grocery store with a list of everything you shouldn't buy; how long would it take you to shop?

I prefer not to use any form of verbal harshness in training. It has always seemed ridiculous to me to hear a person turn to his dog and say "Bad dog! Shame on you!" as if a dog could really feel shame. Have you ever seen a dog blush? Besides, the dog is not bad, he is only wrong, and I have already discussed why it is "wonderful to be wrong."

Almost all training corrections given to a dog should be physical. The only thing he should ever hear from your voice is how wonderful he is for trying or for succeeding. This approach gives the dog security and a positive attitude. The dog never fears that you are rejecting *him* but understands that there are certain actions of which you do not approve. Your positive, happy, encouraging voice immediately following all physical corrections keeps the dog willing to try. An example: If your boss told you that you should feel ashamed of a letter you wrote for him, you might take it personally or feel very low. If, on the other hand, your boss told you that you were a wonderful secretary but that you had made a number of mistakes on a letter that needed correcting, you would be more willing to continue to work for this person. While most dogs are extremely sensitive to voice, they can easily accept unemotional physical corrections when followed with praise. The mother dog corrects her puppies by biting or snapping at them. Dogs don't yell or lecture their offspring!

By the time most people say "No," it's too late. Have you seen the person who pushes the dog off the couch and then yells "No"? By the time the dog hears "No," he is off the couch and has now been corrected for doing the right thing. I prefer to physically remove the dog from the couch (stop the bad behavior) and then praise the dog verbally. Forget about "no." You really don't need it! I have often said to new students, "If 'no' worked, I'd be out of business!"

While verbal harshness hinders training, it can be effective if you are intentionally trying to intimidate a dog. For example, if a dog is about to attack you—by all means, yell "No!"

11

Understanding Corrections vs. Help

A correction is something a dog chooses to avoid. Help is an aid to the dog. Knowing when to use which can make a big difference in your training.

What is a correction for one dog may not be a correction for all dogs. I once had a student with a Poodle who hated to have her face touched. "Good," I said, "then we can use that as a correction for her." But for another dog, touching the face might be considered praise if the dog likes it! A correction is totally determined by the dog, not the trainer. A correction is something the dog doesn't want to happen.

There are really only four distinct reasons why a dog does not respond to a command. He is either confused, afraid, distracted or feels he has a choice. If the dog is confused or afraid, I prefer to help him rather than correct him. This is the time to simplify the exercise, encourage the dog and perhaps explain it to him by using extra body language. If the dog is distracted or feels he has a choice, he deserves a correction such as a lead snap, ear pinch, or physical positioning. Corrections must be carefully taught before they can be used; in other words, the dog is taught why his ear is being pinched before the correction is ever used. (See Chapter 38, Teaching the Retrieve.)

For example, a dog is learning the Broad Jump. He has done hundreds of jumps with his owner running with him and then jumping toward his owner. However, every time the owner attempts to stand at the side of the jump, the dog goes directly to him rather than over the jump. Does this dog deserve to be *corrected?* I think not. The dog is exhibiting confusion. The owner has neglected to teach the dog where to focus his eyes before jumping. The trainer has moved too quickly in training and the dog has missed an important point. If the dog is now corrected for the trainer's mistake, what does this do to the trust, the bond, the teamwork needed to produce top performance?

If, on the other hand, this same dog (after he has successfully done the Broad Jump numerous times with his owner standing at the side of the jump) is not performing because he is distracted by a pretty little bitch across the room, should he be corrected? You bet! How you correct depends on how you taught the exercise and is really not the important part of this example. As a general rule of thumb, if your dog is confused or afraid, you help him, and when he is distracted or feels he has a choice, you correct him.

How do you know when your dog is confused and when he feels he has a choice? This, my friends, is what makes one person a better trainer than another. It is called "reading a dog," and when you learn to read canine body language, you are on your way to becoming a very good trainer. You can learn to read canine body language if you are willing to spend the time. Observing dogs is probably the best way to realize that ears, eyes, head, tail carriage and overall stance of a dog reveal what he is thinking. Working with a trainer who is proficient at "reading dogs" is how most of us develop this ability.

When one of my students says to me, "My dog did . . . What is the correction?" my answer is always another question: "Why did he make the mistake and why are you so sure he is deserving of a correction?" When you are not sure why a dog did or did not perform, it is always safe to give the dog the benefit and assume he was confused or afraid. You will never do any harm by trying to help the dog before resorting to corrections. But then again, if the dog knows what you want and is choosing not to obey or if he is distracted, helping him will not solve the problem. Relax, there is always time to correct.

How do you know when your evaluation of why the dog was not performing is wrong? When your approach makes the problem worse. The dog may not even try or may attempt to run away from the entire situation. Knowing *when* to correct a dog can be more important than knowing *how* to correct him.

Reasons a Dog Does Not Obey	Method of Correction
Dog is confused.	Help! *No harsh corrections!*
Dog is afraid.	Set up a situation where the dog cannot make a mistake. Give lots of praise when the dog succeeds. Break exercise down into simple steps. Repetition!
Dog is distracted.	*Correct!*
Dog feels he has a choice.	Proof the exercise. Set up a situation where the dog will make a mistake and correct. Repetition in unique situations.

When a dog is *afraid,* he should usually be helped, but there are some dogs who will allow you to help them through their fears forever. After repeatedly helping a frightened dog, the trainer must decide when the dog *feels he has a choice.* The choice the dog makes is to remain afraid. When you feel that the dog has made this choice, start administering mild corrections.

A phrase that repeatedly upsets me is, "He knows better, he's done it right many times before." Folks, things are not always as they appear. Years ago I took my new Utility dog out into the back yard for a simple practice session. Since she had just finished her Utility degree, we were learning nothing new. I decided to begin with a long, happy, simple Recall, and left my dog sitting contentedly as I walked 50 feet away. I turned to face her, and with a beaming smile and a clear, happy voice, I commanded, "Charo, come." She stared straight at me and sat there! I was in shock! My Utility dog was not coming when I called her!

I regained my composure and decided to give her the benefit of the doubt (perhaps she didn't hear me because of the wind) and called her again. Again I smiled and in a loud, crisp, happy tone, I called, "Charo, come." She flinched slightly but held her sitting position.

Now at this point a pattern trainer possibly would have been marching in to correct or snap a long line on the dog, but *I* knew better. I had to know *why* the dog was not responding before I would know how or if I should correct her. I ruled out fear because the dog's body language did not show any form of cowering or submission. Distraction was not the problem, either, because there was nothing going on and she was intently watching me. That left me with confusion or feeling she had a choice. While you would think it unlikely for a Utility dog to be confused on Recall, it was also very unlike Charo to refuse to do something because she felt she had a choice not to.

Still at a loss, I decided to walk over to where she was still sitting and look at things from her point of view. I did not get five feet from her when I realized what was wrong. She was sitting at the Go-Out spot and my Utility jumps were both still set up! We had spent so much time doing Directed Jumping (where the dog is not permitted to go directly to its owner between the "jumps") that Charo was confused. She was waiting for a jump signal and didn't think that coming to me between the "jumps" was permitted. Once I knew the confusion, the answer was obvious. I would help her. I slowly walked up to her and gently guided her to me between the jumps and praised her all the way. I then repeated the exercise. This time when I commanded, "Charo, come!" she flew to me, relieved that it was permissible to come in between the jumps. Would the correction or long line have worked? I'm sure it would have, but what would have been the long-term effect of correcting (punishing) a dog who was confused? You guessed it, panic and fear!

The Recall problem might have been fixed with a correction, but at what long-term expense? What would have happened to the directed jumping exercise? By working to understand Charo's problem, the training relationship was strengthened and the problem resolved with no apprehension that might appear later in another aspect of training.

Later in this book a Compulsive Retrieve is explained. The trainer learns how to teach a dog that if he chooses not to retrieve, he will be corrected. Please keep in mind that not *all* refusals to retrieve are corrected. The dog is only corrected if he is refusing to retrieve because he feels he has a choice or if he is distracted.

It is not uncommon for a dog who has been performing correctly for weeks to suddenly become confused. There are different reasons a dog gets confused about an exercise he appeared to know. Any time you put new information on top of old information, you stir up the old information! For example, a dog knows how to do a Recall, until you teach a Drop on Recall. Learning to drop confuses the dog, and there may come a time when he isn't sure about how to do a simple Recall.

As we train dogs, we notice that their behavior often precedes learning. In other words, they do things long before they really understand what they are doing. Dogs often start scenting articles and bringing back the correct article before they realize *how* they are able to accomplish this. Four weeks into training articles, the dog can't do it anymore because he is beginning to think about *how* he does it! Once a dog actually learns it, confusion is gone.

12
Praise

Praise is one of the few things in life that has not yet been taxed, so by all means *use it!* I have never understood why people are stingy with praise, as if there is a limited source. You can never over praise, provided you praise at the right time.

To each dog, praise is different. Some dogs will wag their tails if you say the right words in the right tone. For other dogs, physical contact in the form of stroking or patting will bring a joyful response. Anything that builds a dog's ego is considered praise. It is absolutely critical that you discover what words and gestures bring a tail wag from your dog if you are to train him to work happily.

Whenever possible in early training, refrain from using physical contact for praise. Too often the dog does the right thing and the owner pets the dog, which gets the dog so excited that he then does the wrong thing, for example, break a "sit" command. The dog becomes so distracted by the praise that he forgets what he did that was so great.

There are different degrees of praise. Your vocabulary may vary, but the idea is that as training progresses, so does the praise. For example, a dog does a Sit Stay with no distractions and is praised: "Good dog!" When the dog does a longer Sit Stay, he might be "Very good!" As the dog works to avoid distractions on a Sit Stay, he might be "Super" or "Great kid." Exceptional accomplishments may warrant a "Terrific" or "Excellent." If everything done well brings a simple "Good dog," why should the dog try harder?

Do not take your dog for granted. Praise all desired responses, even a simple, casual sit that was only intended to set the dog up for the next exercise.

Dogs must be taught to accept praise without becoming crazy about it. (No, you cannot omit the praise to avoid the "crazies.") Command your dog to sit. Now turn to him and tell him how wonderful he is, how he is the best dog ever. Use a very high, happy tone. His tail should start to wag, which is fine, but if he gets up, gently put him back into the "sit" and say nothing! Keep praising. If the dog continues to move from the excitement of the praise, reposition him less gently, say nothing and continue to praise.

Petting a dog into your leg (right) teaches the dog to lean on you. It is much more useful to pet the dog on the chest (left) when encouraging a straight sit in the heel position.

BOHM MARRAZZO PHOTOGRAPHY

It is important that the dog understands the difference between praise and release. In advanced training, you will want to praise him while he is away from you (for example, on a drop from Drop on Recall). If he gets up every time you praise him, you can't accomplish the exercise. If you find that you withhold praise at certain times in training because you fear the dog will get so excited that he will break the exercise, stop avoiding a problem and go back and teach the dog to accept praise. It will be worth your while. You cannot have happy working dogs if your ability to praise is limited.

If you are planning to use praise (building the dog's ego) as a positive reinforcer, you must learn to reserve it for the purpose of training. There are people who cannot walk past their dogs in the house without petting them and/or praising them for simply being alive. If your dog is going to receive your approval for doing nothing, then why should he obey commands to earn praise? An ideal training situation would be one in which the dog was confined to a run or crate away from the trainer for a period of two to four hours before each training session. The dog would then look forward to training for a chance to exercise and receive attention from his person. After training, the dog can then return to a normal family environment. I do not believe that "good obedience dogs" need to live outside so that they will appreciate attention. On the other hand, praise for doing nothing breaks down a dog's motivation to perform.

A dog should be rewarded for having a good, willing attitude to try new exercises as well as for the perfect completion of an exercise. Here again degrees of praise are important. For example, a dog's first attempt at doing scent discrimination in a new surrounding may be clumsy at best. He may have hesitated in going out to the articles. His insecurity may have caused him to move slowly and tentatively toward the pile. While scenting, he may have been briefly distracted or stress may have caused him to hesitate. All of these represent imperfections that we work to correct before showing the dog, but for the moment, he finds the correct article and gathers the courage to return with it. This task, which the dog found very stressful, is deserving of great praise. The attempt and the courage, not the mechanics of the exercise, are what should be praised.

Most of the point-losing errors made by the dog in this case will correct themselves as the dog gains confidence, but such is not always the case. It is the better trainer who reads his dog and knows when effort alone is praiseworthy and when the dog is not working to his capacity.

This "praising an attempt" is difficult for some very experienced trainers to swallow. It is almost as if the more you know, the harder it gets to see point-costing errors and not fix them immediately in a new dog. But the fact remains that you cannot fix everything at once, and if you point out too many mistakes to the dog first learning, he throws up his paws as if to say, "I give up! This is just too difficult for my poor little canine brain!"

Accomplished dog trainers, people who have trained one or more OTCHs or even multiple UDs (in which category I must include myself), need to be very careful. It is only by consciously disciplining ourselves that we can avoid the traps of expertise.

Have you ever noticed that each successive dog you train learns Novice through Utility in less time? As you become a more confident, experienced trainer, you demand more from a dog and you demand it sooner. As we grow as trainers, the quality of dogs we train must improve to withstand the pressure of being trained by someone who "knows what he's doing."

It is sometimes helpful to record the day you begin to teach a new exercise to your dog. This way, when you feel like it is taking forever for the new dog to learn the Broad Jump, you can refer to your notes and realize that "forever" is actually six weeks.

Experienced trainers are not necessarily harsher. In fact, the longer I train, the less force I find it necessary to use, but the dog is nonetheless pressured by my confident demands and proficiency. Since I am no longer the awkward, klutzy handler with two left feet, the dog is expected to be able to perform smoothly as well.

Most new, promising Novice dogs are sensitive and willing. Let us not destroy these qualities by withholding praise because we see the imperfections so vividly. So what if a slightly crooked sit goes uncorrected in the beginning? Was it fast? Is he attentive? If yes, be sure to praise him! The "polish of perfection" may be added after the dog masters the major part of the exercises.

13

Training Equipment

Each dog is an individual, and the choice of training equipment should be based on each dog's personality, coat, previous life experiences and his handler's abilities. For example, a dog who has been tied out on a choke chain collar (which is an extremely dangerous thing to do) is likely to have built up a tolerance to the choking sensation and will probably need a different kind of collar for training. The basic rule of thumb is that we want to apply as little force as is necessary to elicit a desired response from the dog. No one collar or leash is the best choice for every dog.

If I am using a flexible lead, I prefer to train with leather. The widest leather leash the trainer can comfortably handle works best. Some people feel that it is impressive to train a 90-pound German Shorthair (for example) on a quarter-inch piece of leather that I refer to as "spaghetti." Not only is it not impressive, but the handler will work much harder to achieve desired results than if he had a wider lead. It would be like trying to cut a lawn with a pair of scissors as opposed to a lawn mower!

The reason behind using the wider lead is as follows: You, the trainer, give a dog a correction by snapping or jerking the leash. This correction must then travel to the dog. The less the correction is dissipated in travel, the more correction a dog receives. Imagine, if you will, a broomstick between you and the dog. As soon as you pull your end of the stick, the dog moves because the solid wood has no "give" to it. Now look at the opposite extreme. If you hold one end of an elastic string and the dog is attached to the other end, how much is the dog affected by you pulling on your end of the string? Very little because the elastic string has so much "give" that your motion at one end is barely reaching the other end. This same principle, when applied to leashes and training, demonstrates that the denser the material between you and the dog, the faster and stronger the dog will feel a jerk.

In recent years many trainers have started using braided leashes. Since a braided leash is another way of putting more leather between you and the dog, the braided leash has proven very effective and is growing in popularity.

Train with a three-foot leash! For years trainers have recommended a six-foot training leash, but now we see little reason for burdening a handler with six feet of leash when 90 percent of the time (except for stays), he uses only two feet of leash. Besides, if you only give a beginning handler a three-foot leash, how far will the dog ever be able to lag or forge?

For toy dogs and dogs of similar size, train with a solid lead and a back scratcher, otherwise known as an "arm extender." The solid lead allows you to hold the dog in position without looming over him, and corrections, when needed, are given at the dog's eye level without any warning that they are coming. The back scratcher allows you the freedom to position your dog without bending. In addition to the back problems a trainer of small dogs faces, every time you bend down to the dog, you are projecting that a correction is coming and changing your position. Back scratchers praise and pet as well as position and correct.

There are many alternatives when it comes to training collars. I like to start all dogs with a buckle collar. For the long-coated dogs, a rolled-leather collar works best, and for the smooth-coated breeds, I like a wide nylon buckle collar. As long as you get the desired response when you snap a leash attached to a buckle collar, why go to anything more severe? I know of many OTCH small dogs that have been entirely trained on buckle collars. You can even trial a dog in a buckle collar!

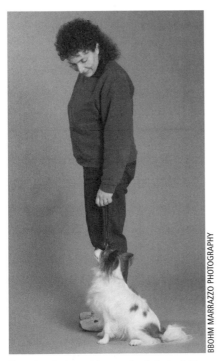

BBOHM MARRAZZO PHOTOGRAPHY

Use a handle to avoid excess leash that might allow a dog to lag or forge ahead.

BBOHM MARRAZZO PHOTOGRAPHY

Use a solid lead and back scratcher to position the small dog into a straight sit.

A rolled-leather collar.

A wide buckle collar.

When the buckle collar is not effective, the next step is a prong collar (also called a "pinch collar" or a "German collar"). The prong collar is a valuable training tool when used properly. Unfortunately, this collar looks like some sort of medieval torture, and the uneducated owner is often afraid of it. The prong collar should fit snugly around the dog's neck, up high and behind the ears. The individual prongs come apart to fit the collar as well as to adjust the size of the collar. When worn properly, the collar does not slide; put the collar on the dog so that the part that attaches to the leash is on the right side of the dog's neck. The part of the collar without prongs should be under the dog's throat, where the neck is most vulnerable.

The prong collar works on an entirely different principle than the choke collar. It is designed to pinch skin evenly all around the neck. Since the prongs are dull, no harm is done to the dog's skin. By distributing the correction all around the dog's neck (instead of in one place as with the choke collar), less force is needed on the leash to impress the dog. The prong collar is particularly effective on dogs who are immune to being choked because they have been tied on choke collars or permitted to pull on choke collars for months.

There are other dogs who, for whatever reason, cannot tolerate a choking sensation and panic, gag and cough when pressure from a simple choke chain collar is applied to their necks. These dogs tolerate the pinch from the prong collar very well. I once owned a Border Collie who had been snapped so hard on a choke chain as a puppy that her throat was damaged. The slightest pressure on her trachea from a chain sent her into a gagging fit. Luckily, she had no problem tolerating a small prong collar.

It is preferable to see large, heavy dogs who may lunge on a prong collar because you will never harm a dog with a prong collar. A large, heavy dog lunging on a choke collar, where all the pressure is at one point, could damage his

RON REAGAN

The prong collar is positioned on the dog's neck so the part that attaches to the leash is on the right side of the dog's neck.

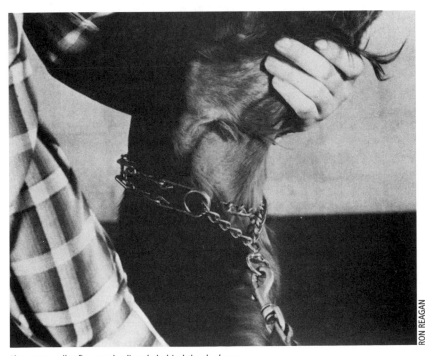

RON REAGAN

The prong collar fits snugly, directly behind the dog's ears.

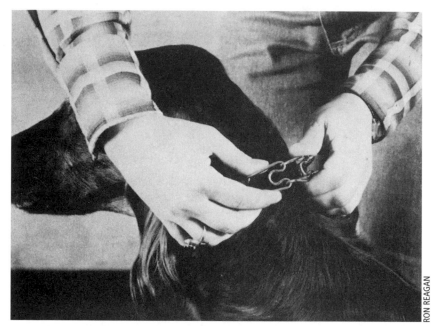

Step one in removing the prong collar is to squeeze an individual link as you slide an adjoining link up and out of the collar.

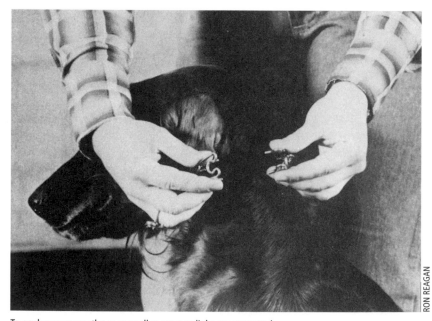

To apply or remove the prong collar, any two links are separated.

trachea. The prong collar is also preferred when you are trying to preserve a dog's coat. The chain and nylon collars will break and rip out the hair on the neck. When a dog comes into class with all of the hair on one side of his neck worn off, he is a candidate for a prong collar!

Prong collars come in four sizes of links, termed toy, small, medium and large. I have never had to use the large size and don't recommend it because the links are too stiff to open and close easily.

We often refer to the prong collar as "power steering" since you need less force to give an effective correction. Small people with large dogs welcome this advantage!

A prong collar should not be used in the case of an aggressive dog who may bite. You cannot successfully hang a dog on a prong collar when trying to keep him from getting close enough to bite you. With aggressive dogs that are too strong to control on a choke collar, use two collars and two leashes. If the dog lunges, restrain with the prong collar. Then if he tries to bite, hang him with a choke collar. Muzzles are also useful when dealing with aggressive dogs.

The only problem trainers ever have with using the prong collar is that people fear what looks horrible and what they don't understand. Because of this understandable apprehension, it helps to put a prong collar on the owner's arm or leg first and snap it so that he experiences what the dog will feel. So far I have yet to have any owner scream in pain from being corrected with a prong collar. In fact, when compared to the snap from a choke chain collar, owners prefer the prong collar. It is important that you explain to owners that their dogs might yelp when this collar is first used but that this is because they are surprised by the new feeling and they are capable of verbalizing as the collar is not choking them. Since the prong collar is used less harshly and less frequently to control a dog, it is often much kinder than the choke chain collar.

If you notice the absence of the nylon and chain choke collar from my writing, it is because I have never been happy with the results from a choke collar. After years of training different breeds, I have realized that it is not necessary to choke a dog in order to teach him something. Many dogs resent or fear the choking sensation. This does not put the dog in a good frame of mind to learn. With the training methods described in this book, the collar is used primarily to guide the dog, not to correct him. By allowing a dog a chance to respond on a buckle collar, you preserve his sensitivity. When the prong collar is needed, it should be used only until the dog learns the lesson, and it is then removed immediately. In the end, the dog must respond because you told him to, not because of what collar he is wearing. Once the dog is off leash, the collar is useless.

The innocuous choke collar (also called a strangle collar) is a potentially dangerous tool. Since its uses are limited, I do not view the choke as a collar of choice.

Any piece of training equipment is only effective and unabusive when used properly and applied to the right dog. There is nothing that prohibits you from using different collars on the same dog for different problems. Some of my dogs only feel a prong collar once in their lives, and that's when they need motivation to move faster.

A good trainer is an open-minded, flexible person who reacts to the individual dog and to the moment in training.

14

Choosing and Raising the Future OTCH

Puppy testing to find the "good obedience dogs" is the current fad. While I have no doubt that you can test puppies to predict their future personality, keep in mind that any test is only as valid as the person performing the test and evaluating the results. If you are not experienced with testing puppies, you would probably be better off trusting the judgment of a reputable breeder who is involved with showing and training for obedience.

Keep in mind that the great obedience dogs of the past, present and future are really great dog-and-handler *teams*. It is the combination of dog and handler personalities that leads to OTCHs. What might be the perfect obedience prospect for one person might be a reject in the hands of another. Analyze yourself and your training style. Are your needs better met with a dominant dog, very resilient to bouncing back after a correction, or does your personality blend better with an outgoing, sensitive sweetheart? Good breeders know their puppies and can help find the best prospect *for you*.

Can you breed OTCHs? I believe you can, but two OTCH dogs bred together do not necessarily produce top obedience prospects. Certain lines do seem to carry more genes that produce driving (energetic), willing dogs with the structure to sit squarely and jump easily.

When choosing a puppy for obedience, look for the pup who chooses to make eye contact, the people-oriented puppy who willingly follows you. You want the puppy who is outgoing, friendly, inquisitive, energetic and likes to show off—a "group winner."

Taking a puppy home at seven weeks seems to be the preferred age as documented by laboratory tests, which indicate that the eighth through eleventh weeks begin a critical period where the puppy should experience no trauma.

What often makes the difference between a good dog and a great dog is early socialization. Take the puppy (inoculated, of course) everywhere! Visit friends, go shopping, audit training classes, spectate at matches, stay in hotel rooms! The more people, dogs, sights and sounds you expose your puppy to early on in life, the easier it will be to demand attention from him later in training and the more secure he will be.

Teach your puppy to play. Games of retrieve, tug of war (alternate who wins), hide and seek and tag help develop a relationship between you and your dog and later on will serve as a release from the stress of learning. Pups should have the opportunity to play with metal objects in preparation for scent articles.

Quiet times alone with your puppy are also important. Take walks (on leash) in the woods, sit together in the sun and take time to stroke and talk to your puppy. This helps him understand your tones of voice and builds a bond between you two that will grow into a working team. Whenever possible, make eye contact.

Be fair and honest with your pup. Never put him in uncomfortable situations, for example with young children who might hurt or tease him. You want your dog to trust that you will protect him. Never do anything to jeopardize this trust. Later on he must trust that if you command him to stay or jump that it is safe to do so.

If you want your dog to respect you, begin by respecting him. Respond to his affection. Be alert to his needs, that is, mealtime, grooming and housebreaking. Make sure to take a lot of time from your schedule to spend alone with your puppy.

Your pup will learn to be handled and will appreciate your attention if you groom him regularly. Learn to clean ears and teeth and to cut his nails and care for his coat. Admiration and love grow on a grooming table!

While time spent with your puppy is important, be careful not to make him overly dependent. There should be time during the day for the puppy to be by himself, either in a pen or crate. This helps the dog develop independence. As the pup gets a little older, occasionally hand his leash to a responsible person from time to time and walk away. Dogs who are never left when they are young may have anxiety to overcome on out-of-sight stays later on in training.

In preparation for Straight Fronts, always greet your dog from in front and pet him toward you and evenly on both sides of his face as you encourage eye contact. Petting a dog on his side causes the dog to turn his side to you, which is not desired in obedience. When feeding your dog his daily meal, talk to him just before you put his food down in front of him. The bowl of food draws the pup's eyes up to your face, so take advantage of the attention.

Whenever possible, pet your dog under his chin and toward you, which will encourage him to lift his head. Handle your dog from his head to his toes to his tail. Your pup should be comfortable with being handled all over in preparation for the Stand for Examination.

Occasionally "rough house" with your pup. Some loving, rough handling will help him to learn to accept corrections later in training.

Never put a choke collar (nylon or chain) on your puppy! (see Chapter 13, Training Equipment).

Your dog's health is your responsibility. A healthy dog trains easier and performs better. Keep your pup free of internal and external parasites, lean, well muscled and free of mats and excess hair. If you have a hairy breed, work to keep his eyes clean so that he can maintain eye contact. Short nails help a dog jump easier and move more freely. A clean, brushed coat never hurt any dog's score in the obedience ring!

Building a bond with your puppy is setting a strong foundation on which to build a good training relationship. The end result is a dog and handler team who works like they belong together.

Training should be incorporated into a puppy's life in a natural way. It is impossible to state an age at which formal training should begin. Smaller breeds tend to mature faster physically and are thus able to handle the physical demands of training (for example, sitting squarely) at an earlier age. In general, smaller dogs can be started younger.

From the moment you get your puppy, attention should be encouraged and praised but not demanded until such time as you begin a formal training program.

Young puppies (three to six months) can and should learn to sit, down, stand and come on command, taught gently and carefully. (In the case of a large-breed puppy who will not yet sit up straight on his haunches, omit the sit until such time as he is physically capable of doing it.) Come at this point is done randomly, from wherever the pup is standing, and there is no Sit Front required.

Heeling and stays are best left until the dog is older (6 to 12 months). While a puppy can learn to walk next to you attentively, it is of little value to attempt to teach him foot cues or rhythm since as he grows his stride will change and his ability to concentrate is limited. Stays require extreme discipline for some overzealous obedience prospects, and to ask a young pup to sit perfectly still is often more than he can emotionally handle. So, wait a few months until he has some of the "ants out of his pants." In early training, the only truly important thing you need to accomplish is teaching the dog to pay attention to you! Once you have his attention, the rest will fall into place.

To be most effective, a trainer should be aware of the various growth stages a dog is likely to experience. Much has already been written about "critical periods" in a dog's life. How these periods affect a dog's ability to learn can be most enlightening. In the book *Training Your Dog, The Step-by-Step Manual* by Joachim Volhard and Gail Tamases Fisher, critical periods are defined to be:

> Birth to Seven Weeks (0–49 days)
>
> Socialization Period (7–12 weeks)
>
> Fear Imprint Period (8–11 weeks)
>
> Seniority Classification Period (12–16 weeks)
>
> Flight Instinct Period (4–8 months)
>
> Second Fear Imprint Period (6–14 months)
>
> Maturity (1–4 years)

While much has been written about young puppies, I am particularly interested in the periods of a dog's life I refer to as Pre-adolescence (9–13 months) and Adolescence (13–24 months), for it is during these times that dogs receive most of their formal training in preparation for a show career. While each dog and breed of dog must be considered an individual, you cannot help but see recurring patterns as you continue to raise and train dogs in obedience.

The adolescent dog has two paws in adulthood and two paws in puppyhood. While at times he appears calm and secure, there are other times when, if left unsupervised, he will have a "pillow party." (That's where you come home after a brief jaunt to find that it has snowed pillow stuffing all over your house!) Your young, aspiring show dog is once again returned to his crate whenever you need to depart.

Erratic behavior, such as running away and not coming when called one day (even in a dog who has been trained to come) and then clinging to mommy or daddy the next day, is not uncommon. I have heard trainers say, "He was such a socialized puppy. We did all the good things like walking him through town and banging on shopping carts, and now at 10 months he's spooking at a garbage dumpster!" This is not at all unusual, as Volhard and Fisher describe in their Second Fear Imprint Period, 6–14 months.

Astute trainers may also notice a difficulty to concentrate and that the adolescent dog is more easily distracted and almost "spacey." At a time in their lives when sexual thoughts dance in their heads, and other dogs seem much more important, we as trainers are concerned with Figure 8s! Gawky, distracted, bodies changing, often overly energetic, the adolescent dog is not always in the best frame of mind to learn. Not yet sure of who he is or where he fits in, the confused 9–24-month-old can find training too stressful to enjoy. Parents report horror stories about raising teenagers, and dog owners rant and rave about their one-and-a-half-year-old dog who looks mature but is still undisciplined and unpredictable.

In my experience with large breeds, two seems to be the magic age where the dog finally starts working with you instead of against you. It is also around two that the dog exhibits a certain "presence" when exhibited in the obedience ring, as if to say, "Look at me! I know who I am and what I'm doing!" I like to show dogs in Novice right around two years of age.

A good trainer is concerned with the dog at the end of the leash—his mental and physical status. We can only teach as much as our student is ready to learn. This learning rate will change throughout the dog's developmental stages. More than once I have doubted the potential of a dog I was training when the dog was about one-and-a-half years old. Experience has taught me to reserve judgment until after 24 months.

As puppies grow up, they might reach a stage where training is not a pleasant experience and the pup appears disinterested. There is nothing wrong with interrupting the training process for a month or more until the dog is again receptive. The ideal trainer trains instinctively, giving the dog as much as he can handle while at the same time watching for signs of stress, and then removing the pressure. There must not be a rush if your goal is to be a top dog-and-handler *team*.

15

Anticipation

Anticipation, when the dog does something before he's told to do so, is a predictable stage of learning. Many obedience exercises as we know them are nothing more than a series of anticipations that we allow. On the Retrieve-Over-High-Jump exercise, we give the dog a single command to jump. He then anticipates that we will ask him to pick up the dumbbell, return over the jump and sit front. He has anticipated three commands. It is easy to see why dogs go directly to heel position in anticipation of the next command.

In the learning stages, anticipation should be permitted, and with some insecure dogs, encouraged. However, once the dog understands the exercise, improper anticipation must be stopped. Since most anticipation is caused by confusion, help the dog understand rather than correct him for being confused.

If a dog is anticipating a Recall or any exercise where he is *coming to you,* put him on a leash and hand the leash to someone standing behind the dog. When the dog gets up, the leash holder gently repositions the dog while saying nothing. When the dog is called, the person holding the leash simply drops it. The dog will eventually realize that he should not come until called.

If the dog is anticipating a retrieve, or any exercise where he is *going away from you,* put a six-foot leash on the dog and drop it on the floor. Step on the leash with your left foot. Now do everything you can to encourage the dog to anticipate. Use his name as if you were going to command him to take it, flinch your body with sharp movements, lean forward and so on. When the dog anticipates, say nothing. He will be stopped by your weight on the leash. After he gets caught, reposition him gently and begin again as if nothing happened. Remember, *do not correct* confusion. When you finally do send the dog, simply lift your weight off the leash. This method is more effective than holding the dog by the collar because the dog never knows when you are standing on the leash and he is forced to *think* about what you say that allows him to retrieve.

If a dog anticipates the finish, sit him in front of you on leash. Command his name, flinch, do everything you can to cause him to anticipate, then gently stop him with the leash. He will soon understand that he is only to move on the finish command.

For anticipation of the Drop on Recall, see Chapter 35.

For anticipated signals on the Signal Exercise, allow more time between the signals to help cause the anticipation. Then, when the dog anticipates, give him the verbal command (not a threatening shout) for what he should be doing. By practicing signals out of order, you will also counteract the anticipation.

Certain breeds of dogs are more prone to anticipation than others. If you are training one of these breeds—for example, Border Collies, Poodles, some Golden Retrievers—allow the learning stage, which includes anticipation, to go on for less time than you would with another breed.

As a rule, dogs trained to listen carefully and to think about what they are doing have fewer incidents of anticipated exercises.

Never correct anticipation of something new that the dog is learning! Anticipation is one of the first signs of understanding.

16
Creatures Big and Small

Each dog and each handler are individual. To attempt to train each team the same way is to be unfairly simplistic. While I certainly advocate group classes, there must be individualization within the classes if dogs are going to have an opportunity to reach potential. What may be an effective method on a dog the size of a Golden Retriever or German Shepherd is not necessarily the best choice for a dog the size of a Yorkie or Papillon. With some of our giant and toy breeds, it takes a lot of imagination to modify training methods. If you are the owner of a toy or giant breed of dog and instinctively feel that methods offered by your instructor are not appropriate for your dog, trust your instincts and don't use them!

It never ceases to amaze me that people will do things to their dogs—although they don't feel comfortable with them—simply because some well-known winning trainer said it was the thing to do. An owner should always have the courage to take responsibility for the specific training methods he uses on his dogs. If you do not feel comfortable with a method, don't use it! If a method makes no sense to you, don't use it, for if it doesn't make sense to you, how in the world is it going to make sense to the dog?

If we agree that each dog and handler is unique, then we must accept that each team has different physical and mental limitations. For example, each dog and each handler has a different energy level. It is not the energy level itself that is so important as it is the combination of the dog's and owner's energy levels. For a dog to be a top-performing dog, he must be teamed up with a compatible handler. A very energetic Golden in the hands of a sweet old gentleman or a very over-weight lady will not fare as well as the same energetic Golden in the hands of a slim, active, person. This does not mean that the sweet old gentleman or over-weight lady will never have the ability to train a superb obedience dog, but I suggest there is a better choice of dog for them. Notice I said "dog" and not "breed." I believe you can find the right dog for you in the breed of your choice, although you might have to search for a while. I have seen exceptional dogs of all breeds.

At the moment, I have a young lady in class with a female Saint Bernard who is as fast and agile and alert and willing and accurate as any Golden Retriever I have seen! No one will ever tell her she's a Saint Bernard.

To ask more from a dog than it is capable of giving is cruel. Not all dogs are fast by nature. To constantly correct or attempt to frighten a dog for the sake of speed in obedience is, to me, abusive. If speed for the sake of speed is what is important to you, then I recommend you get a faster dog. Spectators watch outside the rings at obedience trials and see very fast, high scoring dogs, and for some reason they attribute this speed to how the dogs were trained. While I agree that training plays a part, I maintain that these dogs are naturally energetic and that training has channeled the energy rather than created it.

Dogs and people are limited by their structure. I once owned a very limited dog. After weeks of working on straight sits, I was so exasperated one day that I decided to try an experiment. On a quiet afternoon, I took my little furry friend into the living room and gently commanded, "Sit." Then, one by one, I carefully positioned each foot where it should be for a perfectly straight sit. Just as I let go of the fourth paw, perfectly in position, the dog fell over! Her structure was such that it was impossible for her to sit squarely. I still loved her but gave up on the idea of ever getting her to do a straight sit.

You train each dog a little differently, and each dog you train will teach you something new about dog training. Let us understand and deal with our limitations and not ignore them. To pretend that a Great Dane can be trained the same as a Chihuahua is not logical!

If a 200 score is what you are after, then you must begin with a dog who is physically and mentally capable of perfection. Then, if you train it perfectly and you become a 200 handler, all you need is a judge who will score a 200 if he or she sees it!

17

Special Small Dog and Big Dog Techniques

To be successful training toys or giant breeds, you must be more creative than the average handler. The obedience world was not designed for the extremes. If you are choosing a dog for obedience, always look for a large toy or a small giant within the breed of your choice.

Toy dogs, while fragile, are not helpless. Refrain from carrying them all over, overprotecting them from the real world. In early training, work with the small dog on a table and in your lap to encourage eye contact. Did you know you could start to teach heeling with the dog at your side on an oval table? Raising the dog up to table level also helps start the Signal Exercises. For heeling toy dogs, use the solid lead (see Chapter 13, Training Equipment) and a back scratcher to correct and pet. To make fronts and finishes, make use of 12-inch rulers as guides for the dog to line up with. If Directed Jumping is a problem, put the jumps close together and get down on your knees to give the signals. If you're having trouble keeping your small dog's attention, try dangling a toy or food from a string to start your dog looking up. Lagging can be a problem as many of the toy dogs lack stamina. Rather than snapping forward with your solid lead, "goose" the little guy from behind with your back scratcher.

While the "littles" require a lot of creative, sensitive training, giant breeds are often a case of brute force. Have you ever noticed that it's always little people who buy big dogs? A common large dog problem is speed, especially on a Recall. While you might get response snapping a Golden on a long line, good luck with a Newfie! To motivate large dogs, throwing things from behind works best. While we often begin by throwing chains (a circle of heavy chain) at a giant breed, we have been known to throw metal chairs (not at the dog but behind him to evoke a response) at very large, unresponsive dogs. Make sure the dog is on a long line when you use throw chains or other objects. This is to ensure that the dog comes to you rather than panicking and running away from you.

Use the solid lead and back scratcher to hold the small dog in the Heel position so that he learns where it is.

Use the solid lead and back scratcher to teach a straight sit at heel without having to bend over, which would change the dog's view of the handler.

Use the leash as a sling to teach the small dog the stand signal.

Crowding from a large dog is more than a problem; it can be hazardous to your health! Swinging your right arm across your body works for many dogs. With the giants, you might want to hold a metal dustpan and make contact with the dog's face as you sweetly command, "Off." It may sound something like *The Gong Show*. For the Drop-in-Motion exercise, instead of using your arm as the "windmill" signal, try a plastic wiffle ball bat! The bat makes a lot of noise but wouldn't hurt the big guy.

When it comes to training very large and very small dogs, the secret is to think—be imaginative! If it makes sense, try it! Do not be afraid of what others might think—you can always hand them the leash and tell them to see if they can get results the conventional way!

18
Proofing

"**P**roofing" is a term used to describe a technique of testing a dog's understanding of an exercise. Proofing clarifies concepts while strengthening the dog's concentration and confidence. Every exercise you ever teach your dog to perform in obedience should be proofed before you ever consider taking him to shows. Proofing gives the owner the confidence he needs to show off his dog at a trial. When devising new ways to proof your dog, both you and the dog become inspired and challenged. It is a good way to keep from becoming bored.

There are different degrees of proofing a given exercise. That is to say, some forms of proofing are more difficult for the dog to withstand. For example, petting a dog on a Sit-Stay might be easier for the dog to tolerate and remain sitting than the temptation of offering him a hamburger. Different proofs are more challenging to different dogs. The "chow hound" finds food proofs very difficult, while the noneater is hardly tempted by the food. A good trainer is aware of his dog's weaknesses (food, touch, sound, sight) and works to gradually increase the difficulty of the proof test. For example, with a noise-sensitive dog, it would not be wise to start introducing loud applause until the dog was comfortable with the noise of a single handclap.

EXAMPLES OF PROOFING
Sit-Stays

Put the dog on a Sit-Stay and throw balls and toys in front of him.

Have others give him alternate commands like "down" and "come."

Spray him with water to simulate a rain shower.

Have him hear applause.

Take him to distracting, busy, noisy places and practice your Sit-Stay.

Tempt him to move for food or other dogs.

In general, try anything other than calling his name to get him to make a mistake.

Recalls

Leave your dog with his back to you.

Leave your dog and have someone pet him or feed him as you call him.

Call him and disappear around a corner.

Have him go around obstacles or through people to get to you.

Stands

Stand your dog, leave him, and put slow, steady pressure against the leash.

Does he resist, demonstrating an understanding of stay? (This is good for all "stay" positions; that is, sit and down.)

Step over him.

Have different kinds of people examine him. Have people examining him wear raincoats, hats, beards, umbrellas.

If possible, try crawling under him.

Stand him on various surfaces, for example, plastic, wood, stone, wire.

A Border Collie is being proofed for hand signals using the distraction of a donut. If the dog focuses his attention on the distraction, a correction for a missed signal will follow.

Finishes

Finish your dog and have someone behind you tempt the dog with food or toys.

Finish standing close to a wall.

Finish, and just before the dog sits, make a minor move forward, backward, or sideways.

Does the dog adjust?

Finish your dog from a down position in front of you.

Heeling

Heel in all different places with all kinds of distractions.

Have someone tempt the dog with food or toys while you are heeling.

Head toward an open door or any other distraction, and do a sudden about turn.

Is the dog distracted?

Teach the dog to heel sideways and backward.

Do 360-degree and 270-degree turns.

Practice Figure 8s at a slow pace. Alternate your Figure 8 patterns; for example, two of one post and then one of another.

Turn just before you halt.

Halt facing walls and baby gates.

Practice fast to slow to fast.

Have someone play Frisbee over you while you are heeling.

Retrieving

Retrieve all different kinds of objects from all different places. Put your dumbbell up high, under a chair, under a jacket, in a pot of water, on top of another person lying on the floor, next to another dog, next to food, under another animal, off the cage of a guinea pig, and so on.

Test every possible situation until you are convinced that the dog will retrieve his dumbbell from anywhere.

Jumps

Change the location of jumps.

Change the appearance of jumps, for example, put coats, flowers or balloons on them.

Simulate shadows on the jumps.

Broad Jump: Use fewer boards at the same distance to tempt a mistake.

Gloves

Turn to a glove, give a signal, praise for looking, but don't send the dog.

Turn to one glove, and send to another.

Use brown gloves, which may not be as obvious on dark surfaces (see Chapter 40, Directed Retrieve).

Articles

Use two or more sets of articles.

Stand articles up on end.

Put some articles on a chair or coffee table and some underneath. Alternate where the scented one is.

Have all kinds of noise distractions while your dog works the articles.

Have two dogs work the same pile of articles. (Make sure you are using a third scent on your pile of articles.)

Put food and other unscented objects out in between your articles. Is the dog distracted or does he keep working?

A Golden Retriever is being proofed on scent articles. If the dog is distracted by the turtles and stops working the articles, he will be corrected. This teaches the dog to focus his attention on what he is being commanded to do and to block out distractions.

Go Outs

Do them at all different distances.

Do them in different places.

Throw objects before and during to distract the dog.

Tempt him to go off center by having a person or other dog behind barrier off center.

Stop your dog short. The next time, send him past where you stopped him.

Anticipation

You can proof all anticipation by setting up the exercise and saying the dog's name only. Help him back into position if he moves.

Say his name, followed by an extraneous command like "listen" or "bananas." Help him if he moves.

Flinch with sudden body motions. Reposition him if he responds as if it were a command.

Proofing should be fun and imaginative. It requires that you want the dog to be wrong so that you can show him (not necessarily correct him) what right is. Remember, "wrong is wonderful!" If you can't bear to proof because you are encouraging a mistake, you will end up doing a lot less training and a lot more praying. Proofing causes and solves mistakes *before* the dog starts making them up on his own.

It is not bad to be wrong–it is only wrong. When the dog has exhausted all wrong possibilities, then and only then does he understand what right is. Trainers who do not proof are often heard to say, "My dog works great at home!" or "He never did that before." Trainers who proof cause all their mistakes in practice and get reliable performances in the ring.

As with most good techniques, anything can be taken too far, or, as the cliché goes, "too much of a good thing is no good." The object of proofing is to test the dog's understanding of an exercise, not to drive him crazy!

Weak links in training should be proofed more frequently as in the case of the dog who tends to forget what he is doing on the Long Sit and lies down. It would not be excessive to proof the Long Sit just prior to doing sits and downs every time you show the dog. (Of course, you will have to leave the show grounds to do this, as proofing is considered training.) On the other hand, if you have no problem with the Retrieve exercise, while an occasional challenge will keep the exercise interesting, there is no reason to make every single Retrieve a monumental proofing test.

How extensively you proof should also depend on your dog's personality. Some dogs thrive on challenges, while others are easily stressed by having to perform and, if pushed, may have a nervous breakdown. By reading the anxiety level in your dog, you will know whether to proof further or simplify an exercise.

Good training provides the dog with a balance between the confidence of knowing he can do an exercise by just doing it and the proofing, which keeps him thinking about what he is doing while stretching his level of confidence. A shy Sheltie who is made to retrieve a dumbbell from next to a person's leg gains the confidence he needs to retrieve from anywhere in the ring. This same shy Sheltie need not be made to retrieve his dumbbell from next to a vicious dog as this might traumatize the Sheltie to a point where he would no longer even attempt the exercise.

A basic rule of proofing is that if you set a dog up to be wrong, and he is, you do not correct, but rather *help* him to be right. Only after repetition, if you feel the dog is not trying, should mild correction be introduced.

Do not proof every exercise you train in one session. Strengthen and test one exercise at a time. This way, you don't upset a dog's confidence in several areas of training at once.

19

Homework Counts– When It's Done Right!

Beginning students are instructed to do 10 minutes of homework with their dogs every day. What exactly is homework?

1. A 10-minute session, or two 5-minute sessions, is really all that is required to effectively train a dog, provided the handler is making full use of the 10 minutes.

2. Choose a time of the day when you are in good spirits and when your dog is awake. Don't drag him out of a sound sleep, throw the collar on and expect response. Some low-energy dogs respond better if confined to a crate for a couple of hours before practice.

3. Before you start to work, write down on a piece of paper exactly what you plan to work on. You need not practice *everything* every day. Concentrate on no more than three exercises when in the learning stages. Choose an exercise that you enjoy, an exercise the dog enjoys and then something you both need to work on!

4. Always begin with a short (two-minute) warm-up of heeling or play for your dog. Vary your patterns. One day you might concentrate on only right turns. Do a lot of happy talking and get him excited about what he is going to do next. Avoid any major corrections for the first few minutes of training. This allows the dog to ready his mind and body in preparation for work without the anxiety of a correction. This helps you establish a positive working attitude with the dog.

5. If you have a particular problem exercise or an exercise that the dog has just recently learned, work that exercise briefly, then do something the dog understands well and then return to the problem exercise.

6. Do *not* become patterned. That is to say, do not work things in the same order or in the same place every time. If you did a Recall in one direction one day, do it in another direction the next.

7. Work briskly while correcting deliberately without running or diving at the dog.

8. Keep it fun! Play ball between exercises if necessary if you find the dog is not alert and motivated. If you or your dog gets bored, stop and think about how you can make the exercises more challenging (see Chapter 18, Proofing).

9. Always end each session on a positive note. The last thing a dog does should be something he does well. Always leave him with the feeling that he has succeeded. If he has done nothing well, just play a favorite game or roll on the ground to let him know that you still love him. End training before the dog is too tired to perform.

10. As the dog gains experience and you have been training for a few months, you can extend the training sessions in an effort to help the dog build stamina. Train as long as you want to, but stop before the dog is too tired to learn.

11. If, while teaching or proofing, you get into a session with your dog where he is repeatedly unsuccessful, either stop what you are doing and come back to it tomorrow, or simplify the exercise so that the dog has a small success to end on. If a dog is confused about an exercise and you don't work through it, have no fear—he will still be confused tomorrow. Then you can both come back to it rested and ready to try again. Sometimes, with a fresh outlook, the dog has sorted through the confusion while you were *not* working on it! It's a lot like "sleeping on something," and when you wake up, the answer is suddenly apparent. Dogs learn things as they think about them, not only during training sessions. I think of it this way: During training I plant seeds and then I let them grow as the dog has time to rest and think about what I tried to teach him.

20

The Fifth-Week Plateau

As a trainer of dogs, it is important for you to know as much as possible about how dogs learn.

My experience training dogs seems to suggest a distinct learning pattern. When learning a new command, dogs demonstrate progress daily for a few weeks. After approximately 4 weeks or 32 days, something very unusual happens. The dog acts as if he has never heard the command before! He appears confused and makes a poor, if any, attempt to respond. For the naïve trainer, this can be a devastating, depressing, not to mention frustrating experience.

Interestingly enough, whether you train the dog or not for the next few days, approximately 5 to 10 days later the dog's memory of the desired response has returned! I have heard this phenomenon referred to as "the fifth-week plateau."

There are various theories as to why this occurs. Some suggest that when a dog first learns something, the information goes into his short-term memory. It is hypothesized that when the information is in transit from short-term memory to long-term memory, the dog is unable to recall it.

Similar observations have been documented by other trainers.

Karen Pryor, in her book *Don't Shoot the Dog,* refers to a "pre-learning dip." She explains:

> *You have just shaped a behavior, and now you are bringing it under stimulus control. But just as the subject seems to be showing signs of responding to the stimulus, it suddenly not only stops responding to the stimulus, but stops responding altogether. It acts as if it had never heard of the thing you shaped it to do.*

Pryor has a theory about why this strange learning behavior occurs. She writes:

> *What is going on in my opinion is that at first the subject is learning a cue without really being aware of doing so; the trainer sees only a heartening tendency toward slowly increasing correct performance. But then as the subject notices the cue and becomes aware that the signal has something to do with whether it gets reinforced. At that point it attends to the signal rather than offering the behavior.*

As trainers, this phenomenon helps explain some strange behavior. Any time we teach a dog something, there appears to be a period of time when he acts as if he never learned it. We can theorize why this happens, but perhaps this is not as important as simply expecting it to occur and avoiding our own frustrations.

Plateaus are easily recognized. A dog who, for example, has been going down for four weeks on command only, suddenly becomes totally bewildered, for no apparent reason, like he has never heard the word before in his life. This is a plateau. As the trainer, you should proceed as if you were first teaching the exercise.

The dog's learning process is further complicated by the fact that a dog will probably reach a plateau for every step of the exercise you ever teach him! Rather than trying to keep track of which plateaus have been reached, you are better off to train through these periods and understand why the dog is not responding like he once was.

Different dogs reach plateaus at different rates. The 32 days is only an average. I have also noticed that the length of time spent at a plateau varies from dog to dog. Some dogs pass through a plateau in as little as 3 days, others go for as long as 14 days. There are people who observe that their dogs train and learn better if they are not worked every day. Could it be that they miss having to deal with some of the learning plateaus?

21

Using Food in Obedience Training

In the past 10 years, it has become very popular to use food (that is, treats) along with traditional approaches to dog training. Food can be used in different ways, and the trainer must learn to use it correctly if the food is to enhance training and not detract from it. Let's take a look at how food can be used to train dogs:

- **Lure:** In the teaching phase of any exercise, a treat can be used as a lure to show the dog where and how he should move his body. We initially lure dogs into "front" and "finish" positions and even along our left side to first teach heeling.

- **Target:** Food can be used as a target to get a dog to look to a specific spot. It is very useful to put a piece of food in your mouth to get a big dog to look up to a spot (your mouth) in the middle of your body. For a small dog, put the food between your knees. (Note: I never use food as a target for Go Outs. See Chapter 46, Go Out, to understand why.)

- **Distraction:** Food can be used as a distraction to teach a dog to focus on Recalls, signals and scent articles.

- **Reward:** In most cases food is given to the dog as a reward. Always remember to praise the dog verbally first and then give the treat. If you reverse this order and give the dog a treat followed by verbal praise, you have essentially praised the dog for swallowing the food!

- **Motivation:** Food is often used to motivate dogs to want to work with you and to keep boring repetitions of exercises interesting. I use food repeatedly when teaching and perfecting fronts and finishes because these movements make no sense to a dog and require constant drilling to get them accurate. A hungry dog will willingly work with you on fronts and finishes without losing interest if food is offered.

- **Bribe:** Food should never be used as a bribe to get the dog to decide to do something in training. This is where many trainers get into trouble. Let's look at the Recall exercise as an example. When first teaching a Recall, it is perfectly acceptable to lure a dog to you with a treat. But at some point, the trainer must stop using the treat and enforce the Recall, which the dog now understands, with a correction. I will even go as far as to use the food, held by someone else, as a distraction, and call the dog away from the food to me. You must get a Recall (or any exercise) that is based on understanding and respect for the trainer and is not dependent on a dog being hungry and a treat being in the trainer's hand.

FOOD IS A PRIMARY REINFORCER

Food is considered by behaviorists to be a primary reinforcer. This means food is of major importance to a dog because he cannot live without eating. (Toys are considered to be secondary reinforcers because dogs can live without them.) While it is true that some dogs are more motivated by food than others, all dogs will die if deprived of food. When you choose to use food in training, be aware that you are using a powerful tool. When and how you reinforce a behavior with food carries a lot of weight. Studies have proven that if you reward a behavior with food, the dog will be more likely to repeat that behavior. Be careful what you reinforce!

WHERE TO FEED

If you read that someone is handing out $100 bills at 42nd Street and 5th Avenue in New York City and you are planning to go to the city, where would you go? If you are motivated by money, I bet you'd go to 42nd Street and 5th Avenue—certainly not to 43rd Street and 5th Avenue! What does all this have to do with dog training?

When a dog receives a treat for sitting in heel position, he is more likely to return to "heel" position. If, as I've observed many people do, you give a treat to your dog when he is standing crooked in front of you, the chances of the dog repeating that position increase. You may think you are rewarding an exercise that the dog has just completed, but to the dog, who learns in the context of situations, you have rewarded him for exactly what he was doing when he ate the treat.

If you are teaching your dog to heel, reward with your left hand on the left side of your body, palm facing the dog and your hand straight up over the dog's head. If you attempt to reward with your right hand, you teach your dog to wrap around your leg. We use this technique (feeding with your right hand) when we teach the about turn and we want the dog to wrap around our legs!

For fronts, always point to the food and deliver the food with both hands simultaneously so the dog doesn't look at one hand as being more important, thus throwing off the concept of finding the center of your body.

WHAT KIND OF TREATS

Treats should be very small pieces of healthy, moist, easily swallowed tidbits of food. Try to avoid very salty foods if you are using a lot of treats. I like to use pieces of meat, chicken and string cheese. Figure the amount you are feeding during training into your dog's daily rations so he doesn't gain weight. Vary the treats you use in one training session to maintain the dog's interest. Make sure your dog is hungry, or treats won't work.

HOW TO PHASE OUT TREATS

I phase out food as lures or targets as soon as the dog demonstrates that he can move his body into the desired position. Treats used to motivate and reward continue throughout training. The goal is to ask more and more of the dog before he gets his reward. Initially, a dog may heel a few steps and get a treat. Eventually, the dog must do an entire heeling pattern before he gets a treat. In the end, the dog does an entire class of multiple exercises before he leaves the ring, goes to his crate and gets a treat.

Pointing to food for a straight front. Remember to deliver the food with both hands!

Whenever you are drilling exercises that are not really fun for the dog, use more treats. Fade out the treats on the exercises the dog likes to do. Certain breeds of dogs are born with more desire to play the game of obedience than others. It is therefore common sense that you will probably need to use more food when training an Afghan Hound than if you are working a high-drive Border Collie!

WHEN NOT TO USE FOOD

There are some very high-drive dogs who are willing to work for the sake of being able to run, jump and get your attention. There is no need to use food to motivate dogs like these. In fact, you can over motivate them to the point where the dog is so excited that he can't learn what you are trying to teach. Some dogs get so crazed when there is food around that it actually slows down their thinking and becomes a major distraction. Since we don't begin teaching amid major distractions, treats for this kind of dog are a disadvantage.

Since food is usually a motivator, I don't use it when working on stays. Dogs don't need to be motivated to stay still, they just need to do it! A dog expecting to receive a treat is more likely to move toward the handler in anticipation of the return. Use the food to teach the positions of sit, down and stand, but use verbal praise as a reward, and correction when necessary, to get a dog to stay in position.

Food carries with it a pleasurable quality of giving and caretaking. I have known handlers who become addicted to giving their dogs treats. The act of becoming a human Pez dispenser becomes so comfortable that the handlers have difficulty weaning their dog (and themselves) away from food treats. There appears to be a real emotional element to feeding dogs when training—so much so that I've even had students cry when I wouldn't let them give treats to their dogs who needed to progress in training. Be careful. To some people, food equals love, and training with treats can get out of control!

22

Cross-Training Your Dog

It is now possible to train and compete with your dog in many different performance events. The AKC has recently created the concept of Versatility Titles. These titles are awarded to dogs who have completed degrees in at least three different canine sports. Now it is common for dogs to be training for the breed ring, obedience, agility, tracking and instinctive areas such as hunting, herding and earthdog, simultaneously. There are both advantages and disadvantages to training a dog for different tasks, and trainers must be careful not to confuse commands. The order in which you teach different concepts is also important, to avoid confusion and maintain motivation in the dog.

ORDER OF TRAINING

With a puppy, I begin teaching the pup to walk on a leash in preparation for show handling if that is part of the puppy's future. Learning to stand, being examined and getting lots of socialization around show environments follows next. I think it is important to expose a young dog to instinctive activities such as herding, hunting, earthdog and so on but not necessarily to start formal training. When a dog understands gaiting and standing, you can begin some basic obedience. Teaching a Recall, sit and down will provide a good foundation for agility and future obedience. I usually don't begin to teach a dog to track, which requires putting their nose to the ground, until after a dog has been taught to heel with attention. It's easier to teach attention (head up) *before* you have taught tracking (head down).

61

COMMANDS

You can use any word in any language to mean anything you want when commanding a dog. The only requirements are that the word sounds unique from the other commands, has only one meaning and both you and the dog understand the meaning.

As you begin to cross-train, be careful of the commands you choose. For example, if "out" is going to mean move away from the handler in agility, then you can't use "out" to mean release the dumbbell. Try using "give" when you want the dog to release something from his mouth.

Dogs never learn to spell. They only learn how words sound. If two words sound similar, it can cause confusion. If you are going to teach your dog to herd, be careful of the commands you use for "stay" or "wait" exercises. The herding flanking command "way to me" (go counterclockwise around the sheep) sounds very similar to "wait." If you teach your dog to "come" in obedience and it means to sit front, then you need to choose a different command for "come" in agility, which means come to my side. (I use the word "here" to mean come to my side in agility.) The herding flank command to go clockwise around the sheep is "come by." If you have already taught "come" in obedience or agility, you might want to use "go by" in herding.

As you can see, it is necessary to work out the language you are going to use *before* you train your dog. Some commands can also be used in different venues. For example, a "jump" command used in obedience is easily understood in agility.

Hand signals used in different activities must also be specific. Directional signals in obedience can often be used in hunting and field work. However, sometimes a "drop" signal in obedience is used to mean "go back" in field work. Be sure you understand exactly what your signals mean before you attempt to teach them to your dog! Be consistent.

DISADVANTAGES OF CROSS TRAINING

As you introduce your dog to different activities, the dog is going to show a preference for some exercises over others. For dogs who are not highly motivated, teaching them fun activities like agility and tracking can make obedience and breed handling seem boring. For dogs who do not have a high energy level, trying to teach several things at once can require too many hours of training for the dog. For low-energy dogs, doing one activity at a time is often a more productive approach.

Any time you add new information to existing information, you cause confusion and/or insecurity about the old information. When cross training, confusion is common. As you continue training, the confusion eventually sorts itself out.

ADVANTAGES OF CROSS TRAINING

There are more advantages than disadvantages to cross training. Most dogs thrive on learning a variety of different things. Often, what is learned in one activity can be used to help a dog understand something in another activity. For example, learning the pause table in agility helps a dog learn to do Utility hand signals without moving out of place. Jumping learned in agility helps all jumping needed in obedience. The lie-down taught in herding helps a dog on contacts in agility and on the Drop on Recall in obedience.

When a dog is worked in different sports, the dog gets more experience and becomes more comfortable in a ring. Cross training improves confidence and the dog's overall physical fitness. The handler gets to meet different groups of people interested in dog activities and to observe his dogs learning in all different settings. Both dog and handler are usually more motivated and have more outlets for success when participating in several canine events.

Finally, all training is based on communication and motivation. Whatever the activity, the principles of good training apply.

23

The On and Off Switch of Dog Attention

No dog or person works all the time. For a dog to be reliable and accurate when he is obeying a command, we must have his undivided attention. It is unrealistic to demand such concentration from a dog indefinitely, so we have created an *On* and *Off* switch that lets the dog know when he is working and when he is not. It is very important that the owner be aware of *when* his dog is on a command and make sure to enforce the command. I have observed handlers at a dog show turn to their dogs and say, "Heel" and then proceed to walk leisurely to the restroom while the dog lags, sniffs and does whatever else six feet of leash will allow. Did the owner really mean "heel"? Does "heel" only count in the ring? How is the dog supposed to know which "heel" is the one where you want his attention? A simple, "Fido, let's go" would have gotten them both to the restroom and would have been a lot less damaging to Fido's training.

Think about what you say and only say what you mean and plan to enforce. If your dog jumps up on you, do you say, "Get *down*"? Do you really mean "down" (as in " . . . on the floor"), or would "off" have been more appropriate? When you leave your house, do you turn to your dog and say, "Now you *stay* there"? Is that the same "stay" that you will use in the ring? How is the dog to know the difference?

The Off switch is very easy to teach. I use the command "okay," throw my hands up over my head, yell, cheer, play with the dog and, by golly, he realizes that he's off duty. Throwing your hands up over your head helps draw the dog's attention up toward your face. Do not bend to pet a dog you have just released. Let the dog come up to you for praise. I like to teach beginners the Off switch first because the dogs learn it so quickly and respond so positively. It helps to generate exuberant praise, which is sometimes difficult to get from beginners. Pleased with themselves for having taught their dogs the Off switch so quickly, handlers are now very motivated to teach the On switch. What they do not realize is that teaching a dog to pay attention and to concentrate is perhaps the most difficult task they have ahead of them.

The word "sit" is the On switch to let the dog know that work is beginning and it's time to pay attention. It really doesn't matter what word you use, but I have found "sit" to be convenient when showing your dog because in every ring you ever walk into and before each exercise in Novice, Open and Utility, you are permitted to turn to your dog and say, "Sit." When "sit" also means "pay attention," you are off to a good start.

In my own classes and with my own dogs, attention is taught *before* heeling. I have yet to understand how a dog who is not paying attention can learn to heel correctly.

Before you can even attempt to get attention, you must have a dog who knows that it is possible to sit and stand (eventually heel) while looking up at his owner, and you must have a dog who has learned to accept eye contact. You can prepare a young dog for attention work by making an effort to look into your dog's eyes, stroking him under the chin and talking to him softly. Looking at his owner should be a pleasant experience for the dog. Part of your petting and grooming time should be devoted to looking into your dog's eyes. Small dogs may be in laps or on tables. Take the time to get down on the floor with your dogs and establish eye contact. Any time your dog looks up at you around the house, acknowledge him with a pleasant word or two.

Before starting formal training, try to establish a one-on-one relationship between your dog and yourself. If your dog lives outside, take the time to do these exercises with your dog as well. All potentially nasty dogs or owners who might fear putting their faces near their dogs should be handled separately and differently! You must first be dominant over your dog before you can expect to establish eye contact and demand attention. Please note that when I refer to eye contact I am talking about a smiling, friendly face. Don't stare or glare at your dog unless you want to get bitten or upset the dog. In dog language, a stare is often interpreted as a challenge.

Attention for the adult dog is started with a dog on a collar and leash, sitting next to you in heel position. After you command "sit," since you really mean "sit and pay attention to me," you must enforce the "pay attention" part. You might find that simply talking to your dog gets him to look up at you. If this works, praise him as soon as he looks up, and then release him with an "okay" (Off switch). Start over. If the dog is still not looking up, you can try gently tapping the top of his head with your left fist. I call this "Knock, knock! Is anybody home?" Often the dog will look up just to see who is doing a tap dance on his head, at which point you praise and release.

Holding food or toys works nicely for some dogs to initially get them to look up, but be honest with yourself and understand that if you are holding a toy or food, the dog is looking at the object and not at you. Used initially the food or toy is helpful in teaching the dog to *lift his head*. Eventually, the dog must learn to look at *you*.

When we use food and toys to get the dog's attention, we refer to it as "artificial attention." Once the dog learns to read the handler's upper body cues, the attention becomes "real attention." The dog is now motivated to watch the handler because the dog gets useful information about heeling from the handler's body cues. This "real attention" is reinforced every time the dog knows where the handler is going next. Now there is no more need for the food and toys that were the initial "artificial attention."

For some really difficult cases, you can get very mechanical and physically lift, turn and hold the dog's head so that he is looking up into your eyes. Praise and release.

After three weeks of encouraging the dog to lift his head and watch you, if he doesn't, it is time to incorporate a correction. The correction comes in the form of a gentle tug on the leash up toward your face. If the dog does not look up, try increasing the strength to a "pop" you give on the leash. After a maximum of three pops on the leash, if the dog has not responded, reach down and lift the dog's head up. Praise and release the dog. Work until the dog's rear goes to the floor and his head looks up at you on the command "sit." Gradually extend the length of the time the dog must look at you before he is released. Whenever the dog looks off, start with a gentle pop on the leash first. When the dog will reliably look up at you for 30 seconds, it is time to add distractions. Start with mild distractions, for example, a person walking past the dog. Gradually increase the distractions to a person offering the dog food or petting the dog. When you begin any new distraction, and the dog looks off, first reach down and help the dog by bringing his head back up to you. After some repetitions, if the dog continues to get distracted, you can correct with a mild leash pop.

As you do this two or three times, you can expect that the dog will try to lean on you when he sits. This is because if he is touching you, he thinks he will avoid a correction. Do not permit him to lean or even put his foot on yours. You will also notice that the dog will glance at a distraction for a brief second and glance back right away. This is part of his learning process. Do not pop until the dog *focuses his eyes* on a distraction. Glancing at this point will be accepted. Eventually you will be able to stop him from glancing away with a quick snap up on the lead. If the dog resists the sit, take your time and enforce the sit before you add the distractions.

If you are not impressing the dog in the least by popping with the leash, I would suggest you try a more effective type of collar or leash. If you are training with a thin leash, try a wide leather leash. If a buckle isn't effective, go to a prong collar. You must reach a point of leverage where the dog works to avoid the correction (see Chapter 13, Training Equipment).

When the dog will sit and look up attentively at his handler, you have mastered the On switch. To maintain attention while heeling, go back to holding the dog's head in the sitting position. Command "heel" and take one step forward as you hold the dog's head up. Then praise and release by throwing your arms upward. Gradually lengthen the number of steps you can take while holding the dog's head up. Increase your speed until the dog is trotting as you are holding his head up. When you can move the dog at a trot in a large circle to the left and the dog is not resisting your holding of his head, you are ready to proceed.

With the pinky of your left hand hooked into the buckle collar, it is easy to lift, turn and hold the dog's head up so that he looks up at you.

An alternate way to hold the dog's head up is to hook the thumb of your left hand into his collar.

Holding the dog's head up as you start walking with a "let's go" command.

Holding the small dog's head up as you walk for a few steps.

Start again with the "sit" command and hold the dog's head as you start walking. When you and the dog are in rhythm and feel relaxed, let go of the dog's head and start talking to the dog. If this holds the dog's attention for a few steps, praise and release! If the dog looks away as soon as you let go, reach down and bring his head back up. After a few repetitions of this, you will be ready to introduce a correction if the dog does not choose to walk with his head up. To teach the dog the correction, start moving as you hold the dog's head. Let go of the dog's head and if he looks away, without stopping your forward movement, pop up on the lead. After a maximum of three pops, if the dog has not looked back up at you, reach down and pull his head back up. If the dog is not willing to hold his head up without your holding it, you may have to increase the severity of the pop or change collars. At any time that you lose dog attention, *do something!* Either help the dog lift his head, encourage him, or correct him, depending on why you lost his attention.

What if every time you took your dog into the obedience ring, he gave you 100 percent of his undivided attention? How low a score could you possibly receive?

I was asked to help a girl with a Gordon Setter who said her dog had a lagging problem. While it was true the dog was five feet behind his owner, the problem, I explained, was not lagging, it *was attention!* The dog didn't even know who his owner was, much less how to heel for her! If you look at the mistakes dogs make in the obedience ring, more than 80 percent of them are due to a lack of attention on the part of the dog or handler (let's be fair about this).

We know that it is possible to get a dog's attention and to keep it in the ring because we see the dogs trained by the top trainers staring adoringly up at their owners, waiting anxiously for their next command. So, what's the secret? How do you get dog attention? Are the stories about bathing in chopped liver really true?

For those of you just beginning to strive for your dog's attention, I suggest the following: First you must show the dog that it is possible for him to walk at your side or sit in front of you while maintaining eye contact (or contact with some part of your body for small dogs). You can trick him into doing this by baiting him with food or with a favorite toy. If this doesn't work, you can be very mechanical and lift or hold his head with your hands. Praise all desired positions. Once the dog knows that it is possible for him to walk with his head up (two to three weeks), then he must be corrected gently for not doing so. Lead snaps or gentle tugs on whiskers or cheeks often convince him to look up. A combination of your voice, the leash and your left hand giving "love pinches" on his cheeks used randomly is effective. Any single approach used repeatedly is soon tuned out by the dog.

Personally, I never say "Watch me." By the time you say "Watch me," the dog has already looked off and you've missed the chance to correct him. I will, however, after a correction say, "Guess what, you weren't watching" or "You've missed it."

The biggest mistake made in training classes today is that first the dogs are taught to heel and months later, when a student expresses interest in showing his dog, someone makes the astute observation that he better get his dog's attention! Heeling cannot happen without attention. Therefore, I strongly recommend that you have the dog's attention *before* you attempt to teach him to heel.

Dog attention in the obedience ring is not optional. It is necessary if you are going to earn degrees. The more attention you have, the easier it is to train the dog and the better the dog performs in the ring. You can teach attention with gimmicks, but in the end it must be enforced with correction. If you never take another step without your dog's attention, you will be on your way to becoming a very good trainer.

We consider a dog to be paying attention when he is looking at some part of your body, not necessarily into your face. For most breeds, for a dog to be in heel position, he would have to look at your left hip or shoulder. If this dog was to try to see your face while heeling, he would be forging or walking sideways (out of heel position). Handlers who twist their upper bodies to stare at their dog while heeling are not heeling in a "natural" manner and can lose points for "guiding the dog with your eyes" under the American Kennel Club rules.

We do ask that the dog look *up* at your body and not down to your shoes. How high up a dog can look will depend on the dog's structure. Good shoulder layback enables a dog to look higher. Every dog can look up in a sitting position. Some cannot look up very high when they are standing next to their handler. This is determined by the height of the dog and the structure of the dog's shoulder.

24

Teaching the Dog to Heel

Before a dog can learn to heel, he must know how to walk looking up at his owner constantly. The dog should be taught to look at some point on the trainer's left side and not necessarily into the trainer's eyes. The point the dog is taught to focus on will vary with the size and structure of the dog and handler (see Chapter 23, The On and Off Switch of Dog Attention).

Before we begin, it's important to understand certain terms.

- **Heel:** To walk at the handler's left side, neither forging ahead nor lagging behind; to sit automatically upon stopping. (This is possible only if the dog is paying attention.)

- **Heel Position:** Have your dog sit at your left side, parallel to you, neither touching your leg nor more than six inches from it. Position him so that the area between his head and shoulders (this usually works out to be his ear!) is even with your left hip. For small dogs, envision an imaginary line from the middle of your hip down to the ground. Keep your dog's ear even with this line. Your dog is now in heel position.

- **Heel on Leash:** This is the first heeling exercise the dog will learn. While remaining in heel position, the dog will learn how to move along with you, to turn right, to turn left, to turn about, to change pace and to sit when you halt. Be patient! This exercise will require much practice over a long period of time to become perfected, even though it may seem very simple to you.

INTRODUCTION TO HEELING

Heeling for the ring is the same as dancing with your dog. It is a preplanned, carefully rehearsed performance designed to appear "natural."

For a dog and handler to heel well, it appears as though both are doing exactly the same thing at exactly the same time, much like two people social dancing. Logic tells us that this is impossible and that one must be leading and one following. A dog learns to heel by learning to read cues from his handler so that he can tell when a turn or change of pace is about to happen, before it actually happens!

THE THEORY OF BALANCE IN HEELING

When you teach a dog to heel, what you are really teaching him is how to maintain a constant position next to you as you increase and decrease speed and change directions. For a dog to be in a perfect heel position, he must be in balance next to you. His weight must be evenly distributed left to right and front to back. If the dog loses his balance, he will either fall into you (called crowding), fall away from you (called going wide), fall forward (called forging) or fall backward (called lagging).

Dogs walk around in everyday life in perfect balance. They rarely fall or trip. It is only when we insist they walk with their heads tilted up to pay attention that balance must be relearned. A dog heeling learns to stay in balance by shifting his weight in response to your heeling cues.

To understand balance, think of riding a bicycle. If you lean too far in one direction, you fall in that direction. Have you ever taught a child to ride a bicycle? How

The dog walks with his head tilted up to pay attention to the left side of the handler's body.

BOHM MARRAZZO PHOTOGRAPHY

The bicycle is off balance, leaning toward the handler.

By lifting straight up, the handler can bring the bicycle back to a point of balance.

The dog is helped into balance by pulling steadily straight up on the leash. This is called a "lift and hold" and lasts for only a second.

did you help the child learn to feel balance? Usually it's done by holding the back of the bicycle seat, and if the bicycle starts to fall off-center, you lift up and help bring it back to center.

The same is true in heeling! If the dog next to you starts to fall in toward you (often on right or left turns), lift straight up over the dog's neck on your buckle collar, hold for a second and then release pressure on the leash and praise the dog. This "lift and hold" can be repeated as often as is necessary. By repeatedly bringing the dog back into balance, he will eventually learn how to maintain it himself. (See the photo on the bottom of page 73.)

Dogs need to learn to move with their heads up while staying balanced left to right (on turns) and front to back (on changes of pace, including halts). To improve balance left to right, practice circles and then turns, lifting up on the leash whenever necessary to bring the dog back into balance. To improve a dog's balance front to back, practice changes of pace and halts. When a dog falls forward, lift up his head and hold him for a second, then release and praise. (Notice this is a "hold" with the collar and leash, not a "pop" as in a correction for attention.)

When a dog lags, it's because his weight is too far back. To fix this, get the dog to lower his head by lowering your hand with the leash. The dog is still capable of paying attention with his head in a lower, attentive position.

If you want a dog to slow down, get him to raise his head. This shortens his stride, resulting in a decrease of speed. When you want a dog to increase his speed, lower his head. This frees up his shoulders and enables him to extend his stride and go faster. All dogs must lower their heads to some degree when they speed up on the fast, the about turn, the right turn and the outside of the Figure 8. That's right, the Figure 8, where so many dogs tend to lag on the outside circle because they need to learn to bend and be encouraged to lower their heads slightly. The Figure 8 is really nothing more than an exercise in raising and lowering the dog's head at appropriate times.

The dog's head is lifted up to prevent forging (falling forward) on a slow heel.

The dog's head is lowered to increase his speed and prevent lagging.

In the extreme case, a decrease in speed is a halt. In the halt, the dog's head is the highest. When the dog goes from the halt back to heeling, he must lower his head slightly to shift his weight forward before he can start moving. Slow starts come from a dog who is not encouraged to lower his head. He cannot maintain the heel position.

CUEING THE SHIFTS OF WEIGHT THAT RESULT IN A CHANGE OF PACE

Heeling, then, is the art of teaching a dog to raise and lower his head to increase and decrease his speed, and to turn his head left and right when needed, enabling him to maintain a constant heel position next to the handler's left leg.

The handler cues the dog (who has already been taught to look up and pay attention) by shifting his own weight and turning his own head to change directions. These cues are natural shifts of weight we use to walk in everyday life, and therefore they meet the requirement of appearing "smooth and natural" in the obedience ring.

Any time you increase your speed from a walk to a run or from a standing position to a walk, you shift your weight forward. Try standing up straight and stationary. Now, lean backward and see how difficult it is to start walking. Start from a stationary position and try leaning forward as you start walking. Which is easier? Which feels more natural? Watch someone who is not training a dog go from a walk to a run. Can you see them shift their weight forward?

Any time you decrease your speed from a walk to a halt or from a run to a walk, you shift your weight backward. Start running and try to stop without standing up! It's not easy to do, is it? And it certainly doesn't feel natural. If you walk down a steep hill, you naturally shift your weight backward to keep from falling forward down the hill. You should have a similar feeling when you go from a fast to a normal, or from a normal to a slow.

THE DOG LEARNS TO FOLLOW THE CUES

The goal now is to teach the dog that when you lean forward, he should lower his head, and when you stand straight, he should raise his head. This is initially taught by holding a piece of food or a toy in your left hand over the dog's head as he is heeling. Any time you lean forward, lower the food out in front of the dog. Any time you stand up and shift your weight back, raise the food over the dog's head, which will cause him to lift his head higher and, in effect, slow his pace. Soon the dog learns to anticipate what he should do in response to your shift of weight. At this point, stop using the food and hold the leash in your left hand. Keep reminding the dog by lowering the hand with the leash every time you increase speed and raising the hand with the leash every time you decrease speed.

While each dog watches his handler in a slightly different way and responds differently to bends, leans and shifts of weight, the easiest way for a handler to standardize his body movements is to be aware of where he puts his feet. Thus, we talk in terms of consistent footwork or *footcues*.

YOU LEARN THE STEPS

Before you can teach a dog to heel, you must be comfortable with your footwork, like learning the dance steps before you try doing it to the music. When learning the steps, it helps to wear comfortable shoes or sneakers with good side support. This prevents your feet from rocking side to side as you step.

A right turn for a large dog. Notice that there is space between the right and left feet. This cues the dog while single tracking the turn. Single tracking keeps your feet out of the dog's lane, so to speak. The space keeps the rhythm of heeling smooth and consistent on the turns.

All footcues for large dogs are done with the left foot, since the left leg and hip are what the dog sees move. Some small dogs shy away when they see a foot coming toward them. For these dogs, since they are below your waist and have their eyes focused on your legs and not your hip, you may cue the left turn and right turn with your right foot.

About Turn

The about turn is twice a right turn, so the cue step is the same, only sharper.

About turns are executed so that you come out on the same line you went in on. This is to say, if you followed a painted line, your about turns would be correct. A keyhole turn, as illustrated below, is incorrect.

All turns must be executed without stopping or pausing. Rhythm should be consistent, even on turns. In the AKC obedience ring, military turns receive a deduction. The rules specify "smooth and natural."

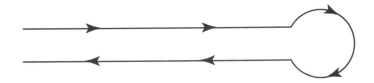

RHYTHM

For you and your dog to appear smooth and natural in the ring, you must have a rhythm between you.

Start by learning a normal rhythm by heeling in a circle to the left with your dog on a snug leash. The dog should be trotting, and you should be moving

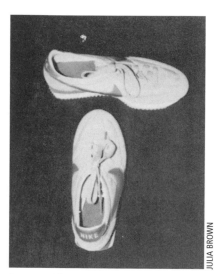

JULIA BROWN

Step one of footwork for the about turn: Make a T with the left foot.

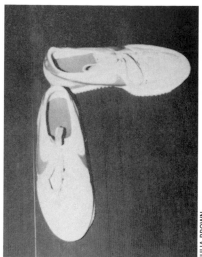

JULIA BROWN

Step two of the about turn: Make a V. Notice that the feet are heel to heel. This ensures that you will come out of the turn on the same line that you walked into it on. Only the right foot has moved since step one.

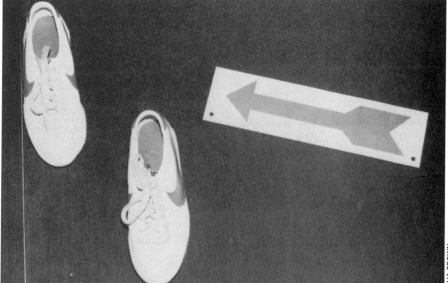

JULIA BROWN

The final step of the about turn: As you walk out of the turn with your left foot, the size of the step you take varies with the speed at which your dog can execute the turn. The faster the dog, the bigger the step.

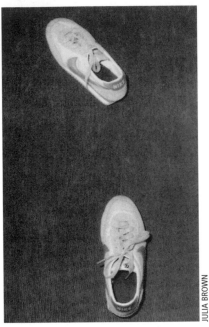

JULIA BROWN

A left turn for a large dog. Notice the space between the steps. Do not shorten your steps on left turns.

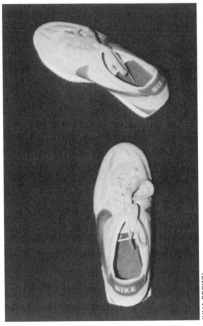

JULIA BROWN

A left turn for a small dog. Because these dogs are below your waist and have their eyes focused on your legs and not your hip, cue the left turn and right turn with your right foot. As the dog sees your right foot come down on an angle, he will learn the cue.

JULIA BROWN

A right turn for a small dog.

briskly. You will be able to feel when you and the dog are "in synch," sort of like walking with another person and being "in step." Try to find a popular song with the same rhythm as your normal speed. This will help you remember the rhythm. If songs are not easily recalled, you might purchase a battery-powered metronome, which can be easily fitted to your belt.

To do a fast, use the same rhythm as your normal pace, but take larger, leaping, running steps. For the slow, count out the same rhythm as the normal, but put a pause between each step. For example, 1 *and* 2 *and* 1 *and* 2. This will drop your pace by half. Be careful *not* to intentionally shorten your steps on the slow. Your steps will naturally shorten slightly as you shift your weight back and stand up. Dogs who start to sit when their handlers go into a slow are doing so because the dog is confusing the cue for the slow with the cue for a halt. On a halt we do not slow down.

You and your dog will score higher if you show the judge that your dog really can perform a slow and a fast. Do not try to fake either pace!

To cue the dog for an increase in speed (either slow to normal or normal to fast), lean forward as you step down on your left foot with a *faster, shorter* step. This alerts the dog to an increase in speed while covering any initial lag. When increasing speed, it is natural to lean forward slightly. Shift your weight forward; do not bend at the waist.

To cue the dog for a decrease in speed (either a fast to a normal or a normal to a slow), step out with your left foot and do a *longer, slower* step. This alerts the dog that the speed is decreasing while covering any initial forge. It is natural to shift your weight backward slightly when slowing down.

TEACHING THE DOG

Forward

Begin with the dog sitting in heel position. Hold the leash short so that the dog cannot get out of position. When you hear "forward," say your dog's name and give him a brisk, happy command to heel. Shift your weight forward and encourage the dog to lower his head. Then step forward on your left foot (that's the one the dog will soon learn to move with). If the dog does *not* get up and move with you as you begin walking, the short leash automatically keeps him with you. *Praise* immediately and continue walking. *Do not snap* the leash! It is not fair to snap (correct) a dog for what he hasn't yet learned.

Halt

As the term implies, the halt means to stop walking. In executing the halt, move *smoothly* to a stop—do not be abrupt. Halt by first standing up straight as you step on your left foot. Stop on the right foot, then bring the left foot up into place (the dog moves with your left foot, remember?). As you step down on your right foot, give your dog the command "sit," bringing your left foot up into place and gently pop upward on the leash. Be sure to guide the dog into a straight Sit-in-Heel position. (See the "opposing forces" photo on the top left of page 94.) Every sit is followed by *praise*. A good way to remember it is when you hear "halt," stand up, then step left, right, left.

CHANGING DIRECTIONS

If you watch people walking under natural conditions, you might notice that they look where they are going! If a person is about to turn a corner, they usually turn their heads first to see where they are going. This head turn causes a natural shift of weight, and the body easily follows. If you have ever led a horse on a halter, you know that wherever you turn the horse's head, his body easily follows.

ABOUT TURN

When you hear "about turn," you will turn 180 degrees to the right (away from the dog) and end up going on the same line in the opposite direction.

The about turn is cued with your eyes and your feet. When you hear "about turn," gently drop your eyes and head down and look at your left foot, which should be making a T. Then, keeping your head down, look at your right pocket (to turn your upper body). Then move your right foot into the V position. Finally, raise your eyes slowly to a spot about three feet in front of you on the floor, and continue walking.

For the dog to maintain heel position as you do an about turn, he must increase his speed and bend his body. In order for the dog to do this, he must lower his head. Encourage his head down the same as you would for any increase in speed. Lower your hand with the leash or bait the dog with food. A dog can and should maintain attention on the handler with his head lowered. There is a brief moment when the dog is actually forging on the about turn. As you look down and make a T, the dog should bend his head around to your right knee (temporarily out of heel position). By the time you finish the turn, the dog will be back in heel position. If you do not allow the dog to forge momentarily during the about turn, he will end up lagging slightly behind you as you come out of the turn.

FINDING THE CORNER TO MAKE A RIGHT TURN OR LEFT TURN

In preparation to cue the dog that you are about to make a 90-degree right or left turn, you must learn where to focus your eyes. Any abrupt head turn just prior to a turn in the ring should be considered to be unnatural and would receive a deduction. While it is natural for a handler to look where he is going, this "look" must be gentle and unobtrusive.

Imagine every turn as a right angle.

Right turn   Left turn

BRIDGET MCKNIGHT

BOHM MARRAZZO PHOTOGRAPHY

Step one of the about turn:
Look down and make a T.

BOHM MARRAZZO PHOTOGRAPHY

Look at your right pants pocket
(your upper body turns).

BOHM MARRAZZO PHOTOGRAPHY

Make a V by moving your right
foot.

BOHM MARRAZZO PHOTOGRAPHY

Bring your eyes up and walk
forward naturally.

What happens as you focus on a spot three feet off the corner and walk straight? Your head slowly and naturally turns. You almost feel as if your body is catching up to your eyes!

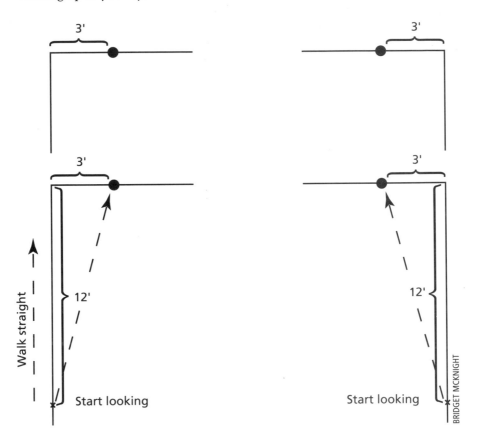

When you turn your head, you naturally shift your weight in preparation to turn. The dog learns to read this cue and also prepares for the turn! As you get ready to turn right, lean forward to cue the dog to speed up. As you prepare to turn left, stand up to cue the dog to slow down. Help the dog understand by raising or lowering your left hand with the leash or by guiding with food.

DOWN-CENTER-LINE EXERCISE

A good way to test your dog's understanding of the cues for right turn, left turn, about turn and halt is to do the Down-Center-Line exercise.

Heel with the dog down the middle of a ring toward a wall or barrier of gates. When you get about 12 feet from the end of the ring, cue with your eyes. Can you feel the dog notice a change? Does he already know what's going to happen at the end of the ring? With practice, he will!

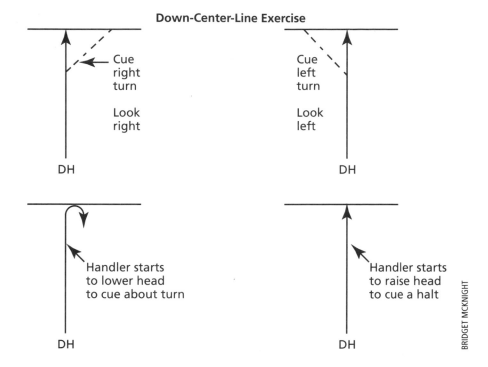

Down-Center-Line Exercise

Cue
right
turn

Look
right

DH

Cue
left
turn

Look
left

DH

Handler starts
to lower head
to cue about turn

DH

Handler starts
to raise head
to cue a halt

DH

BRIDGET MCKNIGHT

CUES IN THE RING

You should always know what the heeling pattern will be before you enter an obedience ring. Either you have watched someone go before you, or you have asked the judge to tell you because you are the first person in the ring. You must know where you are going before you can communicate it to the dog! Do not wait for the judge's command to turn before you cue your dog with your eyes and head. You may not anticipate a turn, but you can begin to gently look in the new direction you will be going, thus shifting your weight and alerting the dog. Remember, it is natural to look where you are going to walk next!

CROWDING

Dogs crowd their handlers for different reasons. Some dogs pay no attention to their trainers and have developed a system of leaning as a way of knowing where their handlers are without watching. I call this "heel by feel!"

I once gave a private lesson to a woman who said she only had one problem with her dog and that was crowding. After watching them heel for a few minutes, I stopped her and said, "I have good news for you and I have bad news. The good news is that we can certainly stop the crowding, but the bad news is that when we do, your dog will no longer be able to heel." Needless to say,

"Sit" means sit and pay attention! No heeling is started without the dog's attention. Notice how high the dog holds his head in the sit position.

this was a leaner, not a heeler. To improve the dog's heeling, the handler would have to start over from the beginning and teach the dog to heel while paying attention.

Some dogs only crowd when the handler stops and the dog sits. This can be caused by a handler who pets the dog into his body as praise for a sit.

Insecurity can cause crowding. A dog who is not confident around other dogs and people will often hug close to his owner. These dogs should be given lots of socialization and help and should not be corrected for hugging close. Sometimes by placing your left hand between the dog's head and your leg, you can gently get the nervous dog off of your leg.

For dogs who are paying attention and are not insecure, crowding may be an honest error of losing balance. Remember that once we teach a dog to walk with his head up paying attention, he must learn a new sense of balance.

RON REAGAN

Teaching the wrap about turn to the dog. By draping the leash at the dog's level in front of your legs you can guide the dog around your body as you do the about turn. The dog is held in place and no lead snaps are necessary. Lowering the leash helps the dog understand to lower his head.

JULIA BROWN

When guiding the dog around on the about turn, encourage the dog to lower his head.

TO CORRECT CROWDING

On Straight Heeling

Heel in a straight line, feet facing straight ahead as you drift left into the dog. This is accomplished by taking a straight step forward on your left foot, then crossing your right foot in front of your left foot, then another step forward with your left foot. Your feet remain facing straight ahead as you sidestep with your right foot. The left foot must go straight because if you sidestepped with it, you would be stepping directly into the dog, which would be unfair. After a few days of this, the dog will start to stay away from you.

For crowding on left turns and the inside circle of the Figure 8, rebalance the dog by pulling straight up on a leash attached to a buckle collar or prong collar. Hold up for one second, and then release the pressure. This "hold up" helps rebalance the dog who is falling into you (crowding). You can repeat the hold as many times as needed, but remember that each hold is only one second long. You can also help a dog balance on left turns and circles left by encouraging the dog to move his head away from you. Guide the dog's head with food so that it turns slightly to the left. He is still paying attention, but his head is not turned to the right. A dog who tries to turn left with his head turned right is very off balance! You try it!

Dogs Who Heel Wide

Heel in a straight line and while facing forward, drift right. You may also try incorporating a step right exercise (see the section on Doodling, page 94). If you are teaching the dog to heel with a short, taut leash, it is difficult for the dog to get too wide away from your leg.

FORGING

A forging dog is a dog whose shoulders are in front of his handler's left hip. Forging is usually a sign of a motivated, happy dog who is not in balance, and is the best of all heeling problems to have to deal with. Nevertheless, a forge will cost the same half point as a lag, and happy or not, the dog must learn proper heel position. If you are bumping your dog repeatedly on left turns, consider that he is probably forging and that his head is cranked to the right as he is trying to turn left.

Many handlers like their dogs to forge because it is easier for a handler to see where his dog is when he is in front. Be careful that you are absolutely certain where correct heel position is on your dog. Have an experienced eye observe you, or heel with your dog in front of mirrors or reflective windows. Even very good heeling dogs who understand the heel position will tend to creep up in heel position as the months go by, if the trainer is not careful to insist on an exact point.

When teaching a dog to heel by holding him on a snug leash in position, we hope he learns *where* to heel. Sometimes, however, when the leash is loosened as in preparation for the ring or Off-Leash Heeling and the dog forges, he must be helped. Begin by enforcing attention to the spot on your hip, leg, shoulder and so on where

RON REAGAN

Pointing out the heel position to the dog. The head and shoulders of the dog are in line with the handler's left hip.

the dog should be watching. This is simply done by pointing with a finger. Point while you heel slowly (it is easier for a dog to think while going slowly) on a loose leash. If the dog starts to forge, pull *up* on your leash in line with where the dog should be watching. This helps to rebalance him. *At no time is a dog snapped back* because this causes erratic heeling and does not teach the dog to maintain heel position.

When you first taught heeling, chances are your upper body was turned toward the dog in an effort to see where he was and if he was paying attention. Now, as you straighten up your posture in preparation for the ring, your right shoulder moves forward, causing a forge in the dog who is cued into your shoulder position. This problem is resolved as you concentrate on heeling with your body pointing straight ahead while learning to sense where the dog is and if he is paying attention.

Exercises that work to counteract forging are circles to the left, left turns, spirals left and teaching your dog to heel backwards.

For severe, chronic forgers who usually forge off leash, you can try to perfect the art of blocking your dog. As you see your dog start to inch forward, swing the side of your right foot into the dog's chest and make contact. Then quickly praise and continue walking. Begin this exercise on leash and slowly to get your coordination so as not to frighten the dog. When your dog is convinced that he might run into a foot, he is likely to stay back in heel position. Swinging a light dowel in front of the dog as you heel is also helpful in adjusting the forged position.

LAGGING

Very few experienced trainers have problems with lagging dogs. This is because their dogs are *never permitted to lag*. When dogs are worked on short, snug leashes and never given enough leash to lag, they never learn that they can.

Lagging is a problem of the new trainer who usually takes the dog off leash too soon to "see what will happen." What happens is that the dog learns how to lag. Lagging is also caused by people who do not permit their dogs to lower their heads, which is necessary for the dog to increase his speed. Do not confuse head position and attention. A dog can pay attention with his head turned to the right, left, and lowered slightly to allow an increase of speed.

When your dog can heel on a loose but short leash at all speeds and perform all turns comfortably, why should he ever lag?

Lagging is frequently caused by attempting to train the dog on a loose leash. When the dog lags, he is snapped forward (punished for what he has not yet learned), and he either fears future snaps or develops a bad, lethargic attitude about heeling. Why should a dog be anxious to do something new when he is likely to get corrected before he is taught?

It should *not* be possible for a dog to lag on leash unless someone allows it to happen! No dog should be asked to heel off leash until he can do it well and easily on leash.

If you have already caused a lagging problem, stop snapping, begging, coaxing and bribing, and start teaching the dog where heel position is with a short lead. Remember that to get a dog to speed up, you must get him to lower his head.

BENDING

If you have ever sat on a horse bareback as he made a turn, you have firsthand knowledge of what happens to a four-legged animal's spine as he bends his body. In order for a dog to make a tight turn, he must learn to bend his body either around the handler (right turn) or away from the handler (left turn).

Bending the spine begins with turning the animal's head and neck. Then the four-legged animal must step underneath himself with his inside hind leg. There are different ways to teach dogs to bend. Most dogs bend better in one direction than the other. Find out which is your dog's weaker direction and work on that one first.

BENDING LEFT

Heel your dog up to and around a barrel or an agility tunnel set on end so that he is forced to bend his body around the object. Another technique is to heel with a dowel held in your left hand. As you make a circle to the left, tap the dog's inside hind leg to get him to move it away from the stick and put it underneath himself.

An excellent exercise to work on bending to the left is to start out heeling in a large circle and gradually spiral into a very small circle.

Getting the dog to bend left (notice that the dog's head is high).

BOHM MARRAZZO PHOTOGRAPHY

Keep in mind that the dog's head cannot be turned to the right if you expect him to bend to the left! Use your hand with the leash or hold food to encourage the dog to move his head away from you slightly so that it is possible for him to turn left.

BENDING RIGHT

For a dog to bend to the right, he must have his head turned slightly toward you (right) and lowered. The bend to the right requires no props because you can actually bend the dog around your own body! The best exercise for teaching the dog to bend right is the "spiral right."

Start by circling in a tight three-foot diameter circle to the right. As you circle, hold the leash tight and slightly in front of you. With each step of the circle right, simultaneously step left into the dog. When the dog can't duck behind you because he's on a tight leash, his only option will be to step away from you and, in effect, bend his body correctly. Make sure your left hand with the leash keeps encouraging his head down, still maintaining attention.

Encouraging the dog to bend to the right (notice that the dog's head is lowered).

BOHM MARRAZZO PHOTOGRAPHY

TEACHING THE DOG TO SIT STRAIGHT

For many people starting out in obedience, teaching a dog to sit straight in heel position seems like a mammoth task. In most early training classes, you are told over and over again to have your dog sit straight, only to find that when you attempt your first match show, most of your points are lost on crooked sits! It appears to the newcomer that his dog will never learn to sit squarely, and often the trainer lowers his standards rather than examining the problem.

All too often novice handlers come to a halt, and when they notice that their dog is sitting at a 45-degree angle to them, they reach down with their left hand and slide the dog's rump into position. Aside from giving the dog hemorrhoids, this does nothing to teach a dog how to line up with your leg and sit squarely. If the dog does not move his own body into position, he never learns how to do it. The dog who has been slid into position learns that he really doesn't have to worry about where he sits because hands will come down from above and fix him.

What is even more ridiculous is the handler who emphasizes "Sit straight" as he slides the dog into position. "Straight" is an abstract term that no canine will ever comprehend regardless how often or loudly you command it. "Straight" is also relative. Straight in line with what? Have you ever pointed out to the dog what he is to be straight with?

Another classic training technique is to haul the dog (on a choke chain, mind you) backward and then to swing him into a straight sit. All this because the dog never noticed that his handler had stopped walking and therefore ended up in a forged, crooked sit. Has the handler here ever considered that perhaps the error is that the dog was not paying attention or that he has never learned the cue that a halt is coming? Does the handler have a way of cueing his dog that he is about to stop? How does swinging a dog back into a straight sit solve an attention or missed cue problem? It doesn't, which is why the dog continues to sit forged and crooked and the handler, in desperation, yells louder, "Sit straight, please, sit straight!" (Sometimes "please" is omitted and other words are substituted.)

In all honesty, good trainers spend very little time fixing crooked sits. In fact, their dogs rarely sit crooked. The reason for this amazing phenomenon is really very simple.

If you teach a dog a cue that you are stopping, and if the dog is paying attention and is in heel position when you stop, and if the dog has been taught a point where he should look to line up with your leg, why would he end up crooked? He wouldn't, but so often a sit is not taught, it is just demanded.

To begin with, do not even attempt to teach an automatic sit while heeling until your dog will heel attentively and maintain heel position. To halt when the dog is not paying attention or when he is out of heel position is asking for a crooked sit.

Sit should first be taught in a stationary position. Plant your left foot (in the direction you are facing). Gather your leash in your right hand all the way to the collar. Now, gently, pull with your right hand as you guide the dog's rump into position in line with your left leg. Slight pressure down on the rump may be required to sit the dog, but most of the force should be in an upward direction, which will induce the dog to sit upon his haunches and not slouch over on one hip. Once the dog is responding and will sit on command, point with one finger of your left hand to the spot where the dog should look to line up a straight sit. This spot might be a seam on your pants, a pocket or your knee if you are training a small dog.

A good cue to your dog that you are stopping is that you have stood up. This will cause you to take a shorter stride. Do not intentionally slow down, as this will confuse the dog with the "slow" pace. Handlers who attempt to cue a dog by taking small baby steps are penalized for aiding the dog because it is not considered natural to stop by taking tiny steps.

To teach your dog what the left foot means, begin with your dog in heel position, "dancing" attentively at your side. Command "sit." as you step out with your right foot. Then bring your left foot up and next to your right foot for a halt. If your dog has not sat by the time your feet are together, snap (not pull) up directly over the dog's head to remind him to sit. Since the dog has heard the command "sit" before you actually stopped moving, the snap correction is justified.

For cues to be effective, they must be used consistently. This means that every time you come to a halt, you must stop on your right foot and bring your left foot into place next to your right foot.

As a prerequisite for teaching a proper sit, you as the trainer must be able to visualize—from your position next to and above the dog—what a straight sit looks like. Train your eye with the help of an experienced person or a mirror. If you get in the habit of looking at your dog after each sit, the dog will be encouraged to look at you, and this will cause him to sit crooked, facing slightly toward you.

Finally, if your goal is to train a dog who always sits straight, you must be working with a dog who is physically capable of sitting squarely. To perfect your dog's ability to line up a straight sit, alternate where the sit appears in the heeling patterns. For example, about-turn halt, then left-turn halt, right-turn halt, slow halt and finally fast halt. Pivoting in place, one step at a time, will also enforce the concept of the straight sit. When practicing, be aware of the surface you are working on. To try to perfect sits on uneven ground is futile.

For a dog to sit straight next to the handler, he must be in balance. If the dog leans in any direction, it will make him sit crooked.

Imagine a dowel standing on end that you want to keep upright. If you apply pressure away from you with one finger and toward you with another finger, the opposing forces keep the dowel upright.

Opposing forces can also help keep a dog sitting straight next to you. The leash applies pressure toward you and the food in your hand pulls the dog away from your leg.

It is really quite easy to teach a dog to sit straight, provided you are willing to *teach* the dog how to do it and not merely correct him for what he never learned. Since straight sits are part of polishing obedience, remember to be fair and to be patient.

There are four things that must happen for a dog to sit straight in heel position. When you get a crooked sit, at least one of these four things has not occurred. It is your job to figure out what part of getting into a straight sit has failed.

Pointing out the straight sit position to a small dog.

Opposing forces keep the dowel upright.

Opposing forces keep the dog sitting straight.

Consider the four ingredients of a straight sit:

1. The dog must be in heel position at the time the handler begins the halt.
2. The handler must cue the halt correctly.
3. The dog must understand what the "halt" cue means.
4. The dog must be paying attention.

Think of the halt as a freeze frame in the video of heeling. If the heeling is off, the sit cannot be correct.

DOODLING

Heeling can be improved by practicing maneuvers other than the heeling you would find in a ring. The following are a group of exercises that you will never be asked to perform in a ring situation. They do, however, offer variety and assist the dog in his understanding of the basic exercises. *Try them!*

Step Right

In class the command to the handler is "step right." This exercise occurs when the dog is in motion at heel. The handler will take a lateral step to the right and then continue forward normally. Upon taking the step right, the handler should be prepared to guide the attentive dog toward his leg, or if the dog is not attentive, to give a leash correction and then praise. As the dog is not expecting the move, he might be left out of heel position. If the dog is paying attention but is confused, help him by guiding him with the leash—*do not snap!* This exercise is particularly good for dogs who tend to heel wide but should not be used too often for dogs who crowd their handlers. Be sure to cue the step with your eyes!

SPIRALS

Spirals may be done either to the right or to the left. For the spiral left, the handler begins by heeling in a wide circle and continues to walk in a circle with each circle getting smaller and smaller. Eventually the circle should be so small that the dog is actually pivoting. For the spiral right, the handler begins with a small circle and gets wider and wider. The dog should be helped to avoid either crowding or lagging. The spiral exercise is particularly good for improving the Figure 8 exercise. Dizzy?

ONE STEP, HALT

In class the command to the handler is "one step, halt." This exercise begins with the dog sitting at heel position. The handler is to command the dog to "heel" and step off on the left foot. The right foot is then lifted, and when the right foot returns to the floor, the handler quickly commands "sit." The handler has actually only taken one step forward. This exercise is particularly good for improving the automatic sit of the dog upon realizing the handler has come to a halt.

RIGHT-TURN SQUARE

This exercise is similar to the One Step, Halt except that with each step the handler is pivoting to the right. After four pivots, the handler should be right back where he started from. The Right-Turn Square should begin with the right foot being lifted and turned to the right. The left foot is then lifted and planted next to the right. The command to the dog is "heel" and then "sit." It is up to the dog to realize that the handler is turning, and if he isn't paying attention, a leash correction should be given. If the dog is paying attention and is reluctant, coax him.

LEFT-TURN SQUARE

The Left-Turn Square is the same as the Right-Turn Square except that the handler is moving to the left and the dog must pivot out of the way. To indicate a backward movement, the command "back" or "off" is used instead of "heel." Begin with the right foot, since it is a pivot, and bring your left knee up at the same time as you step with your left leg, which will encourage the dog to get out of the way. A leash jerk up and back will also help encourage the dog to move out of the way. Placing a snug leash behind your back will help guide the dog back as you pivot.

270 TURN

This exercise is done with the dog in motion at heel position. The command to the handler is "270 turn." The handler does an about turn (to the right, naturally!), immediately followed by a right turn. Since the normal right turn is 90 degrees and an about turn is 180 degrees, when combined it is actually 270 degrees. Most dogs will correct themselves on a tight lead as the handler goes into the last 90 degrees of the turn, because they are not expecting it. This exercise is particularly good for getting the dog's attention and for improving the normal about turn exercise. Be sure to cue with your eyes!

LEFT U

This is the opposite of an about turn. When wishing to change direction in the form of a left U, turn left into the dog and heel back on the same line. The dog must learn to back out of your way. You can help him do this by pulling back on the leash as you swing your right hand and brush his head out of your way. Try putting a snug leash behind your back as you turn. For shorter dogs, use an arm-extender (back scratcher). Left U's are good exercises to use to make left turns easier and to help counteract forging.

FINDING HEEL

Finding Heel is executed the same as the One Step, Halt except that the handler takes one step laterally to the side or backward. The exercise begins with the dog at heel, sitting with the owner at a halt. While we don't necessarily want to teach the dog to heel backward, if he can find heel when we back up, we are sure he knows where it is. Teaching the dog to adjust laterally helps prevent wide or crooked sits in normal heeling. Command "heel" and guide the dog with your left hand and leash as you bring the dog into heel position. (Doodling maneuvers allow a handler to set up his dog for an exercise without excessive movement or circling. This is a valuable tool in the obedience ring.)

HOW TO IMPROVE HEELING

Mistakes in heeling usually occur for one of the following four reasons:

1. Lack of attention on the part of the dog.
2. Lack of knowledge of heeling cues on the part of the dog.
3. Erratic movements on the part of the handler (not smooth).
4. Improper cueing on the part of the handler.

It is easy to say that heeling can be improved with practice, but *what, how* and *when* do you practice?

Practice individual segments with repetition and praise. You may choose to work on any of the following segments.

Starts

Forward, followed immediately with a halt

Right turn, halt

Left turn, halt

About turn, halt

Right turns

Left turns

About turns

Figure 8s

Spirals

"Down-center-line" cueing exercise

Changing pace (speeding up)

Changing pace (slowing down)

Circle right

Circle left

Crowding (move laterally left)

Forging

About turns with distractions

Quick sits, properly timed

Straight sits (lining up)

Off-lead corrections (on specific segments)

Walking into gates and walls

Pivots—right, left, about

Play Find Heel games

270-degree turns to improve about turns

Rhythm

Work on no more than three segments in one session; vary your emphasis. Make sure *you* can execute the maneuver before trying it with the dog. Never *start* without the dog's attention, and then work to keep it. Work in different locations. New places add excitement for both you and the dog as well as providing new distractions.

Think of heeling as dancing with your dog and learn to do it smoothly and in rhythm.

Heeling with the dog's attention. Notice that the dog's head is high as the handler goes left.

How long should you heel? Until the dog shows the first signs of wearing out. An older, experienced dog could heel for up to 10 minutes; a young dog could heel for a few *good* minutes, then rest.

When teaching a dog to heel, your voice is a valuable tool. Your talking helps keep the dog's attention, as well as giving him confidence and helping him to learn the footcues. At some point in the dog's training, however, he must be weaned off your constant chatter if he is to heel well in a quiet ring situation. As the dog's understanding of heel progresses, lower your verbal help to a whisper. Then gradually say less and less as he shows you he is confident enough to heel without your continuous approval. Praise will always come at the end of a heeling pattern. The dog must be weaned off of your talking to him gradually, so as not to destroy his confidence.

25

The Figure 8

The purpose of the Figure 8 is to enable the dog and owner to walk through crowded corridors, around obstacles and in congested areas that require constant direction and gait changes.

Select two posts approximately eight feet apart. These posts may be people or objects such as chairs, trees, garbage cans or whatever suffices. Take a position that places you and your dog at equal distance between the posts, with your dog at the midpoint. Visualize an imaginary straight line running between the posts. Position yourself and your dog, in the heel position, perpendicular to this line, approximately 12 inches away from the line. Begin heeling, as always, by leading with your left foot. The first steps are the same as for a forward, left turn, and after that you are into the Figure 8 pattern. You and your dog will first circle the left post, walk a diagonal line between the two posts and circle the right post as you proceed to walk a Figure 8 pattern. It is easier for the dog to go left first because he is going from a sitting position to a slow around the left post.

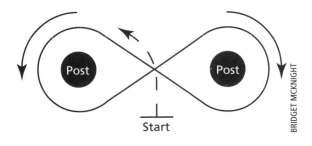

As you and your dog walk this Figure 8 pattern, you will require your dog to maintain the heel position. In order to maintain the heel position, your dog will have to decrease his speed as you circle the first post. This places your dog on the inside track between you and the post. Since he is walking the inside track, in this instance, he will not be covering as much distance as you. His head will need to be high to slow his pace. As you come out of the circle and take up the diagonal track, your dog should increase speed in order to maintain the heel position. As you begin to circle the right post, your dog will now be on the outside track and you will be on the inside track. This time your dog will have to increase speed in order to maintain the heel position since he will be covering the greater distance. To increase his speed, the dog will need to lower his head.

PERFECTING THE FIGURE 8 EXERCISE

The Figure 8 is similar to the circle left and circle right, and yet the pattern is not really two circles.

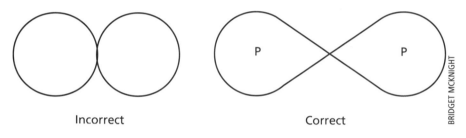

Incorrect   Correct

The Figure 8, while at first glance appearing straightforward, is really a very complex maneuver. The exercise requires the dog to continually change pace from normal to slow" to normal and then to fast and to do all this while walking on a curve!

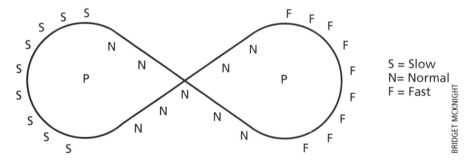

S = Slow
N= Normal
F = Fast

We begin by first teaching the dog that this exercise requires a change of pace. Start with the dog on a tight lead so he cannot forge or lag. Begin to the left at an extremely slow pace and stand up. As you head into the straightaway, pick up speed by leaning forward, pass "normal, and by the time you begin the outside curve you should be walking briskly and encouraging the dog to lower his head. Since the dog is on a tight lead, he cannot lag. You might feel like you are dragging him; this is all right. The dog will eventually learn to bend around the outside curve to keep from being dragged. As you come out of the outside curve, slow your speed back down to normal and then back to slow to go into the left curve. After a few weeks the dog will begin to anticipate the pace changes, and you will be ready to go back to maintaining a steady pace as the dog will make the necessary adjustments to stay in heel position.

WORKING WITH THE DOG

Walking a curve is not as easy as it seems. It is impossible to walk a curve without shifting your weight and leaning slightly. As you walk the curve properly, you will notice that your feet *single track,* which means you will be putting one foot in front of the other. To learn how to properly shift your weight, look where you are going!

To teach the dog to lean into a turn, hold a toy or tidbit in front of his face as you spiral tighter and tighter to the right. Make a game out of this as the dog learns to dig his feet in and lean into the turn to get his reward.

THINK ABOUT YOUR FEET

Until the dog is very in tune with performing a Figure 8, your feet play a critical role in cueing the dog which way to turn. Cues are made with the left foot for large dogs (as in the left turn), with the right foot for small dogs (as in the left turn). To begin the Figure 8, you start with Forward, Left Turn to get you into the Figure 8. It would not be fair to say "heel" and suddenly step left into the dog to begin the exercise!

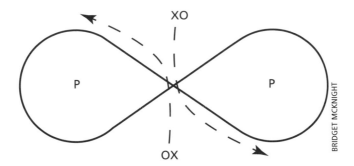

There are four critical points in the Figure 8, as shown in this figure:

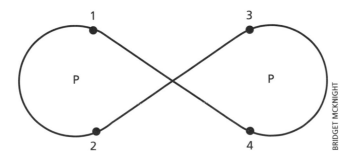

These are critical points because at each point you must cue the dog of a change of direction. To accomplish this, you work to reach each critical point on the foot you cue with (which varies with your dog's size).

Keep the dog (not you) in the center of the Figure 8. This will give the dog room to bend around the post as he goes left.

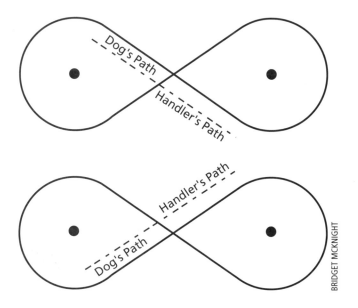

BRIDGET MCKNIGHT

PROOFING

Once the dog and you are together, smoothly floating around the Figure 8 pattern, to keep the dog thinking, vary the exercise by adding about turns, left U's, circling one post more than another, working with strange posts, more than two posts and finally working the exercise simultaneously with another dog and handler!

HIS BODY

In order for the dog to stay in heel position around the curves of the Figure 8, he must learn to bend to keep his spine parallel to the handler's body at all times. As the handler goes to the left, most beginning dogs tend to swing their rears away from the handler. Encouraging the dog to turn his head slightly to the left will help him bend, which will cause the dog's rear to move correctly toward the handler.

When the handler goes to the right and the dog is on the outside, the dog's rear might end up behind the handler, making it very difficult for the dog to stay up in heel position. This is the number one cause for lagging on the outside of the Figure 8. Dogs who lag on the outside of the figure 8 usually have trouble bending on the inside left circle of the figure 8. To teach the dog to move his rear sideways at the appropriate time, use a dowel to tap the dog's leg and get him to bend.

As the dog goes around the outside of the Figure 8, the dowel pushes the dog's rear away from behind the handler's body. This keeps the dog parallel to the handler and in the heel position.

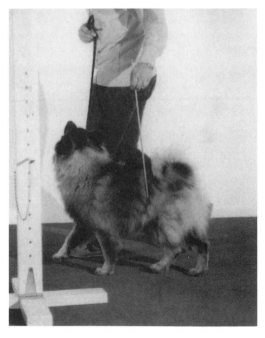

When the dog is on the inside turn of the Figure 8, the dowel pushes the dog's rear closer to the handler to keep the dog's body parallel to the handler and in heel position.

26

Teaching the Dog to Heel Off Leash

The biggest mistake made by beginning trainers is taking the leash off a dog before the dog is ready to work off leash. The second biggest mistake is not knowing what to do when the dog makes a mistake and he's off leash. Good trainers find that the longer they train, the less they choose to remove the leash.

Before you can begin teaching off-leash heeling, you must have you and your dog at the point where you can heel together on a short, loose leash, perform all turns and changes of pace, in rhythm, *with distractions,* and the leash is never tight. Then, and only then, should you consider removing the leash. To give you some guidelines for how long this takes in the hands of an experienced trainer, it takes an above-average dog one full year to learn how to heel! I am not talking about the time it takes a dog to prepare for a CD title, I am talking about really understanding and being proficient at heeling so that in a ring situation, the dog never loses more than one point on heeling.

Every dog knows when he is on leash and when he is off leash. If he didn't, then he'd be too stupid to train in the first place! Many trainers advocate that if a dog makes a mistake off leash, you should put the leash back on and make a correction, then remove the leash. This establishes the leash as a threat. I believe dogs are smart enough to realize that there are times (in the obedience ring) when the leash is not around and is unlikely to be reattached. Rather than making the leash the reason a dog heels, I prefer to use something that is permitted in the ring to enforce the "heel" command. The following is the procedure used to teach heeling off leash with "off-leash help."

1. When you are sure the dog is ready to heel off leash, put him on a light, six-foot leash and tie the leash to your body. (Tying it to your belt or pants loop works well.) The leash is there only to prevent the dog from leaving, as it is

natural for him to attempt to avoid the "off-leash help." At *no* time are you to reach for the leash to correct. It is as if it is not there.

2. Begin with your dog sitting in heel position, with attention, and start your big circles to the left at normal pace. If the dog makes no mistakes, add distractions. (Don't tell me you can't distract him—try a chicken!)

3. When your dog gets out of heel position, reach *in slow motion* with your left hand and take a firm grip on the side of his buckle collar. While heeling, move him gently but deliberately up *into heel position* as you let go and, when he is back to heel position, praise. I cannot impress upon you enough how important it is that you do this *slowly*. Avoid grabbing, and move so that the dog sees what you are doing and is not frightened. Be sure not to let go until the dog is in, or a little ahead of, heel position. (A dog who is a little ahead of heel position will fall into position as soon as you let go and keep moving.)

4. After the dog is back in heel position, praise profusely, continue a few more steps and then release him from the exercise.

The first thing that will happen is that when the dog sees your hand reaching for him, he will duck and pull away. Let him! He is tied to you so he really can't get very far. Keep your left hand extended, reaching for him as he moves away from you. Continue walking slowly toward him. Smile! Eventually (sooner if you are indoors) the dog will reach a barrier. When he does, finish your reach, take hold of him and while *saying nothing* walk him back to the point where he made the mistake and put him in heel position, praise, continue heeling, and then release.

After a few weeks of this, the dog will stop avoiding your arm because he will understand that you are not hurting him and that you are simply moving him back into position.

You will know when the dog understands and accepts the off-leash help because as you reach, he will start to correct himself before you can help him. At this point you are ready to untie the leash and you have a way of helping a dog heel off leash. Since left hands and arms are still permitted in the obedience rings, you have it made! The dog respects the hand and the hand comes into the ring with you.

Another advantage to having off-leash help is that it allows you to practice off-leash heeling. Yes, when you have a way of helping, it pays to practice off-leash heeling.

Heeling off leash is taught step by step, the same as it was on leash. Begin with your big circles to the left, then to the right. Then add the fast and the slow. Next, master about turns, and finally work right and left turns.

To enforce the sit when the leash is off, go back to your verbal sit cue as you step down on your right foot.

When you begin off-leash heeling, your dog will make mistakes for different reasons. Think back to Chapter 11, Understanding Corrections vs. Help. If the dog misses a cue for a turn because he is confused, you should help him by lowering or raising your hand. If the dog is distracted or is lagging because he feels he has a choice (especially now that the leash is off), he should receive an off-leash correction. Reach out and take hold of the collar more forcefully. Just because you now know how to help or correct a dog off leash doesn't mean you should reach for him every time he's out of position. If you reach for the dog and correct him when you should be helping him, he will panic and may even freeze while heeling.

While I have witnessed many top trainers use their hands to correct their dogs off leash, I have never heard anyone else attempt to teach it as a method to students. The reason for this is not really that top trainers hide their best secrets, but rather that it is very difficult for a new handler to learn to read his dog well enough and time the correction perfectly enough to be able to use the method effectively. The danger with using the off-leash correction is that if you do it too quickly, or at the wrong time, you will make the problem much worse. It is also difficult for the beginning handler to watch his dog balking from the hand initially, and few are willing to work to the point where the dog accepts the correction or help. Students have been successful with this technique, but usually they require close supervision while learning it.

For small dogs, one finger slipped into the collar, *very slowly,* works the same as reaching for a dog's collar. Reaching for the left side of the dog's neck helps keep the small dog heeling close.

Always reach for the dog's collar on the right side of the dog's neck. If you take hold of the collar from the back of his neck, you will encourage him to put his head down.

If you feel that when you remove the leash, the dog is unaware of your body cues telling him to speed up on right turns, slow down on left turns, and when to stop, consider that maybe you have been relying on the leash to cue the dog instead of using your body. Go back on leash for a period of time and be very careful not to use the leash to cue. It is common to see handlers pulling up on a leash when they begin a halt. In this case, is it any wonder the dog has learned to wait for the leash tug instead of watching for when the handler stands up?

If you attempt to learn to correct your dog off leash and find it doesn't work, do not become discouraged. It is almost impossible to learn how to train a dog entirely from a book! Chances are, your attempts are not smooth, your timing is off and your dog senses your insecurity. Like anything else you desire to perfect, much time and effort is required. Whenever possible, seek the help of someone who has already perfected this technique.

27

Understanding Difficult Heeling Patterns

The following are heeling patterns you may be asked to perform in a ring. Certain sequences are more difficult than others. You should be aware of these difficult patterns and practice them from time to time.

In preparation for heeling in a ring situation, be sure to practice heeling your dog into walls, gates and ropes, striving for a straight sit each time. It is natural for a dog to want to avoid walking into a barrier. A "forward, fast, normal, halt" into a wall is a common tiebreaker for runoffs in competition.

When watching a heeling pattern in a ring, do not try to memorize it. Make note of the basic pattern, for example, an L shape or a C or a T, and then note any tricky sequences as described in the diagrams.

Also practice "forward, fast, normal, left turn." If the dog does not come out of the fast back to normal quickly, he will bump you on the left turn.

L-Shape

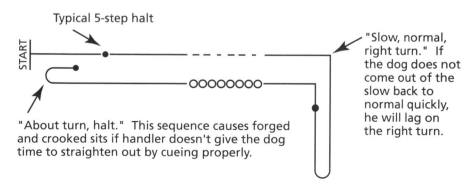

Typical 5-step halt

START

"Slow, normal, right turn." If the dog does not come out of the slow back to normal quickly, he will lag on the right turn.

"About turn, halt." This sequence causes forged and crooked sits if handler doesn't give the dog time to straighten out by cueing properly.

C-Shape

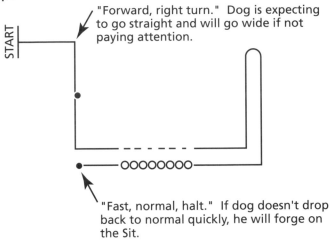

"Forward, right turn." Dog is expecting to go straight and will go wide if not paying attention.

"Fast, normal, halt." If dog doesn't drop back to normal quickly, he will forge on the Sit.

T-Shape

"Forward, slow." Dog just picks up pace when slow is called. If dog is not paying attention, he will forge.

"Halt, forward, about turn." If dog does not start sharply after halt, he will lag on the about turn.

When you understand the theory of balanced heeling, you can see why the sequence of "right turn, halt" is more difficult than a similar sequence of "left turn, halt." On a left turn the dog raises his head and shifts his weight back to slow down. On the halt the dog raises his head even higher and sits. One motion is a continuation of the other. In the sequence of "right turn, halt" the dog must first lower his head and speed up and then dramatically raise his head to stop on the halt. Shifting weight quickly makes the second sequence more difficult to perfect.

Which of these would be more difficult?

1. Forward, right turn, slow
2. Forward, right turn, fast

The answer is number one. The "forward, right turn, slow" requires the dog to lower his head and speed up immediately before he must shift his weight back to slow down.

28

Teaching the Dog to Sit

Goal: to teach the dog to sit on a single command by bringing his hindquarters up to his front quarters, thus avoiding a "rocked back" sit, which is undesirable in obedience.

A dog who rocks back into a sit (which is often a breed characteristic, for example, of German Shepherds, Collies, Shetland Sheepdogs, Doberman Pinschers, Old English Sheepdogs and many other breeds) will never score well in obedience since he will either have to forge on heeling before he sits or he will end up sitting lagged.

IN PREPARATION

1. Place the dog on your left side by moving yourself to his right side, if necessary. (This is easier than lifting the dog!)
2. Hold the bulk of the leash in your right hand. With your left hand, palm down and fingertips pointed away from your body, place the leash between your thumb and forefinger and grab hold. Now you are in position to sit your dog.

TEACHING THE SIT

1. With your right hand, add to the leash you are holding, the snap at the other end. Let go of the leash with your left hand. You are now holding the entire leash and dog in your right hand.
2. Command "sit." gently, quickly, and only one time. Since it is not a moving exercise, there is no need to use the dog's name.
3. Pull up and forward on the collar as you push gently on the dog's rear with your left hand. Be sure to pull up much more than you push down. Maintain forward pressure on the leash to assure that the dog does not rock back. The left hand is used to guide the rear into the exact place you want him to sit.

4. When the dog is sitting, release the pressure on the collar and *verbally* praise him.

5. Should the dog at any time get up without being released, *say nothing* and reposition him back into a sit. Praise when he is back in the sitting position.

Refer to Chapter 23, The On and Off Switch of Dog Attention, to learn how to get the dog to sit and pay attention.

Step one: Hold the leash with your left hand.

Step two: Let go of the leash with your left hand.

Step three: Pull up and forward on the collar as you gently push the rear of the dog to the floor with your left hand.

Step four: Notice the forward pressure on the collar as the dog is placed into a sit. This teaches the dog to sit by tucking his hind end under himself, rather than by rocking back into a sit. The dog is in heel position in line with the left leg.

TEACHING SIT WITH FOOD

For puppies and dogs who are motivated by food, you can teach a dog to sit with food. For a dog to sit he must raise his head and shift his weight onto his rear end. For obedience we ask that the rear come forward and not rock back.

Hold a piece of food between your fingers so that your palm faces the dog. With the dog on your left side, encourage the dog to lift his head by following the food in your hand. By gently baiting the dog's head up, you can usually induce the dog to sit. Some breeds get into a sit easier than others and not all dogs are motivated by food treats. If you have a dog who does respond to this technique, it's an easy way to get the dog sitting *and* looking up at the same time!

BOHM MARRAZZO PHOTOGRAPHY

Getting the dog to tuck sit using food as a lure.

29

Sit-Stay

Goal: to *stay* in the sit position while the handler leaves the heel position and then returns to heel position.

1. Tell your dog "sit" as you guide him into a sitting position at your left leg (the dog's ear is even with the handler's left hip).

2. Place your left hand, palm flat and facing the dog, in front of the dog's nose (without touching him) as you give the command "stay." No name is used since it is not a moving exercise.

3. Holding the leash in your right hand, remove the left hand from in front of the dog's nose and step forward on your *right* foot. (The left foot means heel; the right foot leaving first means stay behind.) Turn and stand directly in front of your dog (no more than six inches from his nose).

IF YOUR DOG STARTS TO GET UP

1. Reposition the dog gently with an upward and backward motion on the leash. If this does not sit the dog, reach over his back (from in front) and push down on his rear. As training continues, you may reposition the dog with a "pop" up on the leash if necessary to return him to the sit position, but initially we are helping him to learn and not correcting him for what we have not taught him.

2. As soon as the dog has regained the sitting position, praise him *verbally* ("good puppy"). Verbal praise is used so as not to encourage him to get up again by your petting him.

3. *Do not* repeat the command "sit." The last command the dog was given was "stay," which means no moving. If you keep reminding him, why should he bother to remember what he is doing?

Repositioning a dog who has
gotten up off a Sit-Stay. Notice
that the handler does not touch
the dog.

BOHM MARRAZZO PHOTOGRAPHY

4. Keep your eyes on your own dog and correct as soon as he begins to move, but do not dive at him too quickly. Our objective is not to frighten or intimidate him, but rather to *teach* him.

THE COMMAND YOU HEAR

Your instructor or judge will have you execute the Sit-Stay by giving *you* the command, "Leave your dog." Make sure you give the command "stay" *before* you move your feet to leave the dog.

After you and your dog have remained in this position for a short period of time, return to heel position. During the early training, this will mean nothing more than pivoting back to the dog's right side, counting to five in your head, and then praising the dog (verbally). If the dog attempts to get up when you praise him, reposition him into a sit and *say nothing*. Eventually you will return to heel position by circling your dog. Do not repeat "sit" and do not repeat "stay"! The first time you return by circling the dog, rest your left hand gently on your dog's head as you walk behind him. This will counteract his desire to get up so that he can see you (also see Chapter 18, Proofing).

When returning around the dog back to heel position for the first few times after doing a Sit-Stay, rest your left hand on the dog's head as you walk around him. This reassures him that you have not disappeared and encourages him to remain sitting.

JULIA BROWN

AS YOU PRACTICE THE SIT-STAY AT HOME

If the dog is not getting up and will sit without moving for one minute, try adding some distractions such as noise, stamping feet, clapping or children walking by. Keep in mind that when your dog gets up and is corrected properly, he has learned something. When he just sits and stays, he is not learning, so we tempt him to get up with distractions. When he is steady with distractions, go a little farther the next time you leave him, until you can go the full extension of a six-foot training leash. Any time the dog moves, you must go back to *in front of him* before you correct him; when you leave again, do not go as far. Eventually you will be required to move up to 30 feet away from your dog. In the learning stages, the correction is no more than repositioning the dog without touching him.

THE DIFFERENCE BETWEEN "STAY" AND "WAIT"

If you decide to train your dog in both obedience and agility, you will probably want to teach a variation of stay that we call "wait." "Stay" is taught to mean remain in one place in a relaxed state until your handler returns to you. "Wait" means remain in one place, ready in a moment's notice to spring into action. For wait, the attitude we want in the dog is akin to "on your mark, get set, *go!*"

Wait can be used in obedience for Recalls, retrieves and any time the handler wants the dog to wait to be released. Wait keeps a dog excited to run agility. The "stay" command lets the dog know he can expect to have his handler return to him, so there is no reason to be ready to be released suddenly.

To teach your dog to wait, put him in a sit position on leash at heel and command "wait." Then take a few steps away from him and pause. In a few seconds, release him with an "okay" release command. Encourage the dog to get up quickly by adding a small tug to the leash or by throwing a toy for him. Continue to do this until the dog is so sure you want him to get up that he breaks the "sit" command as soon as you step away. Having caused the anticipation of a release, gently put the dog back into the sit position and praise him.

It will probably take a few sessions of this before the dog is sitting and waiting with total attention to be released. When the dog shows that he knows to wait and release quickly, go back and alternate between wait and release, and stay and return to the dog.

Dogs learn in the environments in which they are taught. Eventually your dog will learn to associate "stay" with a line of dogs and you returning to him in that line and "wait" with the expectancy of doing something else soon.

Not all dogs seem to understand the subtle difference we draw between "stay" and "wait." When I was only teaching obedience to my dogs, I didn't bother to separate the two commands. Now that my dogs learn agility and obedience, I feel it helps to use the "wait" command on the start line of agility.

For those of you who are also planning to work your dogs in herding, the command "wait" can be confused with the flanking command "way to me." For these dogs, be creative and pick a different word for your obedience or agility "wait." Some people say "pause" or "place." The word you choose is unimportant as long as it doesn't carry with it a different meaning. Dogs respond to all different languages and learn any verbal cues we choose to teach them. I once knew a person who trained his dog with numbers. If he said "twenty-four," the dog sat! Of course, you need to remember what the commands mean, so numbers might not be too realistic!

30

Down and Down-Stay

$\mathbf{T}$he purpose of this lesson is to teach your dog to assume a prone position on command. The command to be used is "down."

There are two different kinds of down in obedience. In the Down-Stay, the dog should be lying comfortably, preferably on one hip with one foot tucked. The tucked foot assures us that the dog will not creep. Later on in training your dog will learn a "drop." In this down, he will be crouched, attentive, and ready to leap up into another position on command.

There are many different ways to teach a dog to Down-Stay. Puppies are taught differently from adult dogs, and dogs with short legs are taught differently from dogs with longer legs. If you find that as you practice the down you are not getting results, try an alternate method of teaching the dog to down.

ADULT DOWN

This is for the average size dog who is not overly tense or nervous.

Sit your dog in heel position. Grasp the lead in the right hand at the point where it attaches to the collar. Give your dog the command "down" (in a firm, short, one-syllable, deep tone) and, immediately following, pull down and off to the side with the lead as you push the dog (with your left hand) from the withers in the same direction you are pulling.

PUPPY DOWN

This is for young puppies or adult dogs who are very frightened.

Sit your dog in heel position. With your left hand, reach across your dog's shoulders and grasp his left elbow. Grasp your dog's right elbow with your right hand. Give your dog the command "down" and slide the dog's front legs forward (out from under him) gently, using your grasp on his elbows. A downward pressure with your left arm across the dog's shoulders keeps the dog from sitting.

116

RON REAGAN

Step one of the adult down.

RON REAGAN

Step two of the adult down.

JULIA BROWN

Step one of the puppy down.

JULIA BROWN

Step two of the puppy down. Gently slide the front feet forward while bringing your left elbow across the dog's back to prevent him from getting up.

SHORT-LEGGED DOWN

Sit your dog in heel position and crouch down next to him. Place your right hand, palm up, behind the dog's front legs. Place your left palm on his withers. Command "down" as you move your right hand forward and push down with your left. Be sure to give the dog a second or two after hearing the "down" command before you position him.

FOOT DROP

This approach is used for very large dogs, resistant dogs or dogs who may bite. It also works well with handlers who have little strength in their arms.

Sit the dog in heel position. Holding the leash in your right hand, make a loop (almost like a stirrup). Command "down." Then, step into the loop with your left foot as you pull up on the leash with your right hand. Your foot will pull the dog to the floor. If the dog resists, just hold the pressure; he will eventually give in and lie down.

As soon as your dog is on the floor, get down with him and praise him (making sure he doesn't get up). Place your left foot on the leash where it attaches to the collar. This will prevent the dog from getting up as you slowly stand up. If your dog should try to get up, a quick jolt on the withers or another snap on the collar should return him to a prone position. When your dog seems content and relaxed, you may remove your foot from the leash.

Step one of the foot drop.

Step two of the foot drop.

When your instructor says, "Exercise finished," you are to tell the dog, "okay" and encourage him to get up. *Do not* pull, drag or snap him up. He must get up of his own free will. If he is content to lie there, you can always break the down with a "heel" command.

TEACHING DOWN FROM A STAND

Encourage your dog or puppy into a standing position. With food in your left hand, lower the dog's head between his front legs. After his head is lowered, command "down" and push his shoulders away from you with your right hand as if to collapse the dog into a down position.

As the dog gets used to getting into a down position from a stand, start saying "down" first, followed by lowering his head, followed by pushing his shoulders away from you.

DOWN-STAY

This exercise is executed in the same manner as the Sit-Stay with one exception: The dog will be in the down position, preferably rolled on one hip and comfortable, before you leave him. The commands to stay (hand signal and verbal) are the same and given to the dog in the same manner. Make sure that the hand signal is given in front of the dog's face. (You will probably have to bend to accomplish this.)

Teaching down from a stand.

BCHM MARRAZZO PHOTOGRAPHY

When the dog breaks a Down-Stay, walk in slowly and push down on his shoulders. You need not sit the dog first. Do not repeat "down" and do not repeat "stay." That's what the dog forgot to remember! When the dog has been repositioned into a down, *praise!*

Caution!

- Because "down" is a separate command from "sit," *never, ever* tell a dog to "sit down" as this is sure to confuse him!
- The "down" command, as with all commands, is only given once, then it is enforced! Do not repeat the command "down" unless you are teaching your dog to count rather than to respond on the first command he hears.

A student who had successfully completed a Novice course once called me with a problem. "Missy is behaving beautifully with one exception," she explained. "She still gets up on the couch, and when I tell her to 'Get down,' she lies down and looks at me wagging her tail!" After a long pause I replied, "Missy is a very smart dog. Be careful what you ask for—you might get it!" Then I suggested, "Try using the command 'off' instead of 'down' next time."

31

Out of Sight,
Out of Mind?

The Out-of-Sight Sit and Down exercises found in the Open class should be taught separately. All too often, trainers assume that if their dogs do a Sit-Stay and a Down-Stay, they will do an Out-of-Sight Stay. Without taking the time to teach the exercise, one day the handler walks out of sight and that's when trouble starts.

As a preliminary exercise, sit your dog and when you leave him, stand directly behind him. If the dog turns his head to see you, do nothing, but if his shoulders move and cause a foot to move, correct the dog from behind by repositioning him. All too often dogs are left on the stays and as the owner leaves the ring, the dog's head swivels around so far to see his owner that he moves out of position. By starting this exercise early in your Novice training, the dog will gain security on stays since he is not facing you but knows you are still there.

To begin the more formal Out-of-Sight Stays, start by leaving your dog and walking all over the room. The dog will eventually stop trying to keep you in sight and will simply relax on the sit. He knows that you are there somewhere but is not totally focused on you like he was in the Novice stays.

Eventually, as you are wandering, drift out of the room for brief moments. As your dog gains confidence, you can be out of sight for longer periods of time.

The final training step is to leave the dog in a formal ring setup and leave the ring in a line of handlers. If you need to make a correction, walk in to the dog slowly and with a smile on your face. Learn to "savor a correction" and avoid rushing in and diving on your dog.

In training and at match shows, make an effort to watch your dog on Out-of-Sight Stays. The object is for you to see him while he cannot see you. All too often, when Open handlers leave the ring in practice, they start to gab and forget to train.

CASUAL STAYS

Many advanced dogs break sits and downs out of sight because they forget what they are doing. You can teach a dog to improve his memory!

Place your dog on a sit or down, stay around your house and, while keeping an eye on him, do something else; cook dinner, talk on the phone, read something. The dog will probably think you have forgotten what he's doing and get up or change position. When this happens, you immediately but calmly step toward the dog and correct him back to his position. Eventually, casual stays become a silent game between you and the dog. It's as if you are saying, "I remember what I told you to do. Do you remember?"

SEPARATION ANXIETY

Separation anxiety is a mental condition where a dog is so fearful of being away from his owner that, when left alone, he experiences tremendous stress. These are dogs who tear up couches when left alone in a house and dogs who come flying across the ring to their handlers when the handler begins to leave for an Out-of-Sight stay. Certain breeds (Cocker Spaniels, Poodles and Daschunds, just to name a few) are very prone to developing separation anxiety.

The best solution is prevention. From the time you get your new puppy, make a point of handing the leash to a responsible friend and walking away. Let a friend keep your pup overnight for you when the dog is about four months of age. Teach the young dog that he can survive without you.

To deal with a dog who is experiencing separation anxiety on the stay exercises, tie the dog in place so he cannot get to you.

32

Stay Problems

Sit, down and Stand-Stay problems can be some of the most difficult training obstacles to overcome. I have observed many severe stay problems caused by handlers who took their dogs to sanctioned matches early in training and the dogs were not corrected for breaking a stay. After a few experiences like this, a dog will be totally confused. He no longer knows what is expected of him.

In teaching the stays, do not rush distance, but rather put your efforts into proofing with distractions.

As with all problems, before you will know the best way to correct the problem you must know what is causing it. A dog who breaks a stay to go sniff another dog is different from a dog who forgets what he is doing, which is different from a dog who is insecure about being left alone.

Whining and crying on stays are usually signs of anxiety. Often the dog is staying but thinking about and wanting to get up. Since the dog knows he will be corrected if he gets up, he stays, but since he has not yet accepted the discipline as mandatory, he whines with indecision and anxiety. To solve this whining problem, help the dog make a decision—the wrong one. Force the dog to break by having someone nudge him or verbally encourage him to get up. Then correct him. When the dog finally resigns himself to staying, the anxious whining should subside.

Some dogs whine regardless of whether they are on stays or not. If the offender is a male (commonly a Malamute, Siberian Husky, Doberman Pinscher or German Shepherd), it is often a matter of "raging hormone imbalance," and neutering might resolve his distress.

For females who whine constantly, it may be a hyper, nervous part of the dog's temperament. For these dogs try a stress vitamin program, along with extreme socialization and exercise. Remove any sugar and most fat from the dog's diet, which may make dogs jittery.

Sometimes whining problems can be corrected with the use of a wide rubber band. Place the rubber band around the dog's muzzle. Correct him with a jerk on the leash if he tries to remove it with his paws. Now, with the band around his muzzle, do a Sit-Stay on leash. The dog may be quiet at this point simply because he is intimidated by this new training method. If the dog remains quiet, return to him, remove the rubber band and praise.

Repeat the exercise while gaining distance. At any time that the dog utters the slightest sound, return slowly and snap the rubber band against his muzzle. (This is done by pulling it slightly away from his muzzle and then suddenly letting go of it.) After the dog has been snapped with the rubber band, praise him for his quiet state.

Once the dog accepts the correction, the presence of the rubber band alone serves as a reminder to the dog to be quiet. The rubber band works to focus the dog's attention directly on the whining or barking problem and can be used on Out-of-Sight Stays as well as for dogs who bark while doing Go Outs.

For some insecure dogs, it helps to get a little more creative. Locate a walkie-talkie set and place one part (with the button taped in the receive position) behind the dog as you leave and go out of sight. Now have someone who can tell you if the dog whines in your absence. When the first sound is uttered, you respond by saying "quiet" into your part of the walkie-talkie. Usually the sudden sound of your voice coming from behind the dog is enough to calm the dog's concerns about your whereabouts and return!

Sometimes stay problems are the result of lazy handlers who fail to correct minor movements because they want the dog to be right! From early training through advanced work, any moving of paws, shifting of hips, swiveling or sloppy sitting should be corrected. If you are clear in communicating your expectations, the dog has an easier time meeting your demands.

If a dog is breaking stays because he is insecure and wants to get to you, there are various approaches you can take. Make a point to hand the dog's leash to responsible strangers from time to time and work to break the dependency the dog has on you. Reteach the stay exercise with a more gradual transition to Out of Sight as described in Chapter 31, Out of Sight, Out of Mind? If none of the above works, you may have to correct the dog to the point where the consequences of coming to you are worse than the fear of being away from you. While fear is usually treated with help and a gentle approach, there comes a time when the fear is so great that the dog must be pushed to overcome it, thus the reason for the correction. Throw chains tossed at a dog who is coming to you often discourage a second attempt.

When a stay is broken because a dog forgets what he is doing, a mistake in training has been made. The dog has not been taught to do an "active" Sit-Stay, where he is very conscious of what he is doing. Go back to Chapter 29, Sit-Stay. Reteach the exercise as described without repetition of commands. Remember, if you keep telling the dog what he should be doing, why should *he* bother to remember?

Doing casual Sit-Stays helps a dog learn to remember what he is doing. By casual I mean that you should find a time in the house during your daily routine when you can casually walk over to the dog and command "sit" and "stay." Then go about your business as if the dog weren't there. When the dog sees you talking on the phone or cutting potatoes or ironing, he will assume you have forgotten what he is doing and break the stay. This is your chance to correct him. Sometimes, because you are not standing and staring at the dog doing a Sit-Stay, he forgets what he is doing. This is another opportunity to help him learn to remember—correct the dog back into a stay and praise. Remember, do not repeat "sit" or "stay" (see Chapter 31).

Proofing teaches a dog to think about what he is doing. Have another person command "down" to your dog while he is on a Sit-Stay. Does the dog respond? Is he aware of what his handler told him to do and what was meant by the command "stay"? If the dog drops, gently reposition him and praise. You may want to put the dog back on leash and stand in close if his confusion persists. (If your dog responded to every "down" command he heard at a show, you would have a big problem.)

Another proof technique for a dog who forgets is to put him on a Sit-Stay on your bed, where there is a temptation to relax. You might even try sitting him and then positioning his front feet stretched out in front of him. While this may be an awkward position, if the dog understands what "stay" means, he will maintain the position. Correct any and all foot or body movements.

Sometimes stay problems begin because trainers are so busy with the other exercises that they forget to practice the group exercises. This is a common problem for people who train by themselves. Discipline yourself to work on "boring" stays.

All stay exercises need to be proofed. See Chapter 18, Proofing, for more ideas.

Stay problems can be very difficult to correct once they start. Take your time teaching the exercise in the beginning and you will have much less to worry about later in training.

33
Come Fore

This exercise aids in teaching the Recall. The dog should already understand what "come" means, as taught with a tidbit of food. The object of the exercise is to get the dog to turn toward you immediately upon hearing the word "come." This is accomplished by making the dog think that if he doesn't respond to the word "come," the *Boogie Dog* will bite him! Since most dogs will come when they have nothing better to do, we work Come Fores to distractions. Distractions include food, animals, open house doors and open car doors.

STEPS OF THE COME FORE

1. Walk briskly with your dog on a loose lead. An informal "let's go" command is used in place of "heel." (You do not want your dog looking at you, which would be the case if you used the "heel" command.)

2. When your dog is distracted and you choose to do a Come Fore, stop, command "Fido, come," followed by a lead snap (not a pull) if he does not respond instantly (put your "motor" in reverse) and then *back up* (without turning around) for five or six steps as quickly as you can. The lead snap is used to convince the dog that he has been bitten by the *Boogie Dog*. This snap is done with both hands and is hard enough to upset the dog. Of course, the dog is not upset with you, only with *Boogie Dog,* who is away from you somewhere. If the dog responds by turning toward you upon hearing "come," no snap is necessary. Try a more tempting distraction until you can get the dog to make the mistake of not responding. Never pull your dog to you. You don't want him to know you are doing it. This will only teach him to come when he is on a leash!

3. Once the dog is coming toward you, keep the leash loose and encourage him with verbal praise and sympathy (because *Boogie Dog* got him). Make

sure the dog touches you first! Do not reach out for the dog! Once the dog has touched you, you may pet him.

4. Should the dog go past you, turn around and snap him again. *Boogie Dog* is all over; the only safe place is by you. Do not repeat "come." Say nothing until he gets to you. Then *praise*.

Important!

- You may only give the command "come" *one* time. After the command is given, however, you may coax the dog to you with words of encouragement.
- The command to come is the dog's name, followed by the word "come."
- At no time is the dog to hear the words "come on." This is *not* a proper command and will only confuse the dog.
- "Come" means to get to you and stay there. A token visit, followed by taking off again, is unacceptable and is cause for *Boogie Dog* to strike.

34
Teaching Fronts

A Straight Sit Front requires that the dog be sitting squarely on his haunches, with his weight evenly distributed (no leaning) and his body positioned in the exact center of your body, facing you within reach, without touching you and without putting his paws on or between your feet.

Teaching fronts is a gradual process. Since it is a precision part of an exercise, it will constantly need fine tuning. Any precision piece of equipment (a watch, a car and so on) will occasionally get out of alignment. A dog who does good fronts is not a dog who never sits crooked but rather a dog who is easily and quickly realigned.

The only way to get a dog to sit at exactly the same spot in the same way consistently is to teach the dog to focus his eyes on a specific point and then teach him what it feels like to position his body squarely.

The dog's point of focus should be above his eye level when he sits in front of the handler. You must focus the dog at a point on the midline of your body that he will see in a ring. For most large dogs, your mouth is a good place to look. Putting food in your mouth that you will eventually give to the dog (with both your hands) will keep him interested in looking at your mouth. With small dogs you can use toys or food placed between your knees. Mid-size dogs can be trained to look at a belt buckle, but only if you use it all the time in training and in the ring.

Fronts are started in conjunction with Come Fores and Recalls. When a dog is responding quickly and confidently to the "come" command, it is time to add a Sit Front.

It is important that the Sit Front be a pleasant experience and that the dog not feel he is being corrected for having come.

TO TEACH THE SIT FRONT

1. Do a Come Fore or Recall. As the dog comes to you, back up. You may back up forever in a circle, so don't let the dog rush you. Take your time backing up as you coil the leash.

2. Coil the leash until you have reached the dog's collar.

3. Your hands, palm down and overlapping, hold the coiled leash, which is under the dog's chin, and cradle his head.

4. Command "sit" sweetly as you stop moving, bend your knees, lean back and put pressure on the collar toward you and slightly up. It is important that the dog is pulled *toward* you for a Sit Front and not snapped away from you.

   When the dog sits between your knees looking up at you (which happens because your dog's head was cradled on your hands and encouraged to look up) on command, it is time to go on.

5. Do a Come Fore with the coiling of the leash, but as you back up, change directions. Step laterally left or right just as you finish coiling the leash and stop; command "sit." Use your knees to gently nudge the dog's rear if he appears to be about to sit crooked. By changing direction just before the dog sits front, you are causing the dog to think about where he is going to sit.

TO TRANSFER FRONT TO OFF-LEASH RECALLS

1. Find a point on the midline of your body that is slightly above the dog's eye level as he sits in front of you. For example, this might be between your knees, the space between your legs, a belt buckle, a pendant that you wear, a V-neck sweater, your mouth or your nose, depending on how large a dog you are training.

2. Leave the dog off leash and go six feet away. Point out the spot on your body that, from now on, will be referred to as a "front" by pointing to it with your hands or by placing food or a toy there initially to draw the dog's attention.

3. Show the dog front. Then replace your hands at your sides. Call the dog with the "come" command. As soon as he is up and moving, emphasize front with your hands. Your goal is to get the dog to point to front with his nose. Do not be concerned with his rear at this point. "Front" is a concept, not a command. The command used is always "come" since that's what the dog will hear in the ring.

Encourage a straight sit front by petting the dog toward you.

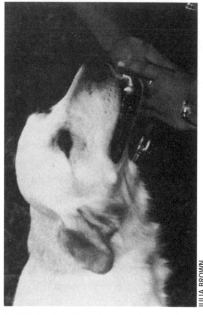

Coil the leash until you have reached the dog's collar. Notice how the dog's head is cradled in your hands.

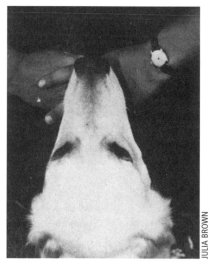

The handler's knees are bent and she is leaning back from the dog. The dog's head is held to look up toward the handler's face.

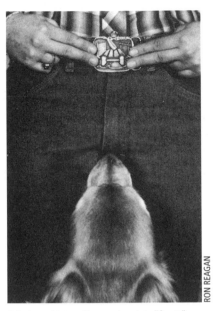

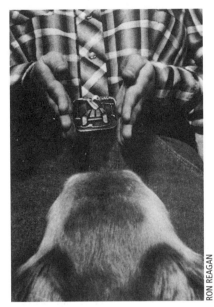

Pointing with two fingers pinpoints "front."

Framing "front" with your hands helps some dogs visualize it better.

4. You may have noticed that the dog has two parts, his front and rear, and that often these appear to be disconnected. To teach the dog what it feels like to line up his front and rear, make a chute out of two broad-jump boards. Teach the dog to comfortably walk into the chute and sit.

5. Stand at one end of the chute. Call the dog and help guide him with your arms into the chute and to the focal point of front.

6. To increase the dog's understanding of front, sit him intentionally off center before you call him and teach him to adjust by insisting he always come in to you via the chutes.

7. As your dog progresses, you will be able to substitute your knees for the chute.

8. For small dogs, 12-inch rulers or large books make good chutes.

It is very important when teaching fronts that the dog learns how to get his body into position without you helping to move him. If a dog sits crooked in front of you and you slide him over straight with your foot, he has no idea how he got there and actually learns that he doesn't have to think about where he sits because a big foot will come and move him to the right place!

The dog learns to look up to the focus point on your body, but how does he learn where to put his rear?

Chutes help the dog place his rear straight while his eyes are focused on the handler's midpoint.

Teach the dog to line up his rear with his front by sitting him between two broad-jump boards. The chute is only wide enough for the dog to sit squarely.

Teach the small dog to focus his eyes on the same point of your body each time he comes into a Sit Front.

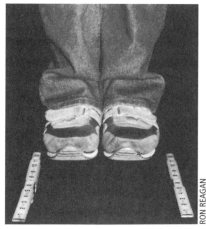

Small rulers work as guides for very small dogs.

Getting the dog used to coming
between dowels.

The dog focuses on food positioned
between your legs.

The dog sits straight in front between
the dowels.

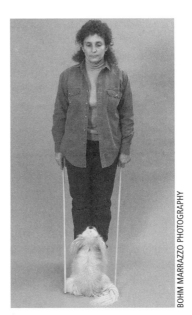

The dog now understands to come and
sit between two dowels that can now be
used to help the small and long-bodied
dog to adjust into a Straight Sit Front.

We teach the dog where to put his rear using our knees for most dogs (very small dogs don't respond to our knees, so we use our toes.) As a dog comes into front, make sure your feet are together and that you are standing straight and not staring at the dog. Especially with small dogs, if you make eye contact with them as they come to you, they will learn to sit out away from you so they can look up into your face. Your eyes don't help the dog on the front. It's done with your focus point (mouth) and your knees.

If the dog comes in to you and sits crooked, bend your knee closest to the side where the dog is angled. Push your knee *straight forward* into the dog's chest until he is forced to back away from you. As soon as the dog backs away, lower your food in both hands, down the middle of your body, and draw the dog back toward you. With the use of this push (with knee) and pull (with food), the dog begins to understand to sit between your knees and look up to the focus point.

Dogs who do nice brisk Recalls and then slow down as they get close to front are worried about sitting in the wrong place and of being punished for what they

Teach the large dog to look at your mouth to find the center of your body.

don't understand. A dog who understands where to look and is helped to line up properly learns to pop into a perfect front with no hesitation.

If a dog sits straight but off center, step sideways to exaggerate his mistake as you use your hands to point to front and your knees to guide his rear. *Never step backward to fix a front!* Most handlers who step backward end up unintentionally stepping in front of their dog so that the dog never learns to adjust sideways. Stepping backward would work to bring a dog *closer* to you but not *straighter*. When asking a dog to find front, please stand still! It is very difficult to line up with something that keeps moving!

Push your knee straight forward into the dog's
chest until he moves away from you.

Lower the food and draw the dog back to
you.

Once a dog is used to tucking himself into a Straight Sit and knows where to focus his eyes, you should not have to work hundreds of fronts to get consistent accuracy in the ring. Be sure to refocus your dog's attention to what you are wearing each day before you enter a ring. This is called "aligning front."

35

Teaching the Drop
on Recall

Keep in mind that a clear, crisp "down" command, without shouting or threatening, is preferred. Any command is only as effective as its enforcement. Dogs have excellent hearing. (It's their listening that isn't always so good!) "Excessively loud" commands in a ring are penalized.

STEP 1: UNDERSTANDING TWO DIFFERENT DOWNS

There are two different down exercises in obedience. The first is the Down-Stay where the dog lies down at your side, preferably on one hip, relaxed and planning to be there for a while. The second is the Down in Motion, where the dog drops as he is facing you in a crouched position, attentively waiting to be called up out of the down position.

STEP 2: DOWN IN MOTION AT YOUR SIDE

Begin with the dog, on a "let's go" command, attentively at your side. Command "down," then drop on your left knee as you slide your left hand down the leash to the collar and push straight down to the floor so that your hand is palm down flat against the floor. If the dog resists and keeps his hind end in the air, maintain your position and wait. With some resistant dogs you can have food in your left hand and encourage them to follow the food to the floor. As the dog relaxes, stop using the food. When the dog is collapsing before your hand gets to the floor, go on to the next step.

Two different kinds of down: The dog on the left is doing a Prone Drop. The dog on the right is doing a Down Stay.

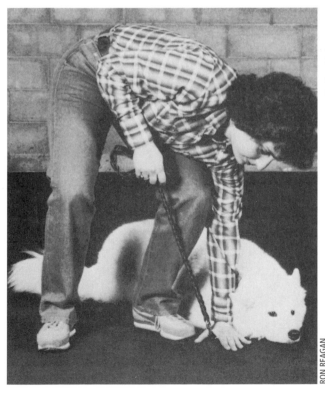

Executing the Down in Motion at your side. Notice that the palm of your hand is flat against the floor and that your elbow is locked in a straight position.

STEP 3: WINDMILL DOWN

From now on you will no longer drop the dog at your side but will do what we call a "windmill down." While walking on a "let's go," command "down" and then pivot in front of the dog to stop his motion, while at the same time swinging your right arm all the way up, around over your head and down onto the dog's neck. (With very large or resistant dogs, you may bring your hand down onto the dog's head or nose, or hold a piece of food in your left hand to lower the dog's head as your right hand comes over his head.) See "Downing a dog from a stand" in the Down-Stay chapter. Your hand is to come down on the dog regardless of whether he drops or not. If the dog beats you to the ground, the hand pets. If the dog does not beat your hand to the ground, the hand will give the dog a jolt to the floor.

This method teaches the dog to drop when he sees the palm of your hand. Never lower your right hand in *front* of the dog on the leash as this teaches the dog to drop when he sees the *back* of your hand. When it comes time to drop your dog on a hand signal, if the dog waits to see the back of your hand, it will be too late. The dog should learn to drop as you raise your arm and show him your palm.

Continue with the windmill down until the dog is beating your hand to the ground and see how fast you can get him to drop.

If your dog is pulling away from your hand so that he ends up lying sideways, you have unintentionally frightened him. Proceed with the same windmill hand signal, but do it in *slow motion* a few times until the dog realizes what is expected of him.

Occasionally use voice only as you pivot in front of the dog. If the dog does not drop, then follow through with your arm.

STEP 4: COME FORE AND DROP

Now it's time to integrate the Down in Motion into a Come Fore. Do a Come Fore and as the dog is coming toward you, command "down." If he does not drop, step into the dog, bring your windmill arm over your head and onto the dog's neck. At any time that the dog rolls over onto one hip, call the dog and pop the leash toward you quickly. This works to give you a crouched down because if the dog thinks he is going to have to get up quickly, he is not going to go down and roll over on one hip. Drop the dog at all different points. Sometimes do a Come Fore and do not drop the dog. If the dog acts like he wants to drop, keep moving backward. Say nothing and *do not* use the leash to correct!

STEP 5: KEEPING THE DOG'S ATTENTION

After the drop, sneak away by slowly backing up as you keep your eyes on the dog. If the dog maintains eye contact after you have gotten to the end of the leash, command "come" and if he gets up with a flying leap, praise him and let him jump on you. If the dog starts to get up slowly, add a sharp snap on the leash after the "come" command. In the event that the dog looks off (gets distracted) as you

The windmill down, step one: Pivot in front of the dog to stop his motion as you bring your right arm over your head and down onto his shoulders.

The windmill down, step two: Your hand makes contact with the dog whether he drops or not. If he drops willingly, your hand pets him. If he is not in a prone position as your hand is about to reach him, use your hand to give him a jolt to the ground.

The windmill down, step three: After the dog has dropped, sneak away slowly by backing up as you maintain eye contact with the dog. At any time that the dog looks off, give a sharp snap on the leash toward yourself and command "come."

are sneaking away, snap him up off the drop immediately as you tease, "Did you miss something? I guess you weren't watching." It is important that you train this exercise so that you have total attention from the dog throughout the exercise. The lead snap off the drop will encourage a fast second part of the drop exercise. Occasionally you should simply release the dog off the drop with an "okay!" and let him leap into your arms, which will add speed and enthusiasm to the Drop-on-Recall exercise.

STEP 6: TEACH UNDERSTANDING

As you work this exercise, the dog will become more and more likely to antici-pate the drop. This is perfectly normal and part of the learning process. We work to cause the dog to anticipate while on leash in a controlled situation before we take him off the leash and work the exercise formally.

Continue working your Come Fore exercise, only now as you are running backward, say meaningless words to the dog before you give the "down" com-mand. For example, say, "Fido, come." and as you back up say, "bananas," "straw-berries," "chocolate" and finally "down." The only word the dog should respond to is "down." If the dog starts to drop on another word, just keep backing up. Do not snap and do not repeat "come." When you can no longer catch the dog responding to the other words, it is time to go on.

STEP 7: DOWN IN THE MIDDLE OF COME

Dogs have a difficult time accepting that a "down" command could cancel out a "come" command. To help them accept this new concept, we change the picture of the Recall when we first take the dog off leash.

Place two to four broad-jump boards on end about 15 feet apart. Call your dog over one board to you, then two, until the dog will recall jumping over all the boards. Most dogs like this simple jump exercise.

Boards placed ready to teach the Drop on Recall.

BOHM MARRAZZO PHOTOGRAPHY

The dog is called over the boards.

BOHM MARRAZZO PHOTOGRAPHY

Next, call your dog and let him come over all the boards until he gets between the two boards closest to you. Command "down" before the last board. The first time you do this, your dog will probably hesitate but still jump the last board. Say nothing and calmly start over. You are making the dog think. Do *not* correct the dog into a down position. Repeat the same sequence and again command "down" before the last board. Do you see any reaction? Is your dog starting to notice that something isn't right? Usually, by the third attempt, your dog actually lies down before the last board or at least considers it as a possibility.

Command "down" before the dog crosses the last board.

When you finally get a drop, praise and then release the dog *to you* over the last board. This helps assure a prompt response after the drop because the dog needs enough energy to jump the board.

Now try to drop your dog between any two boards.

As your dog learns the game, start dropping the dog behind different boards. The use of the broad-jump boards on end teaches the dog a few different things:

1. Drop when I tell you and not five steps later!
2. Get up quickly after the drop.
3. It's okay to stop coming sometimes when doing a Recall (at least when there are boards to run over!).

When you can successfully drop your dog between any two boards or directly in front of any board you choose, you are ready to go to the next step!

STEP 8: OFF LEASH

Take the dog off leash and do a full-distance Recall. Since the dog has never done a formal Drop on Recall off leash, he should expect nothing and come in briskly. If his Recall is not brisk, work on the speed before you worry about adding a drop to it, which will undoubtedly slow it down temporarily.

Remember, the Drop-on-Recall exercise is the first exercise we teach the dog where one command cancels out another command. This is initially a very confusing and upsetting concept for a dog, especially a sweet, willing one who wants very much to please. The dog hears the command "come" and he is briskly heading to you. Now you command "down." While the dog hears and understands the "down" command, he first wants to complete the "come" command. The end result is a dog who comes all the way in to his handler and then drops at the handler's feet. Thinking he has satisfied all the requirements, the dog is very confused to learn that his handler is not happy with his actions. Who knows what the dog thinks now?

To put the dog at ease and help him learn that the "down" command cancels out the "come" command, it is very important that when you first command "down" and the dog is off leash, and there are no boards to jump over, you must immediately walk toward the dog to meet him. Your forward motion (as if to say, "You can stop coming because I will meet you.") encourages the dog to stop and lie down without anxiety over not having completed the Recall.

When you have your brisk Recall, call your dog and command "down" (in a clear, *sweet* tone). Immediately following your command to down, begin walking toward the dog with your windmill hand signal. As you meet, bring your hand down to his neck, either to correct or praise, depending on whether or not the dog is in the prone position. Your walking toward the dog discourages him from continuing toward you. Walk in regardless of how fast he drops in the beginning.

As your dog starts to respond faster and faster to your down command, start giving the command when he is farther and farther away from you, but continue walking in to praise the dog. After the drop, release the dog. There is no need at this point for you to work on the second half of the exercise.

Alternate drops with straight Recalls. At any time that the dog off leash anticipates and actually drops, say nothing, walk slowly to him and gently bring him to you. Praise him when he gets to you. When he is consistently dropping well and responding quickly, alternate between walking in to praise him and not walking in. At any time that the dog slows down because he is thinking about dropping, say nothing and do nothing. Allow the dog to think about the exercise.

PROBLEMS

For dogs who do not stop fast enough in response to a "down" command, you might try the following (listed in order of severity):

1. Stamp your foot immediately after you say "down." (Keep your voice sweet and clear.)
2. Throw a tied-up leash on the ground *next to you* immediately after you command "down."
3. Bounce a tennis ball off the floor right in front of the dog immediately after the "down" command. (Don't worry if he goes to retrieve it, just get him and put him back in position.)
4. Throw a throw-chain or keys on the floor in front of you, or between you and the dog.
5. Tie the dog on a long line to a tree. Measure out where the line ends. Command "down" just as the dog gets to that spot. The line will stop the dog. You may have to go in the first few times and put him down. (Remember not to call him to you after the drop!)
6. For severe cases, hold a water hose in your right hand at your side. Command "down" and then send a stream of water right at the dog.

For frightened and timid dogs, move very slowly and give a slow-motion windmill signal. If your dog turns away from you on the drop, your method of stopping him was too harsh. Back up, slow down and go easier. You probably corrected before you had understanding.

COMMON MISTAKES MADE BY HANDLERS

The most common error made by handlers in teaching the Drop-on-Recall exercise is not letting the dog think. If a dog comes in on a Recall and then slows down because he is thinking about the drop, say nothing and let him think! To shout "hurry!" only stops him from thinking and causes him to rely on you to make all the decisions. When the slow-moving, thinking dog finally gets to you, praise profusely for the correct decision. The only time you intervene is if the dog actually drops and then all you do is slowly walk to him and gently bring him to you. Praise only when he gets to you.

Some handlers will not drop the dog if he is coming in slowly. Why not? The dog is coming slowly because he is thinking about the drop and doesn't want to miss the signal. Give him a clear, smooth signal when he's coming slowly to teach him that he will know when he should drop. Speed returns to your Drop-on-Recall exercise when the dog understands and is not afraid of missing a signal.

If you never drop the dog when he comes in slowly, the dog will eventually realize this. For a dog who doesn't want to deal with the stress of deciding when to drop and when not to drop, you have offered him the perfect solution. He will continue to come in slowly so that you won't drop him! Now, who is training whom?

Some handlers advocate not dropping your dog except in the ring. You cannot work through a problem of confusion if you don't cause the problem and then work on it.

If we believe that the dog is not wrong for thinking, then he is not wrong for coming in slowly in this instance.

PROOFING IDEAS

Drop your dog at all different points of the Recall.

Drop your dog on all different surfaces, that is, wet grass, mats, concrete, plastic, wire, and so on.

Drop your dog three times in a row in the same place, then do a straight Recall. Does he know the difference?

Drop your dog with a hand signal only or with voice only.

Call your dog and say "bananas," "strawberries," "chocolate," his name, then "down." Does he know what word to respond to?

Call your dog and make extraneous body movements. Then give a clear signal. Does he know to wait for a definite signal?

Call your dog and have others command "down." Does he know to respond to only your voice?

When you can successfully complete all of these proofing exercises, you are on your way to having a thinking dog who not only performs the exercise but understands it.

PROOF THE RECALL AFTER THE DROP

Call your dog and drop him. Now say his name as if you were going to call him. If he moves, put him back. Dogs are penalized for moving on their names; it is called "anticipation."

Make all kinds of nonsensical body motions. Any time your dog gets up from the drop, put him back.

Finally, command "come." Make sure that the dog only pops up for the second Recall part of the exercise when he hears the word "come" or sees a clear hand signal.

Practice dropping the dog about six feet in front of you and then call him up off the "drop." To encourage him to leap up at you (even though there is very little distance between you), you may need to give him a snap with the lead immediately following "come" or just release him with an "okay," throw your hands up and/or run away from him. For very large breeds, refer to the techniques used to speed up the Recall exercise mentioned in Chapter 17, Special Small Dog and Big Dog Techniques.

36
The Finish

The purpose of the finish is to teach your dog to go to heel position when sitting in front of you. Upon completion of other exercises, your dog will not always be seated at heel, thus the purpose of the finish is to enable you to have your dog assume the heel position on command. The key to getting a Straight Sit at heel is to teach the dog to complete the finish with his head up and not to look at him as he gets into the sit at heel.

There are two different ways for a dog to finish. From a position sitting in front of you, the dog may go to your right, around your back and up into heel position, or the dog may circle to your left, turn toward you and come along your left side into heel position. Dogs with short backs usually have an easier time finishing to the left. Every dog will prefer to bend in one direction. I usually attempt to teach both finishes initially and then decide which one the dog prefers and perfect that one. Be sure to use two different commands if you are teaching both finishes. Finishes may be taught by using food to guide the dog or by using the leash, or both.

TO TEACH YOUR DOG TO FINISH TO THE RIGHT

1. Tell your dog "wait" and step directly in front of him, so his nose is almost touching you.

2. Gather all the leash in your right hand and position your right hand so that it rests at the back of your right thigh. There should be *very little* slack in the leash. You may also hold a treat in the hand with the leash.

3. Give your dog the command "heel" as you step back with your right foot. If your dog does not respond to the "heel" command, pull gently up and in the same direction that your foot is moving. This will move the dog behind you and encourage him to keep his head up.

145

JULIA BROWN

When teaching the dog to finish, step back with your right foot to encourage the dog to get up, after you command "heel."

4. Switch the leash behind your back into your left hand, while at the same time stepping your right foot back into place and encourage the dog to move up to your left leg and sit. Pass the leash to your right hand, and show the dog with your left hand where to focus his attention to sit straight. Do not snap the dog up into heel position. Encourage, please! A treat in your left hand can also be used to encourage the dog up into heel position.

Large dogs may require two steps backward and two steps forward into position. Small dogs may require no steps back!

Eventually your dog will get up on his own on the command "heel" without the need of the leash or step.

By moving the leash with your right hand in the direction you wish the dog to go, you are also teaching him a hand signal, which you will need later in Utility.

To teach the small dog to walk around you with his head up, try using a toy or food to initially bait him around you. If a dog is not interested in food or toys, a halter type of lead (which looks like a muzzle with a lead attached) can be used. For large dogs or any dog when the other techniques are not working, cradle the dog's head in your right hand. Then as you step back on your right foot, hold the dog's head up as you lead him behind you by his head. Quickly reach back with your left hand and pass the dog's chin from your right hand into your left hand (behind your back). You are now in position to guide the dog up into heel position, which you are pointing to with your right hand. Once the dog is accustomed to moving around behind you with his head up, you can let go and only reach to correct him to bring his head back up, if necessary.

It takes a beginning dog weeks to master the finish. This is because you are asking the dog to do a series of things on one command. On the command "heel," the dog must get up, walk around you, and then sit in heel position. In all other beginning training exercises, one command elicited one response. Be patient with young dogs when teaching the finish.

TO TEACH YOUR DOG TO FINISH TO THE LEFT

Start with the dog sitting in front of you looking up. Command "swing," then take a piece of food in your left hand and guide the dog close to your body and behind you. When the dog's nose is behind your right buttock, change the dog's direction and lead him with the food up along your left side into a sit at heel position.

It is very important when teaching either finish that you give the command ("heel" or "swing") *before* you show the dog where to move and not *as* you move the dog. You *want* the dog to anticipate the movement one day and thus respond to only the verbal command. If you always say the command *as* you move your hand, the dog will never learn to respond on a verbal command!

You can train six dogs to do a finish the same way, and over time each dog will put his own style into the exercise. Some dogs decide to leap up, others swing their rears around, pivoting on their front feet. Give your dog some leeway to express his personality when doing a finish, as long as he moves briskly, attentively and arrives in heel position.

Holding the large dog's head and collar with your right hand, you can guide the dog's head behind your body to begin the finish. Notice that the dog's head is held up.

Switch the dog's head from your right hand to your left hand behind your body.

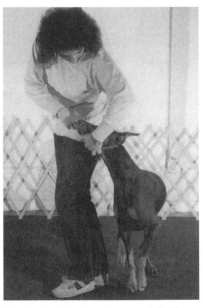

Bring the dog's head up along your left side while pointing out heel position to complete the finish.

The dog should be looking up as he does a finish.

The handler points out heel position as the dog comes around on the finish.

With food in your left hand, command "swing."

Keeping your feet stationary, lure the dog behind you.

The dog's head must go behind your right buttock.

Lure the dog up to sit in the heel position.

37
Stand for Examination

$\mathbf{T}$his exercise teaches your dog to stand on command so that you might bathe him, brush him, pose him or otherwise inspect him for whatever reason. It is also a required obedience exercise.

The dog spends most of his time in a standing position during his daily life, and if his weight is evenly distributed, this should be a very comfortable position for him. Most dogs resist the stand position because they don't understand what the handler wants them to do. It seems too simple. Beginning handlers often handle, grope, and are in general too physical with their dogs when teaching the stand. Dogs resent being pushed, lifted, prodded and so on. Be gentle!

TEACHING THE STAND

1. With your dog in the sitting position, at heel, grasp all of the lead and a treat in the right hand.

2. Step forward on your right foot as you lead him forward with the food, and turn so that you are facing your dog's right side as you simultaneously give him the command "stand." Sliding your left foot under the dog in front of his rear feet will encourage him to stand up, and you don't have to bend! Make sure the dog is comfortable, with his weight evenly distributed on all four feet. This is done by balancing the dog. To balance the dog, push gently left to right on the dog's withers and hips. If he is off balance when you push, he will adjust his stance. Do not push down on the dog, as this will encourage him to sit. If he does not stand up, pull forward on his collar gently with your right hand.

3. When your dog is standing, balance your dog by pushing him gently left to right. When your dog is content to stand still (which may take a week or more), give him the command to "stay" and step directly in front of him, as you did in teaching him the sit.

4. If your dog should start to sit while you are standing in front of him, step forward on the left foot and place your left hand by his stifle. As soon as your dog is again in the standing position, step back on the left foot so that you are back in front of him, and praise.

5. After you have stood him for approximately 30 seconds, return to the heel position in the same manner as returning from a Sit-Stay and Down-Stay (walk all the way around him). If your dog should attempt to sit as you return to the heel position, reach down with your left hand and, by touching his stifle, get him to stand again. (Those of you training small dogs may find it easier to place the instep of your left foot beneath his abdomen to prevent him from sitting. Or you may work the dog on a table and put a brush under him as he stands up.)

Step forward on your right foot as you lure the dog with food up into a standing position.

6. After returning to heel position, praise your dog, then command, "Okay, Let's go" and move your dog briskly to the spot in the ring where he will begin the off-leash heeling. In practice, make up a place to move to. A dog should not be asked to sit following the stand exercise, as this often adds confusion. The dog might be tempted to sit as you return, thinking that you were planning to ask him to sit next anyway.

For dogs who resist being touched by their handler, or for small dogs in general, loop the end of your leash under the dog's flanks and attach the other end to the collar. Now if the dog tries to sit, lift up on the leash.

Be sure not to let your dog take steps forward after he stands up. Stop movement either by lifting his head with your hand under his chin or by placing your right hand on his chest and not allowing him to walk forward.

For dogs who insist on walking and are too big to restrain, stand them facing into a wall so they cannot move, or stand them on the top of a staircase so that if they move they go down the stairs!

For dogs who fidget, stand them with their front paws on a platform or step so that their front feet are raised up 6 to 10 inches.

RON REAGAN

Teaching the small dog to stand. Notice that the signal to stand is also introduced.

Touch your dog as gently as possible when teaching the stand exercise. If you handle him harshly, he will learn to stand with his back humped like a camel. Your leash is only helpful to initially encourage the dog to stand up; after that, drop it because you cannot successfully use your leash to correct a stand unless you have previously draped it around the dog as described before. Move calmly, slowly, gently and deliberately when teaching your dog to stand, and you will achieve the best results.

If the dog tries to walk forward, take hold of his muzzle gently with your right hand and point the dog's nose towards the sky. A dog whose nose is pointed straight up cannot walk forward. This also encourages the dog to stand with his head up!

Before a dog is required to accept being examined by a stranger in the standing position, he should readily accept being touched by a stranger while sitting next to his handler, standing next to his handler, then while sitting in front of his handler and finally while standing in front of his handler. To assure that the first examinations are positive experiences, instruct the person examining the dog to talk approvingly to the dog and to make the exam pleasurable. For nervous dogs, the examiner might even offer the dog a tidbit as a sign of friendship to assure a positive response. If the dog is initially examined with a pat *under* the chin, the dog is less likely to get in the habit of dropping his head as a judge approaches to give an exam.

JULIA BROWN

Standing a dog with his front feet up on a raised board will often stop him from walking forward or making minor foot movements.

TEACHING THE MOVING STAND

If you decide to show your dog in Utility, you will encounter two exercises that require the dog to stand while in motion. The first exercise is the Signal Exercise. On hand signal only, you will heel the dog and then stand him as you stop moving. The second exercise is called the Moving Stand For Examination. In this exercise you command the dog with a hand signal and verbal command and the dog must freeze into a standing position as you continue walking 10 to 12 feet, and then turn to face your dog. The judge examines the dog and then commands you to call the dog directly to heel position. You may use hand and voice to do this. Let's examine these exercises separately.

Heel with your dog at a slow pace. At some point, as you step down on your right foot, simultaneously swing your right hand (which is extended only as far as your right foot is) up and under the dog's chin and use it to stop the dog's forward motion. If the dog tries to sit, place your left foot under him or make use of the leash as a sling (see the photo on page 153). As soon as the dog stops moving, praise him. Eventually the dog learns to stand as soon as he sees the palm of your right hand above his muzzle. It is important that the right foot be coordinated with the right hand because the left foot cues the dog to sit and that is what we don't want him to do in this case.

The handler's right hand gives the hand signal to stand. Notice that the hand signal is no further forward than the handler's right foot is extended.

Lifting the dog's head up with the right hand as you give the stand signal prevents the dog from walking forward. Notice that the right hand and the right foot work together.

To teach the dog to stay in a standing position as you keep walking, command "stay" as you give the stand signal with the right hand. The hand tells the dog to stand and your voice tells him to stay as you keep walking.

The dog stands and is examined by the judge. Then on the command from the judge, you call the dog directly to heel position. This is the more difficult part of the exercise because this is the only time during the obedience routines when the dog goes directly to heel position. It is important to teach this carefully so as not to cause confusion.

To teach the dog to come to heel position, begin with the dog sitting three feet in front and facing you on leash. Command "heel" and with the leash gathered in your right or left hand (depending on which finish you are using), guide the dog around into a finish. This is just an extension of the finish exercise the dog already knows. Now gradually add distance between you and the dog. After a few repetitions, command "come" and do a Recall. Alternate until the dog recognizes that there are two different but similar exercises. Should the dog attempt to do the wrong thing, do not shove him in the right direction! This only makes it look better for the moment, but it does not clarify things to the dog. It is important to realize where the dog made his mistake. He made the wrong decision at the point when he got up and moved. Therefore, it is necessary to go back to the point at which the mistake was made in order to correct it. Put the dog back and redo the entire exercise from the beginning until he makes the right decision in response to the voice and hand signal. If the dog is repeatedly wrong, say nothing and repeat. You may shorten the distance between you and the dog if he makes the mistake again. When the dog is secure with the two different commands, do them from the stand position.

38
Teaching the Retrieve

WHAT KIND OF DUMBBELL TO USE

While it is true that a dog could pick up any small stick if he wanted to, we try to give him an advantage when picking up a dumbbell. Dumbbells should have tapered ends to maximize vision and should have a mouthpiece measured to fit the dog's muzzle exactly, not allowing the bell to shift sideways. The ends should be high enough to allow the dog room to get his jaw under the bar without scraping his chin on the floor. Dumbbells made to order can be purchased from companies specializing in custom obedience equipment. The names and addresses can be found in obedience publications or through your training class.

TEACHING THE RETRIEVE

The Compulsive Retrieve, also called the Forced Retrieve, is often a misunderstood method of training a dog to retrieve. A dog who is taught the Forced Retrieve, in the end, retrieves happily and *reliably*. When executed properly, it is an exercise that is clearly and quickly understood and enjoyed by the dog. If, on the other hand, the Forced Retrieve is not taught properly, it can be unfair and abusive to the dog. Since many of the Utility exercises require a sound retrieve, it is preferable to teach a reliable, Compulsive Retrieve right from the beginning.

The Forced Retrieve is based on the same training principle as housebreaking or learning sit or down. The dog is first carefully taught the exercise and is then expected to perform on command. Retrieve on command is only as compulsory as "sit" is.

A perfect dumbbell fit.

RON REAGAN

There are dogs who naturally like to retrieve. The problem with these dogs is that one day, for some reason (usually a distracting situation), they are not feeling very natural! Since so many obedience exercises are based on the retrieve, it is essential that trainers have a way to enforce a retrieve.

One of the most effective ways to enforce a retrieve is with a technique called the "ear pinch." If you do not wish to pinch your dog's ear, don't do it. For one thing, the correction wouldn't work if your attitude is not positive. When a dog senses that you don't want to correct him, he will resist harder. Usually handlers who avoid teaching a Compulsive Retrieve get so exasperated at some point in training that they do it as a last resort. It works so easily that they wonder why they didn't do it sooner. Do not use any method of training that you do not understand and do not feel comfortable with. Before you get all upset over the ear pinch, take your thumbnail and forefinger and pinch your *own* earlobe. It is annoying–but not excruciating.

Praise: Be sure to praise the dog calmly when the dumbbell is in his mouth, regardless of how it got there. You may give treats, but be careful that the dog doesn't learn to drop the dumbbell to get the food! I have found that using treats in the early stages of teaching the dumbbell causes mouthing of the dumbbell. The dog is trying to encourage you to take it out of his mouth quickly so he can get the treat. I like to wait until the dog has completely learned to retrieve before introducing treats as a reward for this exercise.

TEACHING A COMPULSIVE RETRIEVE HUMANELY

Goal 1

The dog will allow his handler to open his mouth by applying pressure to his lips and place the dumbbell in his mouth just behind the lower canine teeth. (This takes about one week of work, practicing six times in a row one to three times daily.) The dog must not fight the dumbbell; he must be willing to let it sit in his mouth before proceeding.

How to Accomplish Goal 1

The dog is sitting in heel position to begin. You may stand on his leash so that he cannot leave. Begin with the dumbbell held in your right hand by the ends, hidden behind your back. It is important that the dog not see the dumbbell before he has to take it.

Command "take it" as you present the dumbbell to the dog. If he does not open his mouth, apply pressure from under his chin with your fingers pinching his lips. Open his mouth from under his chin so as not to block his vision of the dumbbell. As he opens his mouth, place the dumbbell behind his large front canine teeth and close his mouth gently over the dumbbell. Do not allow the dog to throw his head back as this will cause the dumbbell to roll back to his molars, where he is likely

The dog is taught to hold the dumbbell directly behind his canine teeth and not roll it back to his molars where he might be tempted to chew it.

RON REAGAN

to chew it. Keep your hands on his mouth so that he *cannot drop the dumbbell.* As he holds the dumbbell, talk softly and calmly to him and if possible stroke his head soothingly. Then command "give" and take the dumbbell from him. "Give" should signal the dog to release pressure, not to spit out the dumbbell.

Goal 2

The dog will voluntarily open his mouth upon feeling pressure of the dumbbell on his teeth and accept the dumbbell into his mouth. (It takes about three to six days of work.)

How to Accomplish Goal 2

It is now time to learn how to make a correction in the event that the dog, after having had the dumbbell gently positioned in his mouth approximately 126 times in one week following the "take it" command, still has no idea that you would like the dumbbell in his mouth. With most dogs, the ear-pinch correction works best because it allows the dog complete freedom of his mouth and breathing. If someone was going to put something in my mouth, I would want to have my mouth and throat free to accept it. For some dogs, however, the ear-pinch correction is not sufficient to convince the dog to open his mouth, and then we are forced to use a collar choke approach.

To execute the ear pinch properly, you must first learn to make an "ear sandwich." Place the extra portion of a choke-chain collar (you may need a longer collar for this) over the forefinger of your left hand. Now place the dog's ear with the inside part by the ridges (fairly well inside the ear) over the chain. On top rest your thumbnail. You now have the dog's right ear sandwiched between the chain and your nail, all resting on your forefinger. To pinch, suddenly press down with your nail against the chain. Never pull or twist the ear leather. This is a pinch—not a *pull/twist* technique. Begin your pinch with mild pressure. If the dog screams, you have pinched too hard. If all the dog can think about is the correction, then he isn't thinking about what you want. Try to make the pinch annoying, not painful.

There are dogs who will react to an ear pinch by trying to bite. This is not unusual but certainly not acceptable. If the aggressive response cannot be controlled with a sharp "No!" then the trainer should resort to the choke-collar method initially in teaching this exercise. A dog who is being choked cannot go to bite you. Sometimes dogs snap because they are startled by the ear pinch, and once they realize how to avoid it, there is no more aggression. Sometimes an aggressive response indicates that you have applied too much force. Remember the rule: "Use the mildest effective correction." If you have a sensitive dog, you might start on a buckle collar with an ear that is sandwiched between two fingers without using a nail or chain. On some dogs with very low pain thresholds, all that is necessary is a mild squeeze between two fingers and you never even get to pinch. Be sure that the ear pinch is a correction, that is, something the dog will work to avoid. If the ear pinch is *too* mild, the dog will wait for it to happen, almost as an additional command. The pinch should be annoying, not painful! If the correction is too strong, the dog thinks about the correction and not about what you are asking him to do!

The handler is ready to present the dumbbell and command "take it." The dumbbell is hidden behind the handler's back and the "ear sandwich" is ready to pinch, if necessary.

Making the "ear sandwich" with a chain collar.

Making an ear sandwich with two fingers and a buckle collar.

For dogs who are not impressed with the ear-pinch correction, you may reverse the ear so that your nail is applying pressure to the inside of the ear, which is a little more sensitive. Each dog has a spot on his ear where you will get a better response to your correction. Experiment with different parts of the ear to find the spot that gives you the best results.

WHY IT WORKS

With the dumbbell in your right hand hidden behind your back and with your left hand holding an ear sandwich, slowly and sweetly command "Fido, take it" as you present the dog the dumbbell and press the bar of the dumbbell against the dog's teeth. With any luck, he will clench his teeth shut, at which point you pinch, he says "ouch," you slide the dumbbell into his mouth, let go of his ear and stroke his head as you hold the dumbbell in his mouth. If the dog willingly opens his mouth, let go of the ear and praise. Repeat this a few times hoping the dog will get fed up and hold his mouth shut so that you have an opportunity to pinch him and thus introduce the ear-pinch correction. A dog must learn why his ear is being pinched and understand how to avoid the correction if the training is to remain fair and humane. You should never arbitrarily pinch a dog who is not retrieving unless he has been taught the meaning of the correction. A dog who willingly opens his mouth is still learning that you will let go of his ear when the dumbbell is in his mouth. He is learning how to get you off his ear!

To accomplish the same thing with a dog who is not impressed with an ear pinch, you might use the collar choke approach. Slide the choke-chain collar high behind the dog's ears and hold it snug with your left hand. Command "take it" as you present the dumbbell and press against the dog's clenched teeth. Suddenly pull up on the collar so that the collar is tightening around his throat. He will eventually be forced to open his mouth for air, and when he does, in goes the dumbbell, you release the collar and praise. For the very resistant cases where you must resort to the collar correction, after the dog is opening his mouth for the dumbbell easily you can still go back and use the ear pinch, usually with no resistance. The ear pinch is preferred because while you can choke a dog up by pulling up, eventually the dumbbell is going to be on the floor and it is very awkward to choke a dog down to the floor.

Goal 3

The dog will *reach* one inch for the dumbbell.

How to Accomplish Goal 3

Now it is time to teach the dog to *reach* for the dumbbell. It is essential that the trainer be careful never to put the dumbbell into the dog's mouth, which is very tempting at this point. We cannot teach the dog to reach if we move the dumbbell toward him. The dog must at all times feel that he controls the ear-pinch correction. His reaching to take hold of the dumbbell gets you off his ear.

For this step, when you make your ear sandwich, take hold of the buckle collar with the last three fingers of your left hand (that were previously holding the leash). This will give you better control of the dog's head. Command "take it" as you present the dumbbell one inch in front of the dog's mouth and slightly above his muzzle, where it is easily visible. If, after a moment, your dog makes no effort to reach for the dumbbell, push his head forward with the buckle collar until his teeth are pressing against the bar of the dumbbell. This should remind him of the previous step, which he was able to do, and he should open his mouth. If he does not open his mouth, pinch his ear. After a few days at this step, stop pushing the dog's head toward the dumbbell. If he makes no effort to reach forward one inch himself, pinch his ear. (Remember, at no time does the dumbbell move toward the dog!) The dog may try to move away from this spot: Keep the dumbbell in front of the dog's eyes at all times. You may repeat "take it" slowly in this instance because the dog is often so distracted by the ear pinch that he doesn't remember how to get you off his ear. (It is only until the dumbbell gets to the floor that moderate repetition of a command is permitted and only then because of the stress you are applying with the correction.) No matter how often you repeat the command "take it," it is always said in a saccharin-sweet voice. You can afford to be verbally sweet because you know the dog will eventually respond. He will make the connection between putting the dumbbell in his mouth and getting you off his ear.

Distance is now increased slowly. You are always ready with your sandwich for the ear pinch, *if necessary*.

Since the dog knows what is coming, he is likely at this point to try not to let you make the ear sandwich. If this happens, put your dumbbell away and practice holding his ear. It is not the dog's choice to refuse to let you hold his ear. You own him and his ear!

At any time in training that the dog reaches for the dumbbell, you cannot pinch. This would be unfair.

Use the collar choke approach for dogs who are not responsive to an ear pinch. When they start to respond, go back to the ear pinch.

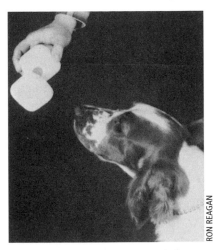

The dog must now reach for the dumbbell. Notice that the dumbbell is held slightly above the dog's eye level.

The dog must move toward the dumbbell to put it in his mouth. Notice that the dog is pulling the handler. The handler never pulls the dog to the dumbbell with the ear. This is the ear-*pinch* method and not the ear-*pull* method!

Goal 4

The dog will *reach* six inches for a dumbbell at eye level with surrounding distractions.

How to Accomplish Goal 4

Apply the same principle that you did for Goal 3.

Goal 5

The dog will *reach* one foot for the dumbbell at eye level, below eye level, and above eye level.

How to Accomplish Goal 5

Apply the same principle that you did for Goal 3.

Goal 6

The dog, after reaching for the dumbbell, will hold it in his mouth, without mouthing or chewing it, for one minute while the handler stands in front of him. (The dog is sitting, the handler is holding the dog's mouth closed. The dog cannot drop the dumbbell.)

How to Accomplish Goal 6

If the dog attempts to mouth the dumbbell, quickly squeeze and release without letting go of his muzzle. If this doesn't work, try a collar correction by popping up on the collar with the leash. When the dog stops mouthing, praise immediately.

The dog jumps up to reach above his head for the dumbbell.

Goal 7

The dog will retrieve the dumbbell from the floor with the handler's hand on it.

How to Accomplish Goal 7

One of the stumbling blocks in teaching the retrieve is teaching the dog to pick the dumbbell up off the floor. Here you might have to assist the dog by pushing up on his lower jaw as he has his mouth hovering over the dumbbell. Believe it or not, some dogs don't realize that they have to bite down before they pick up the dumbbell!

As soon as the dog is retrieving off the floor with or without an ear pinch, a quick "come!" should follow him getting to the dumbbell, ensuring a quick return. Actually you almost run the two commands together: "Take it, come!" You can increase the speed of his pickup of the dumbbell by enforcing your "come" command with a brief lead snap. If the dog comes without the dumbbell, initially you help the dog by pointing to what he forgot. There is no need to repeat the "take it" command. If he does not respond to your help, pinch his ear as you point to the dumbbell. *You never pull a dog by his ear to a dumbbell!* The dog must make his own decision to get the dumbbell in an effort to get you off his ear. To date, no dog has ever decided to live with his owner or trainer attached to and pinching his ear.

The dog is assisted in learning to pick the dumbbell up from the floor. The handler pushes up on the dog's jaw after the dog has put his mouth on the bar of the dumbbell.

The dog must retrieve the dumbbell from the floor with the handler's finger on it. This is an important transition step.

The dog will finally retrieve off the floor with the handler pointing to the dumbbell. Gradually the pointing finger is removed completely.

To help dogs learn to pick up the dumbbell off the floor, try putting it on a step or bench first and encouraging the dog to get his bottom jaw under the dowel of the dumbbell.

Some dogs scream when their ears are pinched, others do not. It has no bearing on how hard the pinch is whether they scream or not; it's just the individual dog's character. It should not be your intention to make the dog scream. But if you know you are not pinching hard, just ignore the theatrics! Some trainers feel that the collar choke or collar twist (which accomplishes the same thing) is a more humane method because when used, the dogs don't scream. Of course they don't—how could a dog scream or complain when he is choking?

A student once came to me and said, "My dog doesn't like it when I pinch his ear." "Good," I replied, "If he did, it wouldn't work!"

There is really very little difference between an ear pinch and a collar jerk as corrections—both are annoying and hopefully the dog works to avoid them. Do we find it easier to accept snapping a collar because we've done it longer? Frankly, I'd rather have my ear pinched.

Goal 8

The dog will retrieve the dumbbell from the floor with one of the handler's fingers touching it.

How to Accomplish Goal 8

Apply the same principle that you did for Goal 7.

Goal 9

The dog will retrieve the dumbbell off the floor when the handler points to it.

How to Accomplish Goal 9

Apply the same principle that you did for Goal 7.

Goal 10

The dog will hold the dumbbell while standing and move with the dumbbell in his mouth.

How to Accomplish Goal 10

If the dog drops the dumbbell, *he* picks it up! Point to the dumbbell, but do not repeat "take it." He must learn to remember. From the time the dog is retrieving off the floor, the handler never again needs to hold the dog's mouth. Let the dog drop it! Command "take it" and if he refuses, then pinch.

RON REAGAN

Having moved forward and retrieved the dumbbell, the handler commands the dog to come. The dumbbell is held in the dog's mouth as he is led on leash into a Sit Front. Notice that the handler's foot is guiding the dog into a Straight Sit Front.

Goal 11

The dog will retrieve the dumbbell a leash length off the ground and return and sit front.

How to Accomplish Goal 11

Use the same principle as for Goal 3. If the dog refuses to retrieve, pinch with your left hand as you point to the dumbbell with your right hand.

Goal 12

The dog will retrieve the dumbbell off the floor at a leash length when the dumbbell is placed next to a distraction (for example, food, another dog or other animal).

How to Accomplish Goal 12

Set up a situation where the dog has a choice of retrieving the dumbbell or getting distracted. For example, place a cookie six feet from where you toss the dumbbell. If the dog heads for the cookie on your command to "take it," prevent him from getting the cookie by use of the leash and then help him by pointing to the dumbbell. If he refuses to pick up the dumbbell at this point, pinch his ear. Every time you introduce a new proof situation, the first time the dog falls for the proof you help him sort it out. In fact, you can continue to help him until you decide that he is not trying to solve the problem and then resort to the pinch as a correction.

WHEN TO LET GO OF THE EAR

You have held the dog's ear in the ear sandwich position in readiness through all of the steps until the dog is retrieving off the floor. It is now time to go back to the beginning and repeat all the steps without your hand on the dog's ear. This should happen quickly and you can usually go through all of the steps in one training session. At any time that you command "take it" and the dog refuses, take your time, make the ear sandwich and point to the dumbbell. Then repeat that step without holding the ear until the dog will respond without your hand on his ear as a reminder of what could happen.

STALEMATES

It is not at all uncommon for a battle of wills to occur during the training of retrieve. Occasionally a dog will attempt to lie down and die with you pinching his ear rather than get the dumbbell. Calmly wait out his stalemate. You may move the dumbbell closer or get someone else to pinch his other ear. This is called a stereo correction! Try using less of a pinch as you wait for the dog to make a decision.

REFUSING TO GIVE UP THE DUMBBELL

At any time that the dog refuses to give up the dumbbell, blow sharply in his ear. Really, it works!

WHEN NOT TO PINCH

The ear-pinch correction is exactly as it states, a *correction*. Just because you now have a way of enforcing a retrieve command does not mean that you pinch the dog's ear every time the dog does not retrieve!

Suppose you toss the dumbbell and it lands next to another dog. You command your dog to "take it," and he trots out briskly toward the dumbbell. As he approaches the dumbbell, you see that he slows down and his eyes focus on the dog lying next to his dumbbell. Your dog slinks back to you without the dumbbell. Do you correct the dog with an ear pinch? Absolutely not. The dog refused to retrieve because he was afraid. Fear is not initially treated with a correction. The good trainer (who had read Chapter 11, Understanding Corrections vs. Help) would help the dog by going with the dog to assure him that it was in fact safe to retrieve the dumbbell next to the dog. Of course, the trainer needs to be sure that it is in fact safe to do so!

Suppose after three or four times of showing the dog that he can safely retrieve the dumbbell, the dog still refuses to retrieve. Do you pinch his ear? Yes, at this point the dog is making a decision based on his belief that he has a choice as to whether or not to retrieve alone, and dogs who feel they have a choice *are corrected*. Of course, you might also look at it as the dog is still afraid to retrieve the dumbbell alone. This may be true, but now we conclude that the dog's decision is not to make an effort to overcome his fear. The correction will convince the dog that it pays to be brave.

Another instance when you would not correct with an ear pinch would be if the dog was confused. Suppose you borrowed a friend's dumbbell and the first time you sent the dog to retrieve it, he went out, smelled that it was not his, and came back without it. This is a time to help the dog, perhaps by going out with him to encourage him or by actually putting the dumbbell in his mouth.

The ear pinch is a valuable training aid when taught properly and applied with understanding. The same is true of most corrections. Be careful that you know why a dog is not responding before you hastily correct. A dog who exhibits fear or confusion does not deserve a correction!

Learning, in general, is stressful; and for some dogs, retrieving is *very* stressful. As long as you are sure that you are being fair to your dog, do not fall victim to feeling guilty about having to correct. Try to ignore temper tantrums and screams as you remind yourself that you have taught the retrieve slowly, step-by-step, and fairly and that the dog is very well aware that all he has to do to get you off his ear is to put the dumbbell in his mouth. For many people, dominance, true ownership and control over a dog are not accomplished until after the dog has agreed to retrieve on command. Following the teaching of the retrieve, there is often a new bond, a respectful, adoring relationship that begins to grow between dog and trainer.

VIDEOTAPE

There is a videotape available that I have made to visually illustrate this approach to teaching a Compulsive Retrieve. It is called *The Obedience Retrieve for All Breeds*. It may be purchased from Max 200 Obedience Equipment Co., J&J Dog Supplies, DogWise Books and other dog-training suppliers.

39

Teaching Scent Discrimination

Premise: This method of teaching Scent Discrimination presumes that the dog has been taught a Compulsive Retrieve in Open work. (See Chapter 38, Teaching the Retrieve.)

EQUIPMENT

1. Unless you have a very small dog, the single-bar type of scent article is preferable because if you have done your work in Open, you should have no mouthing problems with the scent articles.

2. You will need to purchase a wooden peg board, or rubber mat or piece of carpet large enough so that the dog will be unable to retrieve the entire mat or board. Usually three feet by three feet is sufficient. Tie a handle to the board or mat so that you can move it without touching it.

3. Purchase a roll of wire (the same color as the metal articles). Electric fence wire works nicely.

4. Finally, you will need a pair of kitchen tongs and a pair of rubber gloves.

BEFORE YOU BEGIN

1. Understand that the dog already knows how to scent. You are only really teaching him to do it on command.

2. Since you do not have this terrific scenting ability, you must be very careful *not* to overly correct the dog for bringing you the wrong article because you can't smell what he might have smelled. You will learn how to deal with this error properly later on.

The scent-article peg board is prepared with four metal articles tied down. Notice that the handle on the board allows it to be carried without being contaminated with the handler's scent.

The handler is careful to hold the leash high above the dog's head so that it does not drag through the articles and put scent on them.

3. Since you are teaching Scent *Discrimination,* be very careful not to get scent all over the articles, which are supposed to be free from your scent, or to contaminate the board or mat on which you are working. Avoid having your leash drag through the articles. Give common sense a chance, and do not store your board in your clothes closet!

4. Never put the tongs or your Utility gloves *into* the scent-article case, as this will contaminate the articles with your scent.

5. Avoid using Off spray on you or the dog, as well as perfume or perfumed soaps, when you are planning to work scent. In fact, don't even wash your hands immediately before you plan to work scent.

6. When teaching scent work, do not push for speed; work for understanding and confidence on the part of the dog. As the dog gains confidence and succeeds, he will gain speed.

7. Avoid meals heavily seasoned with garlic if you are planning to work scent; the garlic odor may come through the pores of the skin, and some dogs resent this odor.

8. If you or your dog are taking any medication (particularly antibiotics) or supplements, do not be surprised if your dog becomes confused when working "articles." A pharmacist can usually tell you if "odor" is a property of the drug you are taking. If it is, there is a chance it will change your scent, which may confuse your dog.

COMMON MISTAKES HANDLERS MAKE

1. A common mistake is emphatically telling the dog "No" when he brings you the wrong article; consequently, the dog decides to stop trying altogether. For all you know, the article the dog brought might have had some scent left over from a week or two ago when it was last used, and the dog doesn't understand why this is all of a sudden wrong. He often becomes confused and stops trying.

2. Handlers get sloppy about airing their articles and cases and about washing and airing the articles they are using. I like to rinse used articles in cold water and then air them for 24 hours or more before I consider them free of scent. Rinsing articles helps to remove the dog's saliva.

3. A handler should not praise the dog as he indicates a correct article or before the dog has returned with the article. This causes the dog to put his mouth over an article and wait for the praise before he is sure it's the right one. Verbal praise should come only after the dog has made the decision to sit in front of the handler and present the article. The handler must be careful not to use subtle cues, such as smiling, leaning, pointing to front or a change in breathing, that might help the dog make a decision.

4. Some handlers get upset when the dog paws the article to see which one is free. While it is true that he is not using his nose yet, all dogs figure it out

in time. This is a normal learning process. The dog will always choose the easiest path to accomplish a task and will eventually figure out that it's easier just to smell for the right article. Working in a dark room will sometimes encourage the dog to start using his nose.

5. Handlers sometimes forget to place the articles at least six inches apart from one another. Scent travels, and this can be confusing to a dog who is first learning the exercise, especially for Collies and other long-nosed breeds, whose mouth, nose and eyes are relatively far apart from each other.

6. Handlers make the mistake of taking the dog off leash too soon, and then they take the articles off the board before the dog is truly confident or has been proofed.

7. Handlers have even been known to forget which article they scented!

THE STEP-BY-STEP PROCESS

1. Get the dog to retrieve, off the floor, a leather and metal article willingly and with distractions. Treat it as if you were working a flat retrieve of the dumbbell exercise. Make sure the dog is not mouthing and that the pickup of both the metal and leather articles is quick and clean.

2. Prepare the board. If *you* prepare the board, wear the rubber gloves; otherwise enlist the help of someone else. Tie down two metal articles (with numbers) onto the board or mat loosely (in two places) with the metal wire. For small dogs, you may tie down articles with rubber bands. The articles should have some mobility, but they should be unable to be pulled off the board. The tied articles should be very far apart from one another and in different directions. Now you are ready to begin.

3. Position the dog, on leash, approximately six feet from the board in heel position, facing the article board. Scent your metal article by *holding* it (do not rub it vigorously) for one minute. Leave the dog with a stay command and walk out and place it on the board, making sure it is at least six inches from the other two tied articles. (The dog is watching you do this.) Return to the dog. Make a cup out of your right hand and place it three inches in front of the dog's nose. (He will have no idea what you are doing, but this will later become a legal cue to him that you are about to work scent.) Command "take it" or whatever command you have been using for the dumbbell retrieve. Motion forward with your right hand, holding the leash high in the air so that it does not drag through the articles. By motioning forward with the leash, you are saying to the dog, "Go ahead of me, it's all right." Avoid the habit of taking a step backward as the dog picks up the correct article, for this too becomes an extra cue.

4. If the dog attempts to pick up a tied article, say nothing. If he gets distracted or gives up and isn't looking for the free article, treat it as you would a retrieve problem, and go out and point to the scented article. If necessary,

repeat the "take it" command and pinch the dog's ear. Repeat this step until the dog has retrieved three times without the need of a retrieve correction. If you are working with a very insecure, sensitive dog who is exhibiting confusion, *help* the dog by pointing out the scented article rather than correcting a non-retrieve. This is where reading your dog is critical. Why is the dog not attempting to retrieve? Is he confused? Afraid? Distracted? Or does he feel he has a choice? The answer to these questions will determine whether you pinch or just point. We can readily assume that if a dog is smelling the mat or grass *between* the articles, he is distracted and is not working the exercise.

5. Now repeat step three, but change your command to "find it." Most dogs barely notice you changed the command. From now on you will use the "find it" command.

6. Turn the dog so that his back is toward the board. Repeat step three. (Hope he cheats and turns his head to see what you are doing.) Give your cup cue to him, replace your right hand at your side, and then command "Fido, find it." Begin with your left foot and execute an about turn. This is three steps and is the same footwork that you learned for the heeling about turn (see page 77). As you turn around, the dog should fly out to the board. After each "retrieve," rotate the board so as to present the dog with a different picture. Repeat this until the dog has made at least one attempt to pull on a tied article. When the dog is readily leaving your side and finding the correct article (he is probably not scenting yet, just trying or guessing), go on to the next step.

7. Take the leash off. Have a friend—or use your gloves—add two more metal articles randomly (but six inches apart) to the board. Continue as in step six. This is usually the point at which the dog discovers his nose. Each dog figures it out at a different rate—some in a day or two, some in a week or two. Do not become discouraged and do not try to help the dog. If the dog is still cheating (looking to see where you put the article) at this point, then place him around a corner so he can't cheat. (Of course, if he cheats later on in the ring, there is nothing the judge can do about it.) When you are fairly sure the dog is using his nose, get another person to act as a steward and put the article out for you. Make sure the steward does not touch the article with your scent on it. A dog will initially try to bring you any article with your scent on it or any article with his scent on it. Realizing this, be sure to wash all articles the dog has mouthed with water and let them air. As the dog gains more experience, he will be able to discern the difference between his scent and your scent.

8. Have the steward (your assistant or friend) touch each of the tied-down metal articles. Now you are asking the dog to find your scent when there is other scent out there instead of just discriminating between scent and no scent. When the dog has been successful and you have used approximately 10 different people to scent the tied-down articles, go on.

9. The dog still cannot make a mistake because the wrong articles are still tied down. The only thing he might do is get distracted and stop working; this results in a "retrieve" correction with you pointing to the correct article.

Continue to turn the board and change stewards. Intentionally set up distractions around the board—people, barking, noise, stamping feet, alarm clock, other dogs, cat, food and so on. When the dog has made no attempt to refuse to try for one week, go on.

10. Repeat step nine, but add distance (15 feet) between you and the board. By adding distance, you will know if the dog is truly confident. The dog is still off leash. Continue adding distractions to mess up the dog; keep correcting, or helping if the dog shows fear or confusion.

11. Take all the metal articles off the board. Start over back at step three using only leather articles. Usually the leather goes faster because the dog already has an idea what you want. When you reach step nine with the leather articles, go on. Be aware that leather has a strong scent of its own, which may cause initial confusion.

12. Using your gloves, tie three metal and three leather articles (with numbers) down on the board. Start back at step five. When the dog will do both leather and metal off leash confidently at 15 feet, with the use of the steward and the steward's scent, it is time to go on. Add distractions.

13. Retie one of the metal articles on the board using a six-inch string (using gloves). The strings allow you to place the articles off the tie-down board without chancing that the dog could make a mistake. Strings help dogs distinguish between articles that bear your scent versus retrieving the article that the dog might think is loose. If the dog does not make a mistake in three days, do the same for one leather article. These articles are still tied down, but they are on six-inch strings. If the dog is doing well with the one metal and one leather article loosened on the board, go on.

14. Start placing your six-inch tied unscented metal or leather article off the board and the scented one sometimes off and sometimes on the board. If the dog is still getting it right, go on. Add distractions.

15. Retie one more metal and one more leather article on six-inch strings and continue with step 14. *Gradually* you will get them all tied on string and more of them off the board than on the board. They are still tied down, but on loose strings! Add distractions! *See if you can get the dog to panic and grab a wrong article.* When you can no longer get the dog to make a mistake, go on to step 16.

16. Take the board away, but save it because you never know when you might need it to straighten out confusion that you might have caused by going through the steps too quickly. You can always back up and start over to correct confusion. Make sure you always use tongs to put out the articles that you don't want to have your scent on.

17. Once the board is removed, begin with two leather and two metal articles in the pile. As the dog exhibits confidence, add articles. When you start doing "articles" off the board, line them up in an orderly fashion. This helps suggest comparison to the dog. As part of proofing, you might want to build up to a pile of 20 or more articles. By increasing the number of articles the dog must search through, you are teaching the dog to be patient and to work the pile until he is successful. A dog who is used to working 20 articles in a pile is very confident when sorting through nine in a ring situation!

18. If at any time the dog brings you the wrong article, let him start coming back with the article, but before he gets to you point back to the pile. Say nothing and do not move. This point will let the dog know that something is wrong. If he drops the wrong article and goes back to recheck the pile, return the pointing arm to your side. If the dog freezes and stares at you, wait 15 seconds, and then walk right past the dog and point to the correct article. If necessary, call the dog over and command him to "take it." (Notice that it's no longer a "find it" command.) Try to let the dog figure out that he must drop the wrong article in order to pick up the correct article. If necessary, gently knock the wrong article out of his mouth. Never accept or take the wrong article from the dog! Praise only for the correct article. Eventually your pointing finger will cue the dog to go back and recheck the pile because something is wrong.

19. Remove any incorrect article the dog has touched until it has been washed and aired. Beginning dogs will frequently bring an article that has their scent on it as easily as if it had your scent. The only time you correct the dog with an ear pinch is when he refuses to retrieve because he is distracted or feels he has a choice.

20. Be sure to rotate the articles you scent so you don't get some more impregnated with scent than others. It helps to have at least 18 articles, even though a normal set is only 12. Air all new sets of articles and article cases before using them.

BOHM MARRAZZO PHOTOGRAPHY

Articles lined up in an orderly fashion.

PROOFING ARTICLES

Once the dog is doing articles all off the board and is rarely making a mistake, it is again time to proof him. Proofing adds interest and builds dog and handler confidence.

Do articles on all different kinds of surfaces (concrete, freshly cut grass, tall grass, tile, carpet, blacktop and so on).

Stand all articles on end, including the scented ones.

Use two sets of articles at once. This will teach the dog patience because he will have to check through more articles to find the right one.

Do articles in all kinds of weather—rain, heat, cold, snow, wind and so on.

Place the articles in different configurations on the floor (a square, an X, an oblong and so on).

Place articles closer than six inches apart for the experienced dog to teach him to discriminate carefully.

Have two or more dogs work a pile of articles simultaneously!

Put balls and bones and even cookies out among the articles. (Make sure the dog can't actually eat the cookies by putting them in a plastic container or bag.)

These are distractions. Make sure they do not have your scent on them. Allow the dog to sniff them briefly, but if he attempts to pick one up and play with it, treat it as a correction for a "retrieve." If he retrieves it, treat it as a wrong article and send him back without a correction.

Special Note: If the dog brings you the right article, praise him and do the next article. *Do not repeat* a correct performance. Throughout training, if the dog made a mistake, he had to try again to correct his actions. If you repeat a *correct performance,* you run the risk of confusing the dog. He might think it was wrong, which is why he is being asked to repeat it.

OBSERVING DOGS LEARNING ARTICLES

Most dogs eventually develop a system of working a pile of articles. For example, they might always start on the left side and work counterclockwise and toward the center. A dog first learning to do "articles" may become overwhelmed by a scatter of articles and might tend to repeatedly miss checking one corner of the pile. To teach a dog to work articles systematically, start by placing them in a line. Once the dog learns to move from one to another down the line, try a semicircle. Eventually place the articles in a complete circle. As a final step, place one and then eventually more articles in the middle of the circle.

RON REAGAN

The dog is proofed with turtles once he is doing articles off the board.

BAUMAN

Proofing with two dogs and turtles. Notice that the proofing is started while the articles are still on the tie-down peg boards.

Dogs first learning to do Scent Discrimination are often found placing their mouths over each article. This is referred to as "open-mouth scenting" and disappears as the dog becomes confident with the exercise. Some dogs even go so far as to lick the articles as if they were trying to taste the scent. In the early teaching phases, ignore this behavior. Most dogs eventually take the easiest route, which is to briefly sniff each article.

Licking articles is sometimes seen in an experienced dog when the handler is very nervous, has sweaty palms, and overscents the article. In this situation, the dog may indicate the correct article, lick it and then continue to check other articles. This sequence is repeated until some time has passed, allowing the scented article to "cool down," at which point the dog readily retrieves it. It is virtually impossible to scent an article the same amount each time, especially if the handler is the nervous type. Therefore, from the standpoint of training, even though we may understand why the dog is avoiding the correct article, he should be corrected to retrieve the overscented article. It is not up to the dog to decide when to pick up the article. He must learn to pick it up as soon as he indicates it is the correctly scented article. It is true that a dog may initially be confused by the smell of a sweaty, overscented article. If you believe this to be the case, then help the dog by encouraging him to pick it up right away the first few times. If, however, the licking and avoidance pattern continues, a correction is justified.

New Utility dogs, often insecure about doing articles, frequently pick up the correct article, start back with it, and then doubt their choice and either go back and recheck the pile with the article in their mouth or, more often, drop the correct article, recheck the pile and then pick up the dropped, correct article and come in with it. If this occurs in the first few months during which the dog is working off the tie-down board, the best thing a handler can do is to say nothing, not aid the dog, and let the dog work it through. In some rare cases of very insecure dogs, this behavior continues for months and then needs to be stopped. The dog is usually always right, he just doesn't trust himself. For this type of dog, you need to incorporate the following rule: "The one you first touch is the one you take." To accomplish this, correct the dog at the point at which he either drops the correct article or heads back to recheck. A correction at this point in training usually gives the dog the added confidence he is lacking to help him trust his decision.

Some Utility dogs approach a pile of articles, circle the pile, nose high above the articles, two to six times before getting down to the business of discrimination. Handlers who allow this argue that the dogs are air scenting. While it is believed that scent rises off an object in a spiraling fashion, I believe this circling of the pile is an unnecessary bad habit, accidentally learned by the dog. This same dog could just as easily have been taught to go out to the pile with the intent of sniffing each article directly (and not the space between the articles, either). Any time a dog approaches a pile of articles and his nose does not drop in the direction of the articles, assume he is distracted and correct him! You would be surprised how many dogs take advantage of the time they are given to work the scent articles. Don't be fooled!

While it is impossible to determine how long an individual dog will take to master Scent Discrimination, following the procedures outlined in this chapter should take between 5 and 12 months. Most of the training effort will go into proofing and building confidence in the dog. Dogs catch on to the task of scent work in a matter of weeks, but it takes months of proofing and practice for them to gain proficiency and the confidence to do scent work anywhere and any time you say.

A dog's sense of smell is much greater than most Utility handlers are willing to admit. It has been demonstrated that dogs can track six-hour-old tracks and smell gas leaks under miles of frozen ground. Knowing this, how difficult can scent articles be? Most errors in scent work are due to insecure dogs (whose handlers have helped them too much in practice) and to dogs who get distracted as they *pretend* to be working. If you observe your dog looking to you when he is in the pile, you have probably used cues you may not be aware of. Try doing articles for a few sessions with a paper bag over your head with eyeholes cut out. This way you can be sure your face is not signaling the dog which article is correct.

VIDEOTAPE

To purchase a video that illustrates this approach to teaching Scent Discrimination, contact Max 200 Obedience Equipment Co., J&J Dog Supplies, DogWise and other dog training suppliers. Ask for Diane Bauman's video, *Teaching Scent Discrimination and the Directed Retrieve*.

40

Directed Retrieve

For this exercise you will need three predominantly white work gloves and a 20-foot long line.

Before you begin: If you are training a small dog, buy boys' work gloves, then wash them in very hot water and put them in a hot dryer in an attempt to shrink them as small as possible.

Stuff your gloves with rags or paper to give them substance. This will encourage your dog to open his mouth when he goes to pick up the glove instead of holding the tip of a finger of the glove in his teeth. Dogs who do not go out to retrieve with the intention of opening their mouths and stuffing the entire glove into it often drop gloves.

This approach to teaching the glove exercise presumes that the dog has been taught a Compulsive Retrieve (see Chapter 38, Teaching the Retrieve).

STEP ONE: RETRIEVE THE GLOVE

Tell your dog to stay, toss the glove and have your dog retrieve it as if it were a dumbbell. Use the "take it" retrieve command. Correct any mouthing or shaking of the glove. If the dog refuses the glove once he has been introduced to it, make a retrieve correction. **Note:** No signal has been used yet.

STEP TWO: LEARN HOW TO GIVE THE SIGNAL

The AKC Regulations state, "The handler will give his dog direction to the designated glove with a single motion of his left hand and arm along the right side of the dog, and will give the command to retrieve either simultaneously with or immediately following the giving of direction." I prefer to give the command "take it" *immediately following* the direction for it gives the dog more time to focus his attention on the direction.

JULIA BROWN

A proper glove signal. Notice that the fingers are together, the thumb is down and the top of the hand is in line with the bottom of the dog's eye.

To give a clear signal, keep your fingers together and your thumb down. (Otherwise, it may block his vision.) Begin the signal from behind the dog's right ear and bring it forward in a *straight line,* slowly, so that the top of your hand is at the bottom of his eyes.

Be careful that your signal is pointing directly to the glove, which means your hand will be tilted down toward the floor.

As soon as your hand stops moving (although it may move slowly), you must then command "take it" without jerking your arm or hand. As the dog leaves for the glove and is past your hand, you may return your arm to your side and stand up.

STEP THREE: TEACH THE DOG THAT THE SIGNAL MEANS TO LOOK FOR THE GLOVE

Begin with one stuffed glove, held in your right hand, hidden behind your back from the dog.

With your dog sitting in heel position, give him a signal pointing to nothing. As your left arm is extending, toss the glove with your right hand to where your signal is pointing. The tossed glove should get your dog's attention. As soon as he notices the glove, send him to retrieve it immediately. You may give a signal in all different directions as long as you toss the glove in the direction you are pointing.

Do this until, when you start to give a signal, the dog looks straight ahead in anticipation of a glove.

STEP FOUR: TEACH THE DOG THAT THERE IS MORE THAN ONE GLOVE AND THE DIFFERENCE BETWEEN RETRIEVE AND DIRECTED RETRIEVE

Start with the dog sitting in heel position on a long line, and with two stuffed gloves. With the dog watching, throw one glove to your left and then one glove to your right. You and the dog are now facing no glove in the middle.

You pivot left and give the dog a signal to the left glove. If he looks, praise him but don't send him. Then pivot right and give him the signal to the right glove. If he looks, praise him and then send him to retrieve it. (The dog is on a leash long enough to reach the gloves.) Take the glove and again face the middle. Throw the glove the dog just retrieved back to the right. (This will get the dog's attention.) Now, pivot yourself and give him a signal to the left. If he looks, praise him and then send him for the glove.

The dog has been allowed to see both gloves and is seated facing neither glove.

RON REAGAN

Facing neither glove, give a hand signal to one of the gloves and praise the dog for looking. Do not necessarily send him to retrieve the glove. You may pivot to face the glove.

RON REAGAN

If he is still focused on the other glove, wait a few seconds with your signal pointed to the left glove. If his attention is not drawn back to the left glove, command "take it" anyway and walk with your signal all the way to the glove. The dog is on leash for control. This exercise is teaching the dog to retrieve what you point to and not what he sees thrown. It distinguishes retrieve from *directed* retrieve.

Continue alternating between sending the dog for the glove you threw and the one you didn't. Do not get into a pattern—be unpredictable.

Gradually add distance to the two gloves until you are working 25 feet from the two gloves. (You will need a longer leash as you add distance.)

STEP FIVE: ADD CONFUSION

Add the center glove about nine feet from where you and the dog are standing. For the first week, do not send to the center glove at all. If the dog is not trying to pick it up when you send for gloves one and three, you may start giving a signal to the center glove. Praise the dog for looking at the glove, but don't send him to retrieve it. Extend your hand signal to glove two a little farther past the dog's head than the hand signal to the right and left gloves. This will become an added cue to your dog when you want him to retrieve glove two (the center glove). The corner gloves are indicated with a short signal where the dog's nose is even with your wrist. The center glove gets a longer signal where the dog's nose is even almost with your elbow.

When is dog is successfully doing all three gloves (and the number two glove is close), you can then put the center glove back in line with the others.

STEP SIX: LEARN THE PIVOTS

Pivots imply moving in place. Always be sure to give the verbal command before starting the pivot. All pivots are done in three steps. The about turn pivot to glove two is executed in three steps, which are exactly the same as the footwork for the about turn (see Chapter 24, Teaching the Dog to Heel).

Glove two, step one

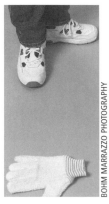
Glove two, step two

Glove two, step three

Whenever you pivot to the right, which is asking the dog to move forward, use the "heel" command. When you pivot left, since the dog is required to back up, use a different command. "Off" or "back" are commonly used, but any command is acceptable as long as it has no other meaning.

To teach the pivots to the right, command "heel." To pivot to glove one, begin by moving your left foot so that the toe of your left foot is touching the toe of your right foot. We refer to this position as "toe to toe." Next move your right foot so that the heel of your right foot touches the heel of your left foot. We call this "heel to heel." Point the toe of your right foot toward the number one glove. Finally, bring your left foot up into place next to your right foot.

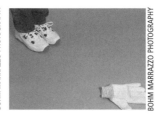

Glove one, step one Glove one, step two Glove one, step three

The pivot to the left requires a little more work as you teach the dog to back up, out of your way, as you pivot left into him. Command "off" or "back," and then begin by placing your right foot (toe to toe) with your left foot. Next, point your left foot toward the glove as you place it heel to heel with your right foot and, finally, bring your right foot up even with your left foot.

Glove three, step one Glove three, step two Glove three, step three

TEACHING THE DOG TO PIVOT BACK

If your dog resists backing up, use a preliminary exercise of circling to the left. Each time, you circle tighter and tighter until you are pivoting in place. By holding the dog in place and commanding "back" or "off," the dog is coaxed into moving his body properly. Many breeds, especially Shelties and Collies, prefer to walk in a circle instead of backing up. Walking a small circle is not always penalized, but some judges deduct points because the dog has moved out of heel position.

RON REAGAN

To help a dog learn to pivot backward, hold a stick in your left hand.

RON REAGAN

As you command "back," hold the leash in your right hand against your left leg. When the dog attempts to move his rump away from your left leg, prevent this by blocking his movement with the stick.

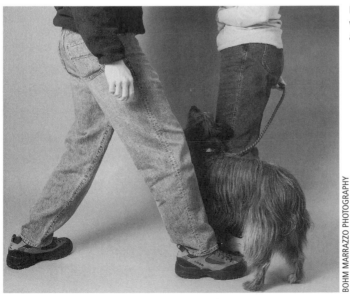

BOHM MARRAZZO PHOTOGRAPHY

Have another person walk toward the dog as you pivot left.

To help your dog learn to back up or jump back, hold a jump stick in your left hand, parallel to your leg but on the side of the dog farthest from you. Begin with a sit at heel and your stick positioned. As you command "back," hold the dog's head with the leash in your right hand against your left leg. When the dog attempts to move his rump away from your left leg, prevent this with the stick. Since you are moving into the dog, he must move somewhere and since he is not permitted to circle, his only alternative is to back up in place.

An alternative way to get a dog to back up in heel position as you pivot is to place the leash behind your back, snug across your rear, and hold it in your right hand. As you pivot left, the dog is held in heel position and only backing will release the tension on the leash. To help the dog figure out that he needs to back up, have another person stand very close to the dog's left side. As you pivot, the other person slowly walks toward the dog (without making eye contact). Most dogs will naturally get up to move when they see someone walking into them!

To pivot to glove one, pivot to the right. To pivot to glove three, pivot left. To pivot to glove two, do the about turn footwork.

STEP SEVEN: ADD PIVOTS

Add your pivots and pivot to the glove you are sending the dog to. Continue to work pivots separately as well and incorporate them into your heeling work. Rotate sending the dog for all different gloves.

STEP EIGHT: PROOFING

Practice pivoting to one glove and sending the dog to another. Be careful when you do this that you are not blocking the dog's vision with your body. If necessary, step back out of the dog's sight line before giving the hand signal.

Tempt the dog to be wrong by moving glove two closer to the dog and then sending the dog to one and three. Then reverse this and move gloves one and three closer, and send the dog to glove two.

Use brown gloves on black mats or white gloves in the snow to teach the dog to follow your signal and take a line regardless of whether the dog sees the glove or not.

Try using five gloves instead of three. Be sure to give a careful signal.

WHAT IF THE DOG GOES TO THE WRONG GLOVE?

If the dog is in the learning stages and is on a long line and heads for the wrong glove, prevent the dog from getting to it by holding back the line (do not snap). Start over and if necessary walk out to the correct glove with your hand signal.

If the dog is working off leash and retrieves the wrong glove, abort the exercise with a "let's go" command. The "let's go" means "whatever you are doing, come with me because we are not doing that!"

Never yell "No!" at a dog who is heading for the wrong glove. Never take a dog from one glove to another to "fix" the mistake. Once a mistake occurs, you must go back to the point where the dog made the mistake before it can be corrected. In the glove exercise, the mistake usually occurs when the dog is sitting next to you and decides which glove to retrieve. This is why if the dog retrieves the wrong glove and realizes he is wrong, you abort the exercise and start over.

When the dog is retrieving nicely, unstuff the glove and practice the command "hold" with the glove. If you reach for the glove and say "hold," the dog should bite down and hold the glove. If you reach for the glove and command "out" or "give," only then should the dog release the glove.

PROBLEMS

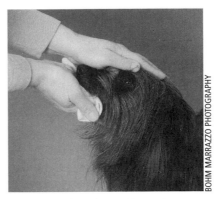

Place your hands gently over his muzzle.

For dogs who insist on "killing" (shaking) the glove, fill the glove one third full of pebbles or fishing weights in the fingers of the glove so the dog ends up hitting himself in the head with the stones. If the dog still wants to "kill" the glove, follow the dog out, and as soon as he retrieves, place your hands gently over his muzzle as he comes back to you.

For the dog who has difficulty getting a good grip on the glove, starch the gloves when you wash them, crumple them up, and let them dry stiff and wrinkled. Practice with the dog retrieving the glove from under a chair leg where he will have to get a good grip to pull it out.

To improve the dog's pickup of the glove, do some retrieves with the glove between you and the dog so the dog is retrieving on his way *to you.*

FOR THE RING

Be sure to present the judge with three *clean* white work gloves before you enter the Utility ring.

Do not look to see where the gloves are placed just before pivoting to send the dog. This is considered an aid to the dog and will be penalized. Be careful to pivot *to the glove.* Underpivoting or overpivoting is considered an aid to the dog and will result in points lost.

With small dogs you are permitted to get down to the dog's eye level (crouch), but you may not put your knee on the floor. The knee on the floor is considered an aid in direction to the dog.

CONSIDER THIS

When you are teaching your dog the directed retrieve exercise and he is still on a long leash, be sure to send the dog as soon as you have completed the signal, even if the dog is looking at the wrong glove! If he heads in the wrong direction, you can always stop him, but if you wait for the dog to look at the correct glove, you are not teaching him to take a line to a glove. You end up teaching him to swivel his head, looking at all gloves until *you* command "take it." Trying to help the dog to be right can really work against you! Remember, dogs learn by trial and error. Do your part correctly and let the dog be wrong until he learns what right is!

Your glove signal should always be given on the imaginary line between the glove and your left hip. Do not adjust your signal for where the dog's head is. Give a correct signal and let the dog learn to move his head to your signal.

VIDEO TAPE

To purchase a video that illustrates this technique for teaching the Directed Retrieve exercise, contact Max 200 Obedience Equipment Co., J&J Supplies, DogWise and other dog training suppliers. Ask for Diane Bauman's video, *Teaching Scent Discrimination and the Directed Retrieve*.

41
Ready to Start Jumping?

Obedience is both an intellectual and physical sport for the canine participant. Before you can attempt to get a dog to jump hurdles, he must, like any athlete, be conditioned.

Top obedience dogs are lean and well muscled. Their trainers work hard to keep them physically fit and sound. A hip X-ray will assure the trainer that the dog is not in pain when jumping and will give the trainer the confidence to insist on a jump response.

I like introducing young puppies to very low jumps. The pup is never commanded but rather encouraged to jump over something so small that it is in no way damaging to his growing bones. A bar jump resting on paper cups is a good beginning. By exposing puppies to jumping, we avoid anxiety later on as the dogs recognize a jump from their early experiences.

A good guideline is to set your jump for a puppy at the height of his elbow. Never ask your dog to jump on a slick surface where he might hurt himself. Remember, you and he are a team and both members of the team must trust each other. To put the dog in a potentially dangerous situation breaks down trust and the bond you are working to form. By the way, long, wet grass can be as slick as a shiny tile surface.

For a dog to be a good, easy jumper, he must have a balanced structure and a confident attitude. Most jumping problems are a combination of poor structure and insecurity. I have seen very poorly built dogs, even dysplastic dogs, appear to be excellent jumpers because they had a positive, enthusiastic, secure attitude about jumping. As a trainer you cannot change structure (although you can search for it in a puppy), but you can work on developing a good jumping attitude by starting the dog young and keeping it easy and fun.

Ground poles spaced evenly teach a dog the coordination and balance he needs to learn if he is to become a fluid jumper. To determine the amount of space between the poles, measure the dog's height once at the withers. This is an approximation and may need to be adjusted two to seven inches, depending on the dog's stride.

Before starting any jumping, teach your dog to trot over the ground poles. Begin on leash at a walk and progress up to a trot. If the dog hits a pole, ignore it and reposition the poles. If the dog hits all the poles, readjust your spacing.

When the dog is trotting over the poles easily on leash, remove the leash and get the dog to trot to you over the poles as in a Recall.

Ground poles make a dog aware of where his feet are. They train the dog to move steadily toward a jump and thus prevent or correct stutter-stepping.

Eventually a low jump is positioned after the ground poles. The distance between the last pole and the jump is twice the space between the poles plus once the height of the jump. Poles may also be placed on an angle for Directed Jumping.

WHAT ABOUT JUMP STICKS?

Jump sticks are black and white dowels that simulate bar jumps. They can be an aid or a hindrance in teaching jumping. If you choose to use a jump stick, be careful to keep it stationary when commanding a dog to jump it. If you move the stick as the dog jumps, you confuse the dog's sense of timing.

The jump stick can be successfully used to teach a dog to kick out after he jumps so as not to "tick" the jump. When using it to teach "clean jumping," have someone who understands the procedure hold the stick just behind the High or Bar Jump and lift up on the stick as the dog's hind legs clear the top of the jump. Be careful not to overdo a good thing or you will soon be teaching your dog to somersault!

SIGNS OF JUMPING PROBLEMS

Some dogs are naturally, instinctively good jumpers—others are not. As a trainer it is important that you detect early signs of jumping problems. While it is true that dogs have different styles of jumping (some tuck and kick, others extend), certain movements are signs of a problem.

A good jumping dog approaches a jump aggressively and smoothly. Stutter-stepping in front of a jump means something is wrong. A dog will stutter-step for different reasons. He might have trouble judging or seeing the height of the jump and by stutter-stepping in front of it, he buys time to decide how high to jump. A dog who is afraid to jump stutter-steps because he is trying to put it off until the last possible minute. While stutter-stepping, the dog is searching for the courage to commit to the jump. At the first sign of stutter-stepping, lower the jump and back up in your training to build the dog's confidence. It would also be advisable to get the dog's eyes examined by a veterinary ophthalmologist who has the equipment to check for eye diseases like PRA (progressive retinal atrophy).

Over the years I have dealt with dogs who have a clean bill of health from a veterinary ophthalmologist, but who clearly have vision problems. How can this be? The ophthalmologist can only tell if the dog's eye is anatomically correct. We cannot ask a dog to read an eye chart, so we really don't know what he sees. As humans we know that as we age, our vision changes. Many people (myself included!) who used to have 20/20 vision find that after 40, they cannot see things close to them. We call this farsighted. It's not difficult to imagine that dogs face similar issues with vision. A dog might see a jump clearly from a distance, but as he approaches the jump, it blurs in his vision, so the dog hesitates or stutters before jumping. Some dogs try to compensate by jumping too early, while they can still see the jump clearly. Be sensitive to anything you see in a dog that is not fluid and natural as he jumps. We can help a dog learn to jump, but we cannot get him glasses!

Another sign of jump trouble is when the dog clears the jump, but in order to do so he twists his rear as he goes over the jump. A twisting rear movement means the dog is straining to clear the jump. He might lack muscle tone, be built poorly for jumping or may just be getting tired and should be rested. Do not raise the height of the jump until he has stopped twisting to clear the jump.

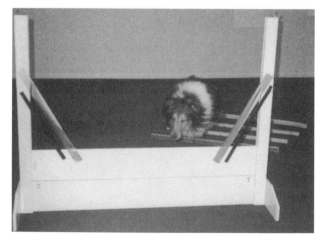

To teach a dog to jump to the middle of a jump, put tape on the two corners as shown here.

PLAY JUMPING

The concept of "play jumping" was first explained to me by Cherie Berger of Meadowpond Goldens. It's a technique used to help teach jumping as well as to relieve stress associated with jumping problems. Most jumping problems start because the dog, for whatever reason, hits a jump and becomes reluctant to jump. The more a dog worries about the jump, the more tense he becomes, the less he is able to jump. It's a difficult problem to solve because it tends to become a cycle that may be difficult to break.

One way to break the cycle is to avoid jumping the dog for a week or more. This may sound contradictory since with most problems, I advise causing the problem and working past it. Because stress makes jumping worse, it is not always the best approach to meet jumping problems head-on. After a week or more of not jumping, much of the stress associated with the exercise has dissipated, simply because of time. When you begin again to cope with the problem, try "play jumping."

To play jump your dog, remove the leash and set the jump at what was once a comfortable height for the dog. Do not put the dog on a stay and avoid any formal commands. Go out with your dog and simply request, "Jump for me." Encourage by running with the dog, tapping the jump or throwing a toy over the jump. If the dog chooses not to jump, there is no correction since you did not command him, you only asked him. Sometimes it takes as many as three sessions before the dog relaxes enough from the absence of pressure to attempt the jump. The dog may jump from any side and at any angle. Failure to jump is ignored. When the dog regains his confidence, you can go back to formal commands.

Play jumping helps the dog learn timing and teaches him to cope with various angles of jumping while avoiding stress.

Food rewards (tidbits) can also be used successfully to relieve the stress caused by anxiety over jumps.

42

Teaching the High and Bar Jumps

Prerequisites: Before teaching the High Jump, or Solid Jump as it is sometimes called, the dog should be able to perform the following exercises:

1. Off-leash Novice Recall of 35 feet.
2. Off-leash Novice Sit-Stay at 35 feet.
3. Pick up a dumbbell off the floor in front of him on command. (If you still need to correct the dog for not retrieving [ear pinch] occasionally, it is acceptable to do so for this level of training.)

PREPARE YOURSELF

1. Build or purchase a High Jump at least four feet wide. Make sure it is painted white. A board or table leaf covered with a white sheet will suffice temporarily. Understand that it is unfair to only jump a dog once a week at school, so you will have to arrange something for him to jump at home in practice.
2. Measure your dog while standing at the withers. (His head need *not* be held high, which tends to raise his withers!) Take this height (including fractions), and check the figure against the required jump height schedule listed in the *AKC Obedience Regulations*. (A few breeds are only required to jump three-fourths their height.)
3. To begin, set your jump to approximately one-third the height your dog will eventually jump, or lower if *you* cannot jump the other height, or if your dog has never jumped before.

CAUTION!

1. Do not pull or snap *up* on a leash to encourage a dog to jump. Dogs do not jump like elevators! If any correction is used, it is always a pull *forward* to start the dog moving.

2. If a dog first learning to jump hits the jump, cheer anyway. You do not want to upset the dog so much that he doesn't want to try again. You encourage the *effort,* even if a mistake is made along the way.

3. Concentrate on achieving confidence and good jumping form. Do not expect a dog to jump his required full height before he has had from four to eight months of training. The specific interval will depend on the dog, his age and how often you train. When increasing height, raise the height one or two inches at a time. To make the jump only one inch higher, use a spacer if you do not have a one-inch board.

4. Make sure your dog is in good physical health, good muscular condition, is not overweight, has short nails and does not have any disabilities such as hip dysplasia or cataracts. Some dogs can overcome these disabilities, but you, as the trainer, must be aware of them and train accordingly.

5. Do not jump a dog who has just eaten, has not had time to limber up with movement or is three or more weeks pregnant.

6. You cannot *force* a dog to jump, so don't try.

7. Be careful not to jump a dog to exhaustion when trying to work out a problem.

8. Most poor jumpers are insecure or frightened. Their owners were undoubtedly impatient. When in doubt as to how to help your dog overcome his insecurity or fear, *lower the jump.*

9. There is a considerable difference to a dog between being able to see and not being able to see over what he is jumping. At the height where the dog can no longer see over the jump and is jumping on faith, you will need to take your time and let the dog gain his confidence. Most Open A dogs believe monsters lurk on the other side of the High Jump.

10. Dogs who approach a jump so fast that they are not thinking or timing the jump must be educated before raising the height of the jump. You can accomplish this by having the dog jump multiple jumps in a line at lower heights. This in-and-out jumping helps a dog learn timing.

11. Dogs have different jumping styles, even within the same breed. Usually dogs will tuck and then kick or extend their hind legs. Do not try to change the way a dog jumps, but if you have a lazy jumper, you can encourage him to tuck tighter or extend higher with the use of a jump stick lifted as the dog goes over the jump (see page 191).

12. It is not advisable to jump a dog with a leash attached to him. The leash inhibits the dog's jumping ability. The less the leash is used, the more fluid jumping will become.

By using two bars on the jump, you can help the dog visualize the height of the jump more easily.

RON REAGAN

STEPS TO TEACH THE HIGH JUMP AND BAR JUMP

1. Have the dog on leash in heel position. The leash should be loose but should not allow the dog to get further than six inches from your side. The only tension on the leash is between the dog and you. Sit the dog next to you about 15 feet in front of a High Jump or Bar Jump set at one-third the full height. Command the dog to "hup" (not "heel") and proceed at a brisk but controlled pace toward the High Jump. Head for the jump so that the dog is aimed at the center of the jump. Try not to slow down at all. Praise the dog as soon as he is *over* the jump. After landing, continue walking in a straight line until about 15 feet past the jump. Then, if you like, you can turn around and jump from the other side. It is important that the dog hears the "hup" command *before* he starts moving. You will know when the dog understands because he will start to forge out ahead of you toward the jump. For the Bar Jump, use the command "bar." By having different commands for the High Jump and the Bar Jump, Directed Jumping will be less confusing.

2. When the dog is jumping confidently and forging ahead of you, take the leash off and do the same as described previously off leash. Do not worry if the dog moves out of heel position. You never told him to heel! If the dog tries to go around the jump, let him, and then put the leash back on and go with him again. When the dog will jump with you off leash, he is confident at this height and is ready to progress.

3. Sit the dog off leash about six feet in front of the jump (closer if the dog is smaller). Leave the dog on a stay, and walk over the jump to the other side; turn and face the dog. With your entire hand, point to the top of the jump. Touch the top of the jump (quietly) if necessary to get the dog's attention.

When you have the dog's attention, command "hup" or "bar" and back up. If the dog anticipates the jump before you command him to, praise anyway and next time do *not* touch the jump. If the dog tries to come around the jump, set him closer to the jump and repeat the touching of the jump. If he still goes around, go back to step two and, if necessary, step one. The only command the dog hears is "hup" or "bar" and he is only to hear it one time. The dog is never stopped or corrected for coming around the jump in the learning stages. When a mistake occurs, praise is withheld. Dogs learn by trial and error and must not be afraid to be wrong.

4. Practice heeling the dog with the dumbbell in his mouth. If at any time the dog drops the dumbbell, *he* is to pick it up with an ear-pinch correction from you if he refuses. Repeat step one now, with the dumbbell in the dog's mouth. Then go on and repeat steps two and three with the dumbbell in the dog's mouth. Yes, the dog can jump a Bar Jump with a dumbbell. In fact, it is a good idea to use the Retrieve Over Bar Jump as often as the Retrieve Over High Jump in preparation for Utility.

5. More dogs tend to go around the jump after having picked up the dumbbell than on the way out to retrieve over the jump. For this reason, we first work on the *return* with the dumbbell before we begin the Retrieve Over High Jump. Sit the dog at various points on the far side of the jump. Give him the dumbbell. Return by stepping over the jump. Turn and point to the jump. Now command "hup" or "bar." This should be done at various angles until the dog has no doubt that regardless of what he is facing, when he

Point out the High Jump to the dog.

The hand signal to jump becomes the palm of your hand.

hears a jump command, he is to return over either the High or Bar Jump. (The jump is still one-third the full height as in the beginning.)

6. Now you are ready to begin the retrieve over the jump. Take the jump down to eight inches. (If you do not have a full-distance Retrieve on Flat yet, do not attempt this!) Put the dog on a six-foot leash. Command the dog to "stay" and toss the dumbbell about three feet to the other side of the eight-inch High Jump. Now command the dog to "hup"; when the dog reaches the other side, command "take it," then again command "hup" and finally command "sit." The jumping often excites the dog, and he may start to mouth, or chew, the dumbbell. If he does, command "hold" and enforce your command with a brief squeeze on his muzzle. The Retrieve Over High Jump is really a multiple of exercises, and initially you are cueing the dog every step of the way. Eventually, because dogs anticipate, you will simply say the first "hup," and the dog will do the remaining parts of the exercise on his own. Remove the leash and gradually raise the height of the jump. Begin proofing the dog as described below.

7. Gradually you will raise the height of the jump, the more gradual, the better. If you work the dog every day, two inches per week is the fastest you should go. When the dog has retrieved successfully seven days at the new height, you may raise the height. Each time you do so, have the dog jump first without the dumbbell as in step three. When the dog is comfortable at the height, build the exercise back up to step six. (Except that the dog is off leash after 16 inches of jump height.)

PROOFING THE DOG ON THE HIGH JUMP

Proofing begins at the low heights and continues through the training process up to the full height of the jump.

ANGLE THROWS

Since you can never be sure that the dumbbell will land and remain exactly opposite you on the other side of the jump, you should intentionally throw it off to one side to teach the dog that if you say "hup," he should jump (even if he can see the dumbbell). Beginning this at low height helps the dog learn the concept of the exercise, when he can jump more often without getting tired.

STRANGE HIGH JUMPS

One High Jump does not always look the same as another to a dog, yet he must have faith and jump them all. Practice jumping different jumps and the same jumps in different places. Put a jacket over the jump, put flowers or balloons on the end of the jump, anything that might appear strange to the dog, and then enforce your command "hup" until nothing frightens or spooks the dog. It is not uncommon to have shadows on a jump in a ring spook a dog. Proof to avoid this problem.

HIGH JUMP–FLAT RETRIEVE CONFUSION

Once the dog has learned the High Jump, there is a stage he will go through where he thinks that any time he sees a jump he is to jump it. Practice doing a Retrieve on Flat next to the High Jump. Your command here is "take it," not "hup." We are teaching the dog at this point to listen to what we say, not to do what he thinks comes next. A good way to improve the dog's listening ability is to sit the dog in front of the jump, toss the dumbbell, then (with the dog on a lead or pull tab) command "heel" and turn away from the jump. The dog will eventually learn to listen, which will help the high-flat confusion. Never yell "no" if the dog is taking the jump when he shouldn't. Simply withhold praise and repeat the exercise, but this time stand where it would be too sharp an angle for the dog to jump. *Help* the dog with your position. Do not correct him for what is only honest confusion.

How does the dog know when he picks up the dumbbell whether he should come back over the jump or not? Does he remember the command given to him just prior to picking up the dumbbell? I doubt it! Dogs need to be taught to look to see where their handler is standing after they pick up the dumbbell. If they see the handler behind a jump, they should return over the jump. If the handler has no jump in front of him, it is a Retrieve on Flat.

To teach your dog to look for you after picking up the dumbbell, try changing your position after you throw the dumbbell. Do not let the dog assume you are glued to one spot!

Try this: Place your dog in a sit with a dumbbell in his mouth in the middle of a ring back by the gate. Put a High Jump on one side of the ring. Now stand away from the jump, facing your dog and call him with a Recall command. When that is successful, put the dog back in the same place with the dumbbell and you stand behind the jump. This time, give your dog a jump command. This exercise will help your dog sort out the Retrieve on Flat–High confusion.

IN-AND-OUT JUMPING

Place two High Jumps approximately 12 feet apart and throw the dumbbell over both of them. Then command "hup" and "hup" again for the second jump. If a dog will jump over two jumps to retrieve a dumbbell, he is unlikely to go around *one*. This is also a good exercise to improve a dog's timing and build confidence.

WHEN THINGS GO WRONG

This chapter explains the procedure for teaching the High Jump. It does not deal with what to do if the dog does not give you the desired response. Each dog is different and each correction is based on the reason the dog didn't perform. Keep in mind that you should not *correct* confusion or a dog who has not learned the exercise yet. You can only correct distraction or a dog who feels he has a choice. Learn to read your dog's reactions.

For a dog who does not jump because he is *afraid,* lower the jump.

If the dog does not jump because he is confused, help him by pointing to the jump and/or standing closer and encouraging.

If the dog is distracted, correct him, possibly with a lead snap toward you over a low (16-inch) jump.

If the dog is not jumping because he feels he has a choice, gently lift him (you might need a helper) and toss him carefully over the jump and praise him. Be sure you are very calm and controlled throughout this procedure. "Sweetheart," you might say, "you can do this on your own or I will do it to you, but one way or another you are going over that jump!" Your objective is to be consistent and deliberate and not to upset or frighten the dog. Most dogs are so utterly embarrassed when this happens that they willingly jump on their own the next time.

43

Directed Jumping

$\mathbf{T}$he purpose of Directed Jumping is to teach the dog to take a designated jump on command or hand signal, or both, from the handler.

This method assumes the dog is familiar with both the High Jump and Bar Jump from the Open jumping work done earlier in training.

Before you begin, you will need two Bar Jumps and two High Jumps.

1. Begin by setting either the two High Jumps or the two Bar Jumps approximately two feet apart, side by side. By using the same jumps, the only variable you introduce is the directional hand signal. Place a baby gate between the two jumps.

2. Position the dog in the middle of the two jumps, about eight feet back from them. Position yourself eight feet away from the jumps.

3. Learn how to give a clear signal. The signal begins as you turn your palm to face the dog while your arm still hangs at your side. (An experienced dog already knows which jump to take!) Now *slowly* and *smoothly* raise your arm, fingers together and palm facing the dog, up and slightly forward until it points to a jump. Your verbal command for the dog to jump should be given toward the end of your hand signal, when the dog is sure which way to go. Flashed signals and rushed commands only lead to mistakes. In the ring you will not be permitted to lean into a signal or turn your head to indicate which jump, but when teaching the exercise, you may begin by using some body language if necessary.

4. To begin teaching the exercise, leave your dog and walk to the other side of the jumps. Stand behind the gate. Turn to face the dog and give a slow, smooth signal to one jump. You may hold a toy in the hand giving the signal. If he sits there, leave your hand signal up as you walk over and touch the jump with the hand holding the toy. Squeaking a toy might encourage him to get up, as well. This should stimulate him to jump as you used the touch to first teach him to go over these jumps. If not, you may encourage

201

him as you touch by saying his name. Alternate jumps and sides. Sometimes use High Jumps, sometimes Bars Jumps. If at any time the dog takes the wrong jump, say nothing and leave your hand signal up. When the dog lands and sees your arm still up, he will know something is wrong. In the teaching stage, this is enough of a correction. Start over and see if he doesn't pay closer attention.

5. Gradually spread the distance between the jumps and remove that gate. As you widen the picture, move the jumps apart as you back the dog and yourself away from center.

6. When the dog is secure at full distance, use one of each jump.

7. You will notice that while teaching, no verbal command to jump is being given. This forces the dog to follow the hand signal, which is what we are trying to teach. If the dog is reluctant to move, it is probably because he is not sure which way to jump (even though it is obvious to you). If you give a verbal command at this point in training, the dog will probably feel he has to do something and he will guess. He will be correct 50 percent of the time because there are only two jumps. However, he will not understand why he is right and this will confuse him. While this approach takes longer to get the dog to respond, when he does commit to a jump, it is usually because he is sure of what he is being asked to jump. Once the dog responds confidently to the hand signal only, you can then add the verbal command of "hup" or "bar" for added clarity in the ring, though it is not really necessary. Directed Jumping is a concept that is easily learned by some breeds of dogs. Most of the sporting dogs grasp the concept easily. I have found that for other breeds, it is a rather abstract concept and that by removing the verbal command to teach it, the dogs are forced to concentrate on the directional signal.

Begin by setting two of the same kind of jumps a few feet apart. To avoid having the dog come between the jumps, block the opening with a gate.

PROOFING THE EXERCISE

In the ring the jumps will be 18 to 20 feet apart. A new Utility dog often doesn't know how to locate the jumps. You can proof against this problem by practicing with jumps 25 to 30 feet apart.

Have someone throw a ball or some other distraction in front of your dog before he jumps.

Have someone tap a jump and then you send the dog over a different jump. This teaches the dog to focus his attention on you and avoid extraneous movements.

Try leaning one way and sending the dog over the other jump. Is he really responding to the signal?

Work to different backgrounds and in different locations.

Stand with your back to your dog and give a hand signal! (Make sure your palm still faces the dog.) This will determine if the dog really understands the concept of a signaled jump or if he is getting extra cues from your face.

Give signals only to direct the dog.

If you are really brave, try sending the dog on verbal commands only. (Since each jump has a different command, this is possible!)

The dog should see the palm of your hand through the middle of the correct jump.

44

Teaching the Broad Jump

The Broad Jump exercise is taught in a step-by-step process. It is absolutely imperative that each step be performed successfully before the next step is attempted. Every dog learns at a different rate. Do not compare your dog's progress; let him learn at his own rate.

The key to the Broad Jump exercise is to get the dog to jump straight over the jump. We accomplish this with the use of guides.

1. Set up the Bar Jump, with the bar at a low height; add two boards from the Broad Jump, placing one directly in front of the bar and the other directly behind it. (One board under the bar is used for extremely small dogs.) Walk briskly with the dog over the boards on leash. Do not snap up on the leash at any time as this will throw the dog off balance. Introduce the dog to the

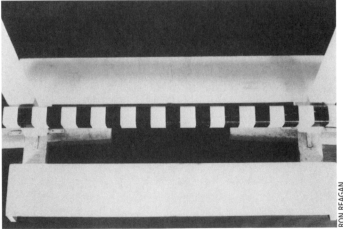

Set up the Bar Jump at a low height and add two boards from the Broad Jump, one directly in front of the bar and the other directly behind.

RON REAGAN

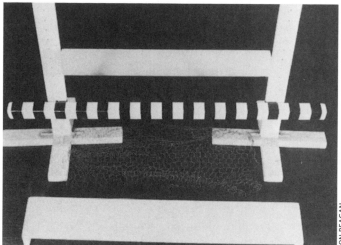

If the dog steps between the boards and the Bar Jump, put chicken wire on the floor.

command "over" by commanding, "Fido, over" *before* you start for the jump. The dog should be told what he is being asked to do before he begins moving. If the dog makes any attempt to walk the boards, set them up on end, put chicken wire over them, or raise them by setting them up on tuna cans! Now take the leash off and again walk with the dog over the jump.

2. Leave your dog on a Sit Stay and walk to the opposite side of the Broad Jump. With the Bar Jump, and possibly chicken wire, over the jump, point to the bar with your hand to show the dog what you want and then give the command "Fido, over." You are now having the dog move toward you over the jump until he is confident. Remember, the command is "Fido, over" not "come." If the dog heads around the jump, put up a barrier so that he can't, or snap him toward you on leash before he can start going around, or go back to step one.

3. Work until the dog will do a Recall on the command "over" (not "come") over the jump off leash without trying to go around or walk the jump. (The Bar Jump is still over the Broad Jump.)

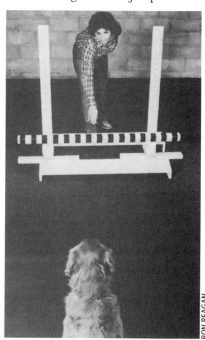

Point to the bar with your hand to show the dog that you want him to jump.

4. Gradually spread the two Broad Jump boards to full distance. (This may take days or weeks.) The Bar Jump is still over the center of the jump. If at any time the dog steps between the boards and the Bar Jump, put chicken wire on the floor.

DOG   YOU

If your dog is not bothered by stepping in chicken wire, you can try sticky-side-up contact paper or double-faced tape. For very large dogs, dig a ditch, fill it with ice and then mark it with two Broad Jump boards!

Once the dog is consistently and confidently jumping full distance (and without using chicken wire), remove the Bar Jump and proceed to step five. You may need to replace the chicken wire temporarily if the dog steps between the boards; you may even need to shorten the distance between the boards initially. Lay the Bar Jump on the ground before removing it

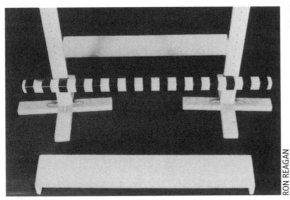

Gradually spread the two boards to full distance.

RON REAGAN

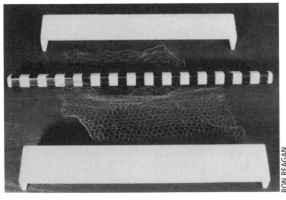

Remove the Bar Jump uprights gradually. Eventually the bar is resting on the floor. Chicken wire may be necessary at this point.

RON REAGAN

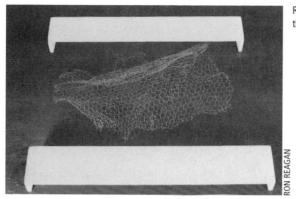

Remove the Bar Jump totally. Leave the wire if necessary.

RON REAGAN

totally. Remove the uprights of the Bar Jump gradually, as these help the dog to focus his attention to the other side of the jump.

The only time a leash helps with a Broad Jump problem is when the dog refuses to attempt the jump, but pulling a dog on a line will not cause him to jump. He can just as easily trot through it.

The first and last boards of the Broad Jump are the ones the dog must learn to focus on if he is to take off and land properly. To avoid confusion, we omit the middle boards until the dog has mastered the concept of jumping from the first to the last board.

BOHM MARRAZZO PHOTOGRAPHY

Guides can be used to teach the dog to jump straight across the Broad Jump.

5. Do a Recall over the jump but stand with your left shoulder facing the dog as you command "over." This gets the dog used to having you give him the command as you stand sideways, which is eventually what he will see. As the dog reaches you, make a 90-degree pivot to the right, away from the dog. This will start to teach the dog to turn and come in to you. Guide the dog around and into a straight Sit Front. (You do not move, only pivot.)

DOG   YOU

Pivot

6. Continue as before until you can do a Recall over the jump off leash with boards spread to full distance. Continue to pivot 90 degrees after the dog lands to teach him to turn.

7. Gradually work your way around to the side of the jump. In a ring situation, you will want to stand almost even with the last board of the Broad Jump (so that your body helps the dog judge the length of the jump) and according to the rule book, "with your toes about two feet from the jump. The handler shall change his position by executing a right-angle turn while the dog is in mid-air, but shall remain in the same spot." This turn is the same as a pivot, started on the right foot. By keeping your heels touching, you will be sure not to move out of position.

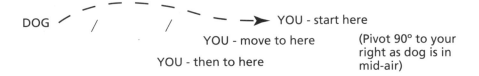

DOG   YOU - start here

           YOU - move to here   (Pivot 90° to your right as dog is in mid-air)

       YOU - then to here

8. When you are actually in line with the jump, put up a gate or some barrier to prevent the dog from turning too soon. You can also place a toy out in front of the broad jump to encourage the dog to travel straight after he jumps. Wean him off the toy by pointing to the floor where you would have placed the toy before sending the dog.

DOG

                   barrier   (Pivot 90° to your right as dog is in mid-air)

                   YOU

9. Now try standing in a normal position at the side of the jump. With the barrier in place, the dog should use up his momentum before he turns tightly to come in to you.

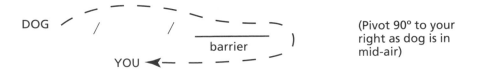

DOG

                   barrier   (Pivot 90° to your right as dog is in mid-air)

       YOU

As the dog turns the corner of the barrier, command "come," and encourage a brisk front. You may even run backward. If the dog attempts to come straight to you now that you are at the side, put up another barrier on his right before the jump and, if necessary, to the side of the jump.

DOG — — — — — — — — ⁄ ⁄ ⁄ — — — — — — ⟩

barrier   barrier   barrier

YOU ⟵ — — — —

10. Add the center board(s) if your dog is required to jump more than two. The dog should have no problems with this if he is jumping confidently the full distance, using only two boards.

11. Remove the barrier, but be ready to run in toward the dog if he starts to turn too quickly. Dogs who turn too quickly use up their momentum with a sweeping wide circle.

DOG ⁄ ⁄ ⁄ ⁄   DOG ⁄ ⁄ ⁄ ⁄

YOU ⟶   YOU   WRONG
Run into dog
if he turns too soon.

12. When the dog is doing a nice Broad Jump, from time to time still run toward the front of the jump. If the dog never knows when you're going to run, he will never cut the corner!

The handler extends her right foot as the dog jumps the broad jump. This prevents the dog from cutting the corner of the jump. Work with the gate (above) gradually prepares the dog not to cut the corner.

A dowel held in your right hand replaces the second set of guides, and the dog still lands straight over the middle of the Broad Jump.

BOHM MARRAZZO PHOTOGRAPHY

13. Another way to ensure the dog will not try to cut the corner of the jump and come to you is to lift your right foot or a dowel up and into the corner of the jump as the dog is in midair. You are now in a perfect position to turn your body to the right as the dog turns and comes in to you. Since the dog never knows when that foot will be in the corner of the jump, he will jump to avoid the corner. A dowel held in your right hand may be used in place of your foot.

14. Dogs often swing wide upon landing. There are several possible reasons for this. If the dog has too much momentum, he needs to be encouraged to travel farther in a straight line before making the turn. Some dogs take a sightseeing tour around the ring. If you are sure that your dog is distracted, set up another person with a throw chain. As the dog starts to swing wide and look around the room, the other person throws the chain at the dog as you command "come." Most dogs swing wide after they land because they don't land straight in the center of the last broad jump board. Their momentum carries them into an arc. Always watch to see exactly where your dog's front feet are landing off the broad jump. If necessary, go back to guides to get the dog to jump straight, or use a dowel.

A dog who understands the Broad Jump exercise will jump on command from the first board to the last board, with no boards in the middle and the handler at the side of the jump.

PROOFING

Do the Broad Jump in many different places.

Face the dog *away* from the jump and command him "over."

Start the dog from a down position.

Have someone else try to distract the dog as he is waiting for the command to jump.

Put toys on or between the boards of the broad jump. (If a dog looks *at* the jump, he will not jump over it!)

45

Teaching Utility Hand Signals

Before you attempt to teach a dog to change positions at a distance with hand signals, you must know that the dog understands how to move his body from a stand to a down to a sit position in place. We begin by teaching the dog to respond first to verbal commands.

Stand your dog and command "wait" as you walk away 6 to 10 feet. Turn to face your dog and command "down" with only your voice. If the dog drops on command, praise. If the dog does not go into a down position, walk toward the dog slowly and when you get to him, push him gently into the down position. Praise and then release the dog. Repeat the exercise (standing closer to the dog if necessary) until the dog will lie down on the verbal command "down" from a distance of 50 feet.

When your dog will drop on a verbal command, begin teaching the dog to sit from a down. Starting with the dog in a drop, stand about six feet away and command "sit." Make sure that your "sit" command sounds distinctly different from your "down" command. Use a high pitch for "sit" and a low tone for "down." If the dog sits up from the down, praise and walk toward him. If your dog acts like he's never heard the word "sit" before, slowly walk in to the dog, without making eye contact. If the dog is still in the down position as you get to him, gently nudge his front feet with your toes as you walk through him. When he finally sits, praise, release and begin again. Work on teaching sit and down separately before you ask the dog to do one and then the other.

It is important that the dog changes position without moving forward toward you. If your dog tries to walk forward before he lies down, place a board or wire in front of him. Try doing the signals at the top of a flight of stairs so that if he walked forward, he would start to come down the stairs. Correct any movement down the stairs by putting the dog back on the top landing and try again.

The stay signal is given with your left hand, palm facing the dog, in front of his eyes.

The stay signal.

To teach the stay signal, simply use it with the verbal command and then enforce the stay.

The heel signal is given with the left hand in a scooping forward motion that should pass both of the dog's eyes. (He has two, so use both!)

To teach the heel signal, hold the dog on a snug leash. Give the hand signal as you say "heel" and *then* step forward on your left leg. After one or two times, give the heel signal only, say nothing and then step forward on your left foot. Praise! A common mistake made in the Utility ring is that the handler gives the hand signal to heel at the *same time* that he steps off with his left foot. This often causes a lag. Just as you should give a verbal "heel" *before* you move, the dog should receive a hand signal to heel *before* you move.

The come signal is taught when learning the Recall. It is modified slightly in Utility as you bring your right arm out to your side away from your body before you bring it in and snap the leash for a correction (if the dog didn't respond).

The come signal. Notice that the handler's palm is facing the dog before it hits the leash and ends up pointing to the front position.

Completing the Recall signal. Notice that the hand ends up at the midpoint of the handler's body, reinforcing the "front" concept.

Whenever possible, we keep signals away from our body, where they are more visible. Make sure your hand ends up pointing to front at the completion of your signal. This is "legal cheating" where you have an opportunity to point out front in the ring just before the dog does a Recall!

The drop or down signal is given with the right arm and is the same as for the Drop on Recall (see Chapter 35, Teaching the Drop on Recall). Handlers either use the entire windmill signal or shorten it to a smooth up-and-down motion with the right palm clearly facing the dog.

The sit signal is perhaps the most difficult to teach. We want the dog to sit by bringing his front feet up and back so as not to move himself out of position. The signal is given with the left hand, palm facing the dog.

The drop signal.

Completing the drop signal. Notice that the hand comes down onto the dog's shoulders so that at no time does the dog ever see the back of the hand.

Put the dog in a crouched down on leash directly in front of you. Command "sit" as you slide your left hand, palm facing the dog, past both of his eyes while pulling back on the leash with your right hand, which allows you to pull the dog up into a sit as you bring the *side* of your right shoe gently against his chest. Eventually, as the dog sees your left palm moving up and away from your body, he will pop up into a sit away from you as he avoids the sneaker against his chest. You can also teach the dog to pull up into a sit by holding food in your left hand and raising the hand over his head. He should already know how to get from a down to a sit because of the work you did to teach verbal signals.

For small dogs, teach this on a table. Your hand is usually enough to ensure that the dog moves his front feet back to his rear.

The stand signal is given with the right hand, palm facing the dog. You raise your right hand over the dog's eyes (encouraging him to look up) and stop his motion by first touching his muzzle with your hand. Initially you may use a verbal command. For small dogs, use the leash looped under the dog's stomach to stand him as the signal is given. You can also bait the dog into a stand (see Chapter 37, Stand for Examination).

The sit signal. The left hand, palm facing the dog, slides up the leash, past the dog's eyes and off to the left of the handler.

The handler's foot steps toward the dog, encouraging him to pull his front feet back into a sit. For the resistant dog, the side of the handler's foot taps the dog in the chest to encourage him to pull his front feet back into a sitting position.

The finish signal is done with either the right or left hand, depending on whether your dog has learned to finish to the right or left. To teach the finish signal, gather the leash under the hand giving the signal. (Your thumb can hold the lead as your hand remains flat.) At first give the verbal command as you move your hand and the leash. Eventually move just your hand and the leash, which will automatically help the dog (see Chapter 36, The Finish). If you taught the finish using food in your hand, the dog probably already knows the signal!

In general, signals should be clear, smooth, consistent and never flashed. Be conscious that your palm faces the dog whenever possible, which adds to the visibility of your signal from a distance. Sloppy signals are often cause for a dog's mistake. By using the left hand for heel, the right for stand, the left for stay, the right for down, the left for sit and the right for come, we are always alternating hands, which helps to keep the signals distinct.

I recommend wearing a plaid or print long-sleeve shirt with contrasting colors and some white to give your dog the best chance to see your arms move at a distance. This theory came about one day in New York as I watched two flags flapping in the wind. One flag was an American flag and the other one was all white except for a round insignia in the center. By watching the flags high above move in the wind, I realized that the contrasting colors of the American flag made its movement much clearer than that of the almost completely white flag. Since then I have always worn prints (usually plaids with some white) in the Utility ring and try to contrast with the background as much as possible. If you don't know what the background will be, bring two shirts!

Good handlers quickly master the act of giving clear, consistent signals away from their bodies with palms facing the dog. Practicing in front of a mirror helps. However, most mistakes made in the Utility signal exercise are the result of a lack of attention on the part of the dog. In practice, if your dog looks off, give him a

The stand signal. Notice that the right hand giving the signal is above the dog's head. This encourages the dog to look up and thus stand with his head high. The right hand and the right foot are moved at the same time.

Using the leash to teach the small dog the stand signal.

To teach the finish signal, gather the leash under the thumb of your right hand.

The finish signal from the dog's point of view.

clear signal, followed by the signal's correction if he misses it. You will never develop dog attention if you are willing to wait for the dog to look back or by saying "watch me," thus doing his work for him. Signals are taught on leash, in close, and the goal after the dog learns the various signals is to try to distract the dog so that he learns what happens if he looks off. Good distractions include: food, toys, people waving hands and someone petting the dog or standing over the dog. When the dog ignores all distractions, you may start to increase your distance. If the dog misses the signal and is corrected for not changing position, when he looks off, it becomes to his advantage to watch you and you never have to tell him to!

Handlers often make the mistake of giving a verbal command simultaneously with a hand signal. This actually works to confuse the dog since he may be listening and not even notice that a hand has moved. If you want a dog to respond to a hand signal, then be quiet and let the dog notice the signal!

Dogs new to Utility training often fail the Signal Exercise. This is usually because of tension in the ring. The Signal Exercise is the first thing the dog must do in Utility A, and he is 30 to 40 feet away from you! I have seen and owned many dogs who understood signals and who were looking straight at me in the ring but who did nothing when a clear signal was given. To help your dog over the anxiety of signals, it is important to attend many practice match shows (see Chapter 49, Using Match Shows to Your Advantage) and do signals under stressful conditions (for example, crowds of people, shopping centers and noisy places). When the dog fails to respond because of stress, help the dog. Help can take the form of a verbal command or going in and gently repositioning the dog. With some dogs, the only way to break their frozen state is to have someone else, preferably someone the dog knows well, walk in, say nothing and gently position the dog as you praise from a distance.

Be sure to practice doing signals in all different orders to avoid patterning the exercise. Dogs learn the signals quickly; the attention training takes a little longer.

46

Go Out

Of all the exercises in AKC obedience, the Go Out is perhaps the most frustrating to teach and difficult to perfect. The reason for this is that the Go-Out exercise makes no sense. There is no intelligent animal that I know of who will at any time, other than in a Utility ring, charge in a straight line toward a brick wall or similar barrier. It would be as if you were in the driver's seat of a car and someone pointed you toward a stone wall and said, "Floor it!" All of your instincts would tell you to veer one way or the other in anticipation of a turn so as not to hit the wall head on. In other words, you would not be inclined to do a straight Go Out either!

It is relatively easy to get a dog to run in a straight line toward open space. The field trainers do it all the time. While it has been said that the Go Out is similar to a Blind Retrieve exercise in the field, I do not find much similarity at all. There is never anything in a ring for a dog to retrieve on a Go Out, and Blind Retrieves in the field are not done toward barriers.

Aside from the fact that the Go-Out exercise makes no sense, its difficulty is increased, as the sight picture of Go Out in a ring is always changing. When you teach a dog to jump a High Jump, you are assured of what the jump will look like in every ring. When you teach a Go Out, you must train for all different kinds of barriers (string, baby gates, walls, solid barriers, other fence-type structures and so on), which makes the process take longer and frequently adds to the dog's confusion.

From what I am told, years ago in the sport of obedience, the Go Out was merely an exercise where the dog left his handler and went to the other side of the ring, approximately to the center. In fact, *approximate center* is still the wording used in the AKC regulations. No points were lost for a dog who was three feet off center. As training has improved and as our top working dogs have gotten so good that at times they are difficult to fault, the only way the judges can split the really top dogs is to pick apart Go Outs. Now, if your dog isn't exactly in the middle of the ring, you can expect to lose points. What began as a reasonable exercise that made little sense is now a ridiculous exercise that makes *no* sense!

There are two things we can count on being consistent in the Utility ring. There will be a High Jump and a Bar Jump about 18 feet apart from each other and positioned halfway down the longest side of the ring, and there will be a gate, wall, string, or some kind of barrier letting the dog and handler know where the ring ends. In an effort to make some sense, the Go Out then becomes an exercise where the dog is taught to split the ring in half by going straight between the two jumps.

Go Out is divided into three separate teaching steps. It is important that when you are working on one step you do not worry that the dog is not doing another step.

The first concept to teach is that on the command "go out" or "go way" the dog is to leave your side. The easiest and most mechanical way to teach a dog to leave your side is to pull him away from you with the use of a pulley. The pulley gets the dog to leave your side in a matter of moments and avoids confusion of any kind. An alternative to using the pulley is to encourage the dog to go to a toy or food. I prefer using the pulley to using bribery because when a dog is going to food or a toy he is thinking about the food or toy and is not thinking about what he is doing. If you send a dog to a target, then when the target is missing in the ring the dog is likely to search for it or become confused. It is important that if you use a pulley, you do not become concerned with the dog going straight since it is normal for a dog to avoid a line and arc away from it. With all breeds of dogs and all temperaments, I have never had to use a pulley for more than two sessions (5 to 15 minutes each time) to teach a dog to leave my side. One pulley at your training location serves all dogs.

The pulley may be set up so that it pulls the dog to a solid wall, or it may be nothing more than a person pulling a line through a gate. In either case, the person pulling the rope must be experienced enough to know when to pull, when to stop pulling, how to pull and what kind of collar to pull with. Sometimes steady pressure on a buckle collar is all that is needed, and sometimes jerks on a prong collar are what it takes initially to get a dog to leave your side.

SETTING UP THE GO-OUT PICTURE

Set up two Board Jump boards on end (wide enough for the dog to sit in) against the barrier in the center of the ring. Attach two 50-foot long lines to the gate and stretch them straight to make a path about 3 feet wide.

TEACHING THE CUE

It has been my experience that many dogs who know how to do a Go Out in training will appear totally confused in a ring when commanded to "go out." There are different explanations for this behavior. It is certainly possible that the dog has only been successful at performing the Go Out in a few familiar places. Now anytime he encounters a new site picture, he's not confident where to run. This is why it is imperative that a dog be exposed to many different rings, with many different barriers, when teaching the Go Out.

Sometimes a dog has been trained to do Go Outs in many different locations, but when he's in a ring and the handler sets up for the Go Out, the dog may not realize it's the Go-Out exercise and may be expecting to heel or do a Stand for Examination. To prevent this kind of confusion, we teach the dog a cue that he is about to do that thing where you run across the ring.

When you move into position to set up for the Go Out, your left arm is at your waist in a "heel" or "let's go" position. As you stop moving, the dog sits and should be looking up attentively. To transfer the dog's attention from you to the Go Out, lower your left hand and arm to your side as you give a verbal cue command. Some popular cue commands are: "look," "focus" and "gate." It is important that as you drop your hand and cue the dog verbally, *you* also look at Go Out. (If you look at the dog, the dog will be encouraged to look back at you and then no one will look at Go Out!)

When teaching the cue command in the beginning, wait for the dog to look straight ahead before sending him. For a dog who is determined to keep his attention on you, have the person pulling the dog out on the pulley gently tap the baby gate until the dog looks to see where the noise is coming from.

BEGINNING THE USE OF THE PULLEY

You have set up your Go-Out picture with a gate, two Broad Jump boards, two 50-foot ropes, an assistant and a dog on a long line attached to a buckle collar.

Sit the dog in heel position between the ropes facing Go Out, about six feet from the gate. The dog should be on the long line, which the assistant is ready to pull through the gate. Cue your dog. Wait for the dog to look straight ahead. Send the dog with your "go out" command. Stand still as the assistant gently pulls the dog to Go Out standing between the Broad Jump boards. Praise the dog when he gets to the barrier and walk out to offer him food from the other side of the gate. Praise and release the dog and then guide him as he turns around in the boards and walks back through the ropes. Gradually lengthen the distance you stand away from the gate until the dog is moving at least 15 feet to get to Go Out.

It usually takes two 15-minute sessions with the dog being pulled out before the dog learns to leave your side on the Go Out command.

The dog is paying attention to his handler in the Go-Out position.

BOHM MARRAZZO PHOTOGRAPHY

The handler has dropped his left arm to cue the dog to look ahead.

Starting close to the Broad Jump boards, the dog hears the command "go out."

Your assistant pulls the dog toward the gate.

When the dog reaches the gate, the handler stands outside the Broad Jump boards and feeds the dog from the far side of the gate.

BOHM MARRAZZO PHOTOGRAPHY

TRANSFER TO OFF-LEASH

When the dog will leave your side on the "go out" command and go 15 feet to the gate and stand between the Broad Jump boards, waiting for you to come out and reward him, it's time to remove the line.

When you first try a Go Out off the pulley, shorten the distance between the dog and the gate to about four feet. If you used an assistant to pull the dog out, have the assistant remain standing on the far side of the gate for your first few attempts.

- Make sure you cue your dog before giving the "go out" command.
- Make sure you look at Go Out and not at the dog.

If the dog moves out away from you, let him go as far as he is willing to go before moving. If the dog goes all the way to the gate, walk out and reward with food on the far side of the gate. If the dog stops before getting to the gate, walk past the dog and offer food from the far side of the gate, as if to say, "This is where I will deliver the food, but you can stop anywhere you want to." The dog will eventually learn to go to the gate and wait for the food to be delivered. If the dog does not move away from you on the command to go out, take hold of the dog's buckle collar with your left hand and push the dog ahead of you, through the ropes, to the gate and then reward with food from your right hand on the far side of the gate.

TEACH "GO TILL I TELL YOU TO STOP"

The second concept is to teach the dog to go until you tell him to stop. This is accomplished with the use of a barrier. Begin with scissor gates and ring stanchions if the dog shows in your area ordinarily use scissor gates as ring barriers. It stands to reason that if most of your shows use stakes and ropes, then that is what you would start with. Eventually you will want to accustom your dog to all kinds of barriers. Along with the scissor gates and stanchions, use two Broad Jump boards that will work to give the dog a place to go to and will get a tight Turn and Sit at the end of the Go Out. When we begin teaching the Go Out, the dog is expected to stand facing the gate. The Turn and Sit is taught later. While it is important to teach the dog to go all the way to a barrier, he must also learn to stop when you command him to sit, and not because he has reached a barrier.

TEACH THE TURN AND SIT

We avoid teaching the Turn and Sit at the end of the Go Out until the dog is confident and willing to stand facing the barrier at the end of the ring. This helps to counteract the dog's natural tendency to anticipate the Turn and Sit. When a dog anticipates the Turn and Sit, it might show up as a short Go Out, or it might cause the dog to arc off the straight line of the Go Out as he prepares to turn.

To teach the Turn and Sit, send the dog on a Go Out and slowly follow him out. He should get to the end of the ring and stand facing the barrier, waiting for a reward. Allow the dog to stand for a moment, and then call his name as you keep walking toward him. The dog should turn to look at you when you call his name. If he doesn't, reach out your hand with food, and lure his head around toward you. As soon as the dog turns toward you, command "sit." By walking toward the dog as you execute the Turn and Sit, you discourage the dog from walking back to you.

As the dog understands that it's okay to turn toward you and sit, (most dogs prefer it to standing facing a barrier), you can start walking up on the dog slower and slower and increase the distance between you and the dog as he sits.

Sometimes walk up and feed the dog for a sit. Sometimes walk up to a dog who has sat and offer the reward from the far side of the gate as you did initially. By alternating where the dog is rewarded, you avoid anticipated Turn and Sits. If the dog's response to "sit" is strong, reward him from the gate. If the response to "go out" is stronger than the sit, reward the dog in the sitting position.

A dog cannot understand the difference between two feet from the gate or four feet from the gate, but he does understand the difference between touching the gate versus not touching it. In the future, any time the dog stops short, he will be corrected by being taken to the gate and will be made to touch it. In training, however, if the dog gets close enough to have touched the gate, we will accept it as close enough.

TEACH GO STRAIGHT

The final step is to teach the dog to run in a straight line. This is more difficult for some dogs than others. There are dogs who, because of structural faults, are not capable of walking in a straight line. Dogs who naturally "crab" must learn to compensate if they are to end up doing straight Go Outs.

A dog will never understand an abstract concept like straight. So far I have been unable to teach a dog to line up two points in order to walk a straight line. A straight line is accomplished by providing the dog with a chute. The chute might be two pieces of white clothesline (which will eventually become a darker color rope) if you work outdoors, or a series of white fold-up rulers (easily transportable) if you work indoors or two 50-foot long lines.

The ropes work as a guide to teach the dog to run straight. If the dog does not honor the ropes and tries to cross them, hold the ropes about six inches up off the floor. If you are outside, you can stake the rope off the ground by tying it to a tomato stake.

In early training, you always put out the ropes. When the dog is willing to do Go Outs in many different places with the ropes out, it's time to progress.

You can use raised ropes to keep the dog going in a straight line.

Use the ropes in a new place for the first Go Out. Then, remove the ropes for the second Go Out. Regardless of the outcome, put the ropes back in the picture for the third Go Out. Keep alternating between ropes and no ropes in new places.

When the dog is successful at imagining where the ropes would be if they were there, move to the final step.

Now go to a new place and do the first Go Out without ropes. Regardless of the outcome, put the ropes in for the second Go Out.

For the entire career of the dog, the ropes should be used intermittently to maintain straight Go Outs. Think of the ropes as you would a leash for heeling. Just because the dog knows how to heel off leash doesn't mean that you don't continue to train heeling using the leash.

This method of teaching Go Out in no way makes use of any retrieve exercises, and a hand signal is not used. Therefore, the confusion often seen between gloves and Go Outs is minimal. A dog seen going to a ring corner is not necessarily confused and looking for a glove. The dog goes back to the glove corner because he has lost his Go-Out target and doesn't know where else *to go*. I refer to this as a "lost Go Out" as opposed to a case of "glove–Go Out confusion."

It is important in the Utility ring that you, as the handler, stop the dog on the Go Out. The judge must not feel that the barrier stopped the dog. Since the dog ideally goes only 20 feet past the "jumps," he would end up 5 feet from the end of a 50-foot ring. While initially we make a point of teaching the dog to go all the way to the end of the ring, we must then teach the dog to stop on our command.

To teach your dog to stop and sit when you tell him to, you must intentionally teach the dog to stop short. (This actually works as a proof against having a dog stop short on his own.)

Send the dog on a Go Out and follow him. Before he passes the jumps, call his name and command "sit." If the dog responds, praise and release him. If the dog ignores you, abort the exercise with a "let's go" command and try again.

If you are having trouble getting the dog to stop short, try holding a squeaky toy and after you command "sit," squeak the toy to get the dog's attention. If you still can't get the dog to stop (and some are persistent), put a long line on the dog and let him drag it. When you command "sit," step on the line.

Once you get your dog to stop short on the Go Out, do another Go Out and send him all the way to the barrier. If the dog stops short in anticipation of your "sit" command, he is confused and you must say nothing and take him by the collar to Go Out. By repeatedly stopping the dog short and then sending him all the way out, you teach the dog to listen and respond to your commands and not to anticipate.

In the final stages, the dog will leave your side, go immediately through a set of ropes and continue in a straight line until you command him to turn and sit. Many things affect Go Outs. If you are working outdoors, be sure you know what straight is before you drive the dog crazy! When you are working indoors, take advantage of the connecting lines made when two rubber mats are placed next to each other. If you place the ropes on the edges of the mats, many dogs will learn to look for the edge of the mat and use it as a guide to walk in a straight line.

It is certainly fun to do Go Outs to wide-open space, and the dogs learn to like it and really pick up speed, but I find that it has little carry-over to a barrier ring situation.

The Go-Out exercise needs constant work since it is always changing. If you know ahead of time what barrier the dog will be sent to in the ring, practice to that kind of barrier the week before in training.

If a dog stops short, take him by a buckle collar (on his two hind legs if necessary) and make him touch his nose to the barrier.

Some dogs tend to walk back toward you before they sit. To prevent the "walk back," do not call your dog to you after the Go Out in early training. This problem can be eliminated if you will quietly walk behind the dog as he goes out. When he turns to face you and starts to walk back, you will be there to enforce the sit. If the dog is too fast for you to get there in time to stop him, throw a rolled-up leash between you and him after you command, "Fido, sit."

IDEAS FOR PROOFING THE GO OUT

It is important that your dog remains focused on the Go Out and not become distracted. This is accomplished by proofing. At any time that the dog loses the concentration and misses the Go Out, he is taken by the collar with only his hind legs touching the ground and made to touch the gate. He is then praised.

> Have people and dogs standing and/or moving behind your barrier.
>
> Have someone throw a ball or Frisbee in front of the dog as he does the Go Out. If he loses his concentration, correct him.
>
> You throw a ball into a corner of the ring, then command, "Go out." If the dog heads for the ball, he is wrong.
>
> Put white pieces of paper that might resemble gloves in the ring corners, and then send your dog. If he heads for the corners, he is wrong.
>
> Have someone try to distract your dog with noise, food or by petting him just before you send him. If he falls for any distraction, correct him!

A correction for Go Out is pushing the dog out ahead of you with a buckle collar. If you need to increase the level of correction, lift the dog off his front legs as you push him out.

47
Secrets of Showing

As a team, you and your dog will strive to give a sharp, neat, accurate performance and appearance in the ring. The appropriate dress can help you accomplish this.

SUGGESTIONS FOR WOMEN

Pants suits or slacks with tops and sometimes even vests make good show wear. Make sure pants legs are not too flared as this might interfere with heel position. Skirts and dresses are also acceptable, but if you haven't worked your dog in a skirt, don't start it at a show.

It is to your advantage to try to match the color of your clothes as closely as possible to the color of your dog. For example, it is very difficult to detect a crooked sit by a black dog sitting next to a black pants leg. Most dancing teams dress alike, so why not a dog-and-handler team? You may even choose to go as far as to dress incorporating your dog's breed or original purpose, for example, wearing feathered earrings with field dogs, rhinestones with Pomeranians or Poodles, sheepskin vests with Border Collies, or red suspenders with Dalmations! Your creative efforts may or may not be appreciated by the judge, but your overall performance will appear costumed to perfection.

Avoid wearing strange perfume, noisy jewelry or long belts where the ends swing freely, as these might distract the dog. Never wear sunglasses in a ring. This frightens some dogs and besides, you need eye contact!

When showing outside, wear warm undergarments and plan to take your heavy coat off before going into the ring. The coat causes interference and covers heel position and front. If your hair is long and tends to fall in your face, tie it back. You don't want to be accused of a second command by unconsciously brushing hair out of your eyes.

SUGGESTIONS FOR MEN

Comfortable sports clothes chosen to match the color of the dog are ideal for the obedience ring. Whenever possible, try to incorporate the purpose or original theme of your dog's breed into your outfit to enhance your overall picture of teamwork. Slacks should permit freedom of movement without appearing baggy or ill fitting. At no time should a sport jacket or suit jacket be worn in the obedience ring. While a neat, formal look is appreciated by some judges, a sport jacket does not benefit the dog. For one thing, you probably don't wear a jacket every time you work with the dog. Your dog has learned to judge front and heel position based on the contour of your body in the clothing you generally wear to train. Now is not the time to cover up the front with a sport jacket! Should you feel that you would like a more formal appearance, a tie can be worn with or without a sleeveless sweater. Even bow ties have made a comeback in the obedience ring.

If you have trained your dog to focus "front" on a belt buckle, be sure the buckle is visible to the dog in the ring. Avoid pockets full of change and keys that might jingle as you do a fast. Both men and women should remember to wear comfortable shoes (the same color as the dog) regardless of costume choice. Make a point to practice heeling the dog in the shoes you plan to wear in the ring. Your footwork is always easier to control when the shoes you wear offer good side support.

DON'T FORGET THE DOG

Your dog should be clean, brushed and groomed in keeping with his breed. You should be as proud of his appearance as his performance. Be sure there are no tags, ribbons or other attachments on your dog's collar before you take him in the ring, as this is prohibited by the rules.

If you are showing a dog who gets clipped, like a Poodle or Cocker Spaniel, keep in mind that the kind of clip you give the dog can affect how straight he looks sitting next to you. It is very difficult for some Poodles to be viewed as straight unless all three pom-poms line up! Kennel clips are usually the best choice for obedience.

Cut, tie or braid hair that might fall in the dog's face so he can see heel position and front position!

Remember, a good appearance doesn't make up for poor training, but a sloppy appearance can hurt the score of a well-trained dog.

WHEN TO ARRIVE AT A SHOW

After you have entered a sanctioned obedience trail, you will receive in the mail a judging schedule and a number for your dog. Bring your schedule and entry pass to the show. You will know from the schedule how many dogs are in the class and how many dogs are supposed to show before yours. The schedule may also tell you if the class will break for lunch, when this break will be, and if the break is mandatory or up to the judge. Keep this in mind when figuring when you will most likely show. It is reasonable to estimate four minutes per dog in Novice, six minutes per dog in Open and eight minutes per dog in Utility. Of course, this will also depend on how many dogs show up and how fast the judge works! When figuring time of showing, include time for group exercises.

Try to get to the show at least an hour to an hour and a half before you might be in the ring. If there is bad weather on the day of the show, keep in mind that more dogs will be absent and be there earlier. The judge is not required to judge you if you are not there when he gets to your number.

WHAT TO DO WHEN YOU ARRIVE AT THE SHOW

Leave your dog in the car (if it's not too hot) and take your blanket or crate, a water dish and water, chair and any other equipment you have with you and investigate the show setup. Locate your ring and check in with the steward. He or she will give you an armband that corresponds to your catalog number. You may also ask at this time if the judge plans to take a break and if so, when. Make sure to notice what number dog is in the ring and which dogs before you have picked up armbands, which indicates they are present. Locate a space to sit and watch your ring, but preferably *not* directly outside the ring. You do not want the dog looking for his blanket or other members of the family when he is in the ring.

Once settled, go get your dog. If you plan to show within the hour, exercise the dog. Then bring him into the show under control and let him get used to the surroundings. Do not let him sniff other dogs or people. You may walk with him, practice and warm up but do not train him on the grounds as this is not permitted at a sanctioned show or match. Locate a place away from the show grounds where you can legally give a correction or two before you show. This should not be done in public on the show grounds. The area considered show grounds should be mapped out in the premium list or catalog, or you can ask the show chairman what area is considered "show grounds."

It is important for you to watch what is happening in your ring. Familiarize yourself with the heeling pattern, from what end of the ring the judge is doing the Recalls, where the Figure 8 is to be done and so on. The same is true for Open and Utility exercises. Before you enter the ring, you should know where each exercise begins so you can get there without having to be told by the judge. Pay attention to difficult parts of the heeling pattern, but do not try to memorize the pattern as this might cause you to anticipate a command and lose points. A general idea that the judge is doing an L-shaped or a T-shaped pattern should be sufficient.

THINGS TO BE AWARE OF WHILE IN THE NOVICE RING

While you are not permitted to talk to the dog during an exercise other than the initial command, you may talk and praise him between the exercises. When ending an exercise the judge will always say, "Exercise finished." Before you begin an exercise, the judge should ask, "Are you ready?" This will let you know when it is safe to talk to the dog, praise him, keep him "up" and demand attention.

In Novice, be sure to go no farther than six feet away from your dog on the Stand for Examination exercise. Six feet is two big steps. You must be in heel position before you leave the dog. When returning to the dog on the Stand exercise, be careful to return to the heel position, your hip even with the dog's head to shoulder. Failure to do this results in a point loss. When you stand your dog for the judge to examine, it is not wise to face him toward the entrance of the ring. No need to tempt him to leave! Be sure your dog is standing comfortably and squarely before you leave him and that your hands are not on the dog when you actually command "stay."

On the Heel-on-Leash exercise, make sure your leash is loose. A loose leash should have the clasp at the end of the leash hanging down. Should you totally lose your dog on the Heel-off-Leash exercise, you may repeat the "heel" command. You will be penalized for a second command, but you will not forfeit the entire exercise if the dog recovers.

On all exercises where the dog is heeling off leash, the *AKC Obedience Regulations* state that "the handler's arms and hands shall move naturally at the handler's sides while in motion, and shall hang naturally at the handler's sides while not in motion; or the right hand and arm must move naturally, while the left hand shall be held against, and centered in the front of the body, in the area of the waist. The left forearm shall be carried, as much as possible, against the body." For many dogs, a swinging left arm would interfere with the dog's point of view of the handler's heel position. Even small dogs can get confused watching a hand swing back and forth as they try to concentrate on watching one spot on your left leg. Judges don't always agree on what a "natural" swing is. Handlers have lost points for not swinging their arms fast enough, high enough or in a constant rhythm. Under these circumstances I recommend heeling off leash with all dogs with your left hand positioned against and centered in front of your body. While this often looks as if you have a stomachache, at least the judge doesn't have to think too hard about whether your arm is swinging naturally!

Make sure that your hands are hanging naturally by your sides when you call your dog on the Recall exercise and that you do *not* move your head, as this is considered a second command. The same is true for bending at the waist or for bending your knees. The dog must respond on voice or hand signal alone to the command "come." All extraneous body movements may be considered an aid to the dog and be penalized accordingly.

In Novice you may gently guide the dog by placing your hand through the collar between exercises. Hopefully, if you are talking to the dog and if he is paying attention, this will not be necessary.

Be alert and at ringside for your group exercises. It is not the responsibility of the judge or stewards to find you. When you position your dog for the group stays, make sure he is not sitting on a crack in the mats or on an anthill, if outdoors. Place your leash far enough behind your dog so that if he wags his tail, he won't hit the leash and scare himself. After you give the "stay" command, place your arms behind your back and leave them there until the judge says, "Exercise finished." Your dog is less likely to confuse the stay with the Recall if your arms are positioned differently for each.

THINGS TO BE AWARE OF WHILE IN THE OPEN RING

Before you enter an Open or Utility ring, check to see that the jump heights are correct.

No guiding of the dog is permitted in the Open and Utility rings, so keep your hands off the dog except for praise.

Be careful not to add any extra body language (bending, bobbing your head and so on) to your Recall and signal for the Drop on Recall. If you are using a verbal command to drop your dog, keep the tone sweet and the volume reasonable. Excessively loud commands may be penalized. If you are using a signal for the drop, be careful that it is a continuous motion. "Held signals" are penalized.

As a handler, it is your job to learn how to throw a dumbbell so that your dog has the advantage of retrieving in a straight line. If you practice and concentrate on where you want the dumbbell to land, you can perfect the art of dumbbell tossing.

For the High Jump, position yourself so that you are standing where the dog is likely to return over the jump. This will help your front. Be sure to give your dog plenty of room to jump. While the rulebook states a minimum of eight feet, you may stand back as far as the ring permits.

When positioning yourself at the Broad Jump, the rulebook states that you are to be two feet from the jump. Two feet is longer than you think. Learn to estimate two feet accurately.

THINGS TO BE AWARE OF WHILE IN THE UTILITY RING

Be sure you know where each exercise begins so that you can move quickly around the ring and give your dog the advantage of seeing the steward put the articles out and a chance to see the Go-Out picture.

Be careful to pivot so that the dog is facing the correct glove. Underpivoting or overpivoting is considered an aid to the dog and is judged accordingly.

Once you give the scented article to the judge, the exercise has begun and you may not talk to the dog, except to give the "find it" and "heel" commands.

If you plan to reuse your articles in the near future, mention to the stewards that you would like the scented articles kept separate from the others. Most stewards are happy to do this if they are aware that you prefer it.

WHAT TO DO AS YOUR CLASS IS ENDING

As you notice the last group of Stays being performed, wake your dog up, exercise him and get ready for a possible runoff. There is nothing more upsetting than to be caught off guard for a runoff. Since you are not the judge, if you qualify, prepare for a possible runoff.

WHAT TO DO AFTER YOUR CLASS HAS ENDED

Shortly after a class is completed, the breakdown of the individual scores of each dog is posted by the superintendent's desk. It is often helpful to find out which exercises cost you the most points. Track down those posted scores so you will know what to work on. If you are displeased with your dog's performance, do not take it out on the dog. He only knows what you taught him or didn't teach him. View every show as a learning experience. There is always tomorrow. If you find that your dog does perfectly at home and blows it at a show, you probably need to work him in more varied places and proof harder. Keep in mind that every dog, even the best, will occasionally "blow it." To err is canine!

UNDERSTANDING SPORTSMANSHIP

This is the way competition works:

If there is a winner, there must be a loser. It is easier to be a winner than to accept defeat graciously.

Your dog should work for *you,* and *you* should be his strictest critic. Sometimes you will be very pleased with your dog's performance and your score will not reflect your opinion. Sometimes you will be unhappy with your dog's performance and you will end up a winner. Actually, it is quite rare that both you and the judge will agree on the dog's caliber of work! You cannot train your dog to please every judge, only to please yourself. When you choose to show under a judge, you are asking for that judge's opinion. Accept the score with the understanding that it is only one person's opinion. If you do not like a particular judge's opinion of your dog, you do not have to show under him again.

To argue with a judge gets you nowhere! It is always viewed in poor taste and accomplishes nothing positive. If you have a legitimate complaint, put it in writing and mail it to: Director of Obedience, American Kennel Club, 51 Madison Avenue, New York, NY 10010.

When you lose, congratulate the winner. If for some reason you cannot bring yourself to congratulate the winner, smile and *say nothing!*

When you win, *accept* congratulations from others. *Do not* say things like, "Well, he really didn't work that well," or "I know that some of his 'sits' were crooked and the judge didn't see them." This is not good sportsmanship and only degrades the judge who thought enough of your dog to select it as the winner. A simple "thank you" is sufficient.

When you feel that you have received a higher score than you deserved, accept it and consider it as a *credit.* When you feel that you have received a lower score than you deserved, accept it and consider it as a *debit.* Understand that, in time, the debits and credits balance out and that obedience as a sport really is quite fair.

Appreciate and applaud a good-working dog and/or handler. Then go home and work hard to beat them! If the other guy is a good sport, he will applaud your performance some day.

48

The Bible

In keeping with the analogy that dog training is like a religion, trainers are forever referring to AKC's rule book, their Bible. Like the Bible, the rule book is, on the surface, simply written but open to varied interpretations. I have been involved with obedience for years, and I still refer to the rule book on occasion in the hopes of finding a new explanation for a judge's ruling.

If you are going to play the game, you should know the rules! A copy of the *AKC Obedience Trial Regulations* and a copy of *Guidelines for Obedience Judging* are available free upon request from the AKC by writing AKC Operations Center, 5580 Centerview Drive, Raleigh, NC 27606 or on the AKC web site at www.akc.org. Unfortunately, after you get done reading both of these booklets, fine points will still elude you. In my classes I "spoon feed" the rules to my students, appraising them of the loopholes and technicalities. What follows is some of the same.

This is not intended to be a recap of the rule book, but there are some things you may not absorb by simply reading the rule book.

While the rule book states that "judges are not permitted to inject their own variations into the exercises," it also gives the judge flexibility by saying, "The judge must carry a mental picture of the theoretically perfect performance in each exercise and score each dog and handler against this visualized standard . . ." It has happened that a dog loses points for no error other than that the dog's performance did not reach the expectations of the judge's mental picture.

No matter how the AKC tries to standardize judging, under the current rules it will always be subject to the judge's opinion. Remember, when you enter a class, you are asking for one person's opinion. If you don't like their opinion, you need not ask for it again.

You are eligible for Novice A only if you have never put a CD title on a dog and have never owned or co-owned a dog who has a CD title and if you are not a judge. I advise my students to avoid husband-and-wife co-ownerships because if a dog is co-owned and the wife puts a CD on it, her husband will have to show the first dog he actually trains in Novice B. However, anyone eligible to show in Novice A may, by choice, enter Novice B as in the case where you prefer one judge to another or already have a leg under the Novice A judge.

If you have earned an OTCH (Obedience Trial Championship) on a dog, you are ineligible to compete in Open A or Utility A.

When you finally decide to show your dog, it is to your advantage to plan the shows carefully. While you only need three legs (qualifying scores under different judges) to earn a CD title, you may show the dog in Novice until you have earned a leg in Open. It is advantageous to show your dog more than three times to help both of you gain ring experience, improve your scores, and maybe even win some prizes. If, on the other hand, your dog is trained through Open and is ready to show, you may enter at the Open level as soon as the third judge has confirmed your third CD leg. The same is true when moving from Open to Utility. The third qualifying score must be received before the closing date of the trial in which the entry in the next level class is made.

The AKC says that praise may be given between exercises and following exercises. While this appears clear, there is another rule that says that any form of training in the ring shall be penalized. Be careful *how* you praise your dog and learn which judges are super sensitive about training in the ring. I was once told that tapping my hip between exercises, to bring the dog to heel position, was "training in the ring." That was one judge's opinion and interpretation of the rules.

On the Stand for Examination exercise, the rules state that the handler may "pose the dog as in the show ring." A student of mine once received a zero for this exercise as she lifted her Miniature Schnauzer up off the ground and placed him into a standing position. Of course, the rules also state, "there shall be a substantial penalty for any dog that is picked up or carried at any time in the obedience ring." Does the second statement include posing the dog for a stand? Most judges don't think so; one did. Either way, the score of zero was incorrect.

While the dog's name may precede any verbal command, an extended pause between the name and command is considered by some judges to be a double command and is penalized.

When calling your dog in Novice, any movement other than your lips (head bob, hands, knees and so on) is considered an aid to the dog and will be penalized under good judging. In fact, in all the classes, any extraneous movement that could be considered an aid to the dog is penalized. For example, stopping on about turns to wait for the dog (even if done unconsciously) or giving two drop signals (one as you raise your arm and another as you lower it) might be penalized. The rules clearly state that "when a signal is permitted and given, it must be a single gesture with one arm and hand only, and the arm must immediately be returned to a natural position."

A dog is ineligible to compete if he "has been changed in appearance by artificial means (except for such changes as are customarily approved for its breed)." This includes dogs who have had accidents and have needed their tails removed or significantly shortened, as well as corrective eye surgery or hip surgery. Spaying and neutering are not included, and a spayed or neutered animal is allowed to compete in obedience trials.

If you enter a show under a particular judge and later learn that the judge has been changed, you are eligible to receive a cash refund, even if entries have closed, if you plan not to show.

On the Long Down exercise, the rule book states that handlers shall "down their dogs to a position facing the opposite side of the ring." The rules do not specify *how* the dog is to lie down, only that he is facing the opposite side of the ring. There was once a judge who interpreted this to mean that any dog not in a crouched down should be penalized. He was soon persuaded to change his opinion about this exercise's requirements.

In the Retrieve-Over-High-Jump exercise, the rules state, "[T]he handler must stand at least eight feet, or any reasonable distance beyond eight feet, from the jump but must remain in the same spot throughout the exercise, and he must throw the dumbbell at least eight feet beyond the jump." Open A handlers have a tendency to want to move their feet *after* they throw the dumbbell. Be careful to *stand still*.

If you throw the dumbbell less than eight feet past the jump or out of the ring or any place else that the judge decides is unacceptable, the judge should return the dumbbell to you and you get a rethrow. While there is nothing in the rules that would indicate a handler should lose points for a rethrow, there are judges who will deduct points, feeling that the handler committed a "handler error" or that the rethrow is in some way an aid to the dog. Here again is a case where interpretation of the written word varies.

Be sure to remove any tags from your dog's collar before showing him.

Judgments and interpretations of the rules seem to run in stages. To keep up with the judging trends, I recommend you subscribe to *Front & Finish, The Dog Trainers News,* P.O. Box 333, Galesburg, IL 61402.

Know the rules of the game and, just in case, keep your "Bible" with you at all times.

49

Using Match Shows to Your Advantage

One of the most valuable training tools available to a show-oriented person is the match show. All too often match shows are misunderstood or not used to the trainer's advantage.

There are many different kinds of match shows. It is important that the trainer understands each type of match and is familiar with what is and is not permitted.

Match shows fall into two basic categories: sanctioned matches and nonsanctioned matches (also referred to as "fun matches" or "show-and-go").

The purpose of a sanctioned match is to give the club putting on the match the experience needed for running an obedience trial. The rules for the sanctioned match are not written to benefit the exhibitor. There are two kinds of sanctioned matches, listed as A and B. (An O preceding the A or B refers to obedience.) The match regulations that the AKC publishes state that "There shall be no drilling or intensive or abusive training of dogs on the grounds of an OA or OB sanctioned match."

The rules for an OB match are a little more lenient than an OA match, which is run just like a trial. "At Plan OB sanctioned matches, while dogs in the ring may receive verbal corrections, such corrections shall be penalized." In addition, "the judge of a Plan OB sanctioned match may, at his own discretion, permit a handler and dog to repeat an exercise; however, only the first performance shall be scored."

In general, sanctioned matches are of little value for the obedience trainer. If you are not in a position to correct your dog, you might as well be showing him at a trial! As far as repeating exercises goes, if your dog made a mistake and, for example, went around the High Jump on the way back with the dumbbell, why would you want to repeat it? If the dog made the mistake the first time, without a correction or some change made (possibly a simplification), why should he do it right the second time?

Sanctioned matches provide an environment in which handlers get an opportunity to practice their mistakes! I cannot in all honesty recommend to anyone that they show their dog at a match where they are unable to correct. Let the clubs practice giving shows with someone else's dogs! Obedience seminars and workshops would be just as good as fundraisers and would do a lot more to help the training of our dogs.

On the other hand, nonsanctioned matches (fun matches or show and gos) are very valuable training experiences. Since these matches are not governed by the AKC, corrections and their restrictions are decided by the group giving the match. I have been to fun matches that permit prong collars, leashes in Open and Utility, food and all kinds of reasonable corrections in the ring. Under these conditions, the performances of the dogs and handlers can be improved. Problems can be encountered and solved! No prizes are awarded, but the conditions are similar to accredited trials, and the dogs learn to obey in ring situations.

If you live in an area where fun matches are not popular, you can work to change this. It only takes a small group of people to get together on a weekend and set up a ring and play show. Little by little as people realize the value of a fun match, there will be enough people in your area to support a larger match.

Under AKC rules, clubs that are sanctioned to give trials are not permitted to hold nonsanctioned matches. However, the AKC does not restrict these clubs from holding training workshops!

I do not believe there is such a thing as a "ring-wise dog," that is to say, the dog who only makes mistakes when he is in the ring. A dog cannot tell which side of the ring gate he is on, but he can tell if you are nervous or not, and whether he is being compelled to perform.

There is no mistake that cannot be created; you just have to work at it. I had a student whose dog, she said, only laid down on the Long Sit in a ring. "Really?" I exclaimed questioningly and asked her to sit the dog and leave it. When she had left, I walked over to the dog, pointed to the floor and commanded "down." The dog dropped immediately. "But that's not fair!" you argue. Sure it is! Is your dog supposed to down because someone in the next ring says "down" and gives a hand signal that your dog sees? It is important that you learn how to cause mistakes because it is only when they occur that you can fix them!

If you walk into a match ring and correct the dog for every little mistake he makes, you have essentially told the dog that this situation is different from a trial. If you have a problem and are using a match to correct the problem, do not correct all the other smaller mistakes the dog might make. Save your correction for the real problem! Most nonsanctioned matches advertise "reasonable corrections permitted." What is considered reasonable? Usually, any correction given without anger, followed by praise to the dog, is acceptable.

Match shows provide an excellent setting in which to train your dog. In fact, some of my best training has been done outside the rings at matches! Training in the midst of show distractions means that when you get results, they will still be there when you cross the gate into the ring.

When training a new dog through titles, match shows help you evaluate your dog's progress and determine when the dog is ready to show. Since match show judges need no special credentials, you are often better off evaluating your own dog or having an instructor evaluate you and your dog than getting a false sense of security from inflated match show scores. Many people who judge matches give out high scores trying to encourage beginners to go on to show. I generally tell my students to subtract five points from their match-show score if they want a more realistic idea of their dog's working ability.

When using a match as a training experience, ask to show FEO (for exhibition only). If the judge understands that you are only for exhibition and are in no way competing, he is more likely to allow you to correct since he doesn't have to worry about how to score you. Showing FEO should also allow you to enter one dog in many levels, for example, Novice, Open and Utility.

While every beginner looks forward to their first ribbon, let it be a blue one from a trial and not a pink one from a match! (Yes, match ribbons are issued in different colors, so you are never going to fool anybody!) Take advantage of your fun matches to have fun improving your dog's performance. Practice makes perfect, *as long as you practice the right way!*

50

The Week Before the Show

The week before you show your dog, take special care to make sure your dog's ears are free from dirt or infection, his anal sacs are not full, his hair is not in his eyes and he is free of external and internal parasites. Any one of these things could cause problems in the ring.

With assured health, now turn your attention toward your dog's attitude. For very hyper, energetic dogs, make sure the dog gets plenty of exercise the week and day of the show. Sometimes with the hyper dogs, we kid about taking them to the show tied to the bumper of the car! Some dogs need to have lots of exercise before they can settle down enough to perform in a ring. I know of one exhibitor who gets to a show four hours early to give his dog time to unwind!

On the other hand, if your dog has limited energy, you will want to keep the dog confined to a crate and resting a good part of the week before the show. For some dogs, no training at all the day before a show is the best way to go. If your dog tires easily, get him to sleep early the night before—no late night TV!

It is my policy to never change anything the week before a show. If you're not happy with your dog's response to a verbal down command, now is not the time to switch to a hand signal.

Be careful not to overtrain or overcorrect your dog just because you have a show coming up. If anything, train in shorter, happy sessions, working on problem areas and on polishing (that is, fronts and finishes). Have you heard people say, "He was doing great until I mailed the entry in"? It is not uncommon to see handlers become tense and panicky because they mailed in an entry, and this is bound to affect the dog. Remember, no one forces you to go to a show, even if you are entered. Since we have to enter weeks in advance, sometimes we miscalculate our dog's readiness, and the week before the show, we find that he is not. If you don't feel confident about taking your dog into the ring, then lose the entry money and stay home. Relax and go back to training. You are never penalized for not showing. Consider it a donation to a worthy cause. Many have made such donations.

Some dogs need food in their stomachs or they get ill. Others work better on a totally empty stomach. As a quick "pick up" or energy boost, try giving your lethargic dog honey water 15 minutes before you show. Experiment with feeding and its effect on your dog's performance at matches before you get to the trials. For fear of bloat, a dog should not eat a full meal and then jump sooner than four hours later.

Experiment with playing with your dog versus drilling your dog before you go into the ring. Each dog will require a different kind of warm-up to get ready for the ring. Match shows offer you a chance to try different kinds of warm-ups to see what works best to put your dog in a good thinking, attentive, alert frame of mind for the ring. You are not going to teach your dog anything new the day of the show, so don't try any crash courses! The best chance you have is to get your dog awake and relaxed so he can recall the information you have already taught him to the best of his ability. Remember: Your best is all you can do!

51
Obedience for Agility

Agility is one of the fastest-growing dog sports in the world. As more and more dogs and people navigate the courses of jumps, weavepoles and contacts, where does obedience play a part? Agility is a high-energy sport where dogs get very excited and are encouraged to run and jump as fast as they can. As with any sport, there are rules, and that's where obedience is important.

In the obedience ring, the dog is very controlled. In the agility ring, the dog is somewhat controlled, or as some like to say, "running on the edge of control."

The most important command for a dog about to do agility is the Recall. In obedience, "come" implies a sit in front of the handler. Since a sit in front of the handler would be useless in agility, we teach a variation of "come" referred to as "here." "Here" means come to my side (the side you are already closest to) and move in the direction I am running in. "Here" enables an agility handler to get his dog to move toward him in whatever direction the handler is running.

TO TEACH "HERE"

Hold a piece of food or a toy in both hands. Command "here" as you turn the palm of your hand toward the dog and move away from the dog, encouraging the dog to move toward you. If your dog is already on your left side, use your left hand. If your dog is already on your right side, use your right hand. Hold your hand close to your hip when commanding "here." Eventually, your hand's distance away from your hip will vary with how close you actually want the dog to come to you. Allow the dog to get to your palm and receive the reward of food or toy. Then turn toward your dog and reverse your direction, commanding "here" again as you encourage your dog to come to your other hand.

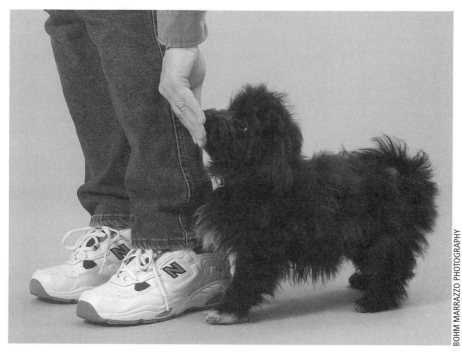

BOHM MARRAZZO PHOTOGRAPHY

Hold a piece of food, palm toward your dog, as you command "here."

A DIFFERENT STAY

In obedience, the command "stay" means remain in one position and location until I return to you or give you another command. In agility, "stay" means "on your mark, get set, go" when I tell you to! In agility, we want the dog's toenails digging into the ground, with the dog ready to leap out of position and over the first obstacle. Many trainers have chosen to distinguish between agility and obedience "stay" commands by using different words to explain when the dog should "stay" and relax and when the dog should "stay," but be ready to move at any moment. Usually, "stay" is used to mean remain in one position and one location until I return to you, and "wait" is used to mean remain in one position and one location until I release you to do the next thing.

To teach stay, see Chapter 29, Sit Stay.

To teach wait, put your dog on leash in a sit in heel position. Command "wait" and give a stay signal with your left hand, palm facing the dog. Walk out to the end of your leash and stand sideways to the dog. If the dog gets up, gently return him to the same position. If the dog remains in position, crouch down as if you are getting ready to run and release the dog with an "okay, get it" command as you throw a toy out in front of him. The dog soon learns that when you say "okay," he can get up and chase the toy. In anticipation of the release to the toy, the dog waits but is ready to suddenly spring up out of position to get the toy.

TEACHING DOWN FOR AGILITY

In both obedience and agility, it is important that the dog learns to assume a down position from a standing position and not from a sit. If you teach a dog to sit, and then teach him to down from the sitting position, he assumes that he must sit before he lies down. This slows down the dog's performance of going into a down position for either the pause table in agility or the drop signal in Utility, or for the Drop on Recall in Open.

Always begin teaching the down in agility from a stand (see Chapter 30, Down and Down Stay).

HEEL AND SIDE

Unlike obedience, in agility the dog learns to work off your right side as well as your left side. If you are thinking about doing agility with your dog, be sure to work stays, Recalls, jumps and even heeling off both your left and right sides. "Heel" always means come up to my left hip with your ear in line with the seam on my pants. In agility, we also use the command "side," which means come to my right hip with your ear even with the seam of my pants on my right leg. If you ask your dog to heel on your right side, use the command "side" in place of "heel."

TO TEACH HEEL TO SIDE

You can easily teach a dog to move from "heel" to "side" behind you. Put your dog in heel position at your left side. Hold a piece of food in your right hand behind your back. Show it to your dog as you command "side" and lead the dog behind your back into "side" position. Now reverse the procedure and guide the dog back to heel position with your left hand.

It is not necessary to teach your dog obedience before you introduce him to agility. The obedience needed for agility can easily be taught as the dog learns to complete the agility obstacles. Actually, the obedience part of agility makes a lot more sense to a dog when it is taught in the context of agility. Dogs seem to understand "here" as a Recall command because now I want you to run through a tunnel. The tunnel actually becomes the reward for having done the Recall. *Wait* until I tell you to jump makes more sense to a dog than *wait* until I choose to release you.

Since agility is a sport that must be played off leash, agility teaches off-leash control in early training. Many pet owners who once went to obedience classes for basic control over their dogs now seek out agility classes and find they have fun teaching their dogs agility and gain off-leash control quickly.

If a dog has had too much formal obedience training, he is likely to try to pace himself to his handler and be slower in his agility performance than if he had never had the initial obedience training. It's difficult to speed a dog up in agility once training has slowed him down. If a dog is slow in agility because of his fears or lack of knowledge, his speed should naturally increase with experience. If he is slow because the handler has encouraged him to stay next to her, it is very difficult to speed him back up!

1. The dog is in heel position at your left side.

2. Hold the food in your right hand, behind your back.

3. Command "side" and lure the dog.

4. Now the dog is sitting in the side position.

52

As You Train Your First Advanced Dog

If you continue on with training past beginners, certain situations are bound to occur:

- You will have good training sessions with your dog where you finish feeling satisfied and happy.
- You will have lousy training sessions with your dog where you finish feeling frustrated and irritated. (Try not to let the dog know it.)
- You will make numerous mistakes in your training.
- You will be corrected by your instructors—some days more than others.
- From time to time you will feel that "you know better" and you will not adhere to the recommendations of your instructors.
- You will find yourself unfairly comparing your dog to others in the class.
- Occasionally you will become angry with your instructors and your classmates.
- There will be days when you feel like giving up, but for some reason you don't. That's because deep down you know you and your dog can do it.
- There will be exercises you don't practice as much as others because *you* don't enjoy doing them.
- There will be days when you wonder if your life really has room for dog training.

I know. I have been a student much longer than I have been an instructor. I am still a student. Anyone who trains has felt all these things at one time or another. Some encouraging words:

- All you have to do is want a degree badly enough and you will achieve it. Your determination is a lot stronger than even the most difficult dog.

- No mistake you ever make while training your dog is irreversible. Dogs retrain very well.

- Your second and third dogs will be better than your first. Each dog will teach you to be a better trainer.

- With every conflict you face in training—whether it is with your dog, your instructor, your classmates or your spouse—you are learning. Of course, you may not realize it at the time.

- Necessity is the mother of invention, especially in dog training.

Dog training is a unique and wonderful sport. It spans all ages, all lifestyles, all economies and includes both sexes. It stimulates the mind as well as the body. It teaches compassion as well as sportsmanship. Dog training strengthens patience and understanding of yourself, your dog and others around you. Once you leave beginners, dog training takes on a new perspective. View the problems and stumbling blocks as growth. Accept the conflicts as learning experiences.

Nothing worth doing is easy. So train on. . . .

53

"As Told by the Dog" or "It's a Dog's Life?"

She told me to sit and stay, and I did. She walked away from me as she had done many times before. She had a long leash in her hand. I sat comfortably, proud of myself for understanding. All of a sudden it happened! My neck hurt and I was propelled across the room. Sometime while flying through the air, I heard her say "come." When I arrived at her feet, she told me I was a "good puppy"; mistreated would have been more appropriate! Still attached to the long leash, I had a horrible thought: She was taking me back to do it again.

***

I was lying relaxed at his feet; the instructor was talking, but I didn't understand the big words. All of a sudden it happened. He snapped me off the floor and took off toward the center of the room. Ouch! That hurt! Why didn't he just tell me to heel? I would have been more than happy to. I guess his sudden move meant that we were next in the class to perform the exercise. Was I supposed to know that?

***

We were working dumbbell. She threw the dumbbell and sent me. The command "take it" rang loud and clear. I trotted right out and found that there were two dumbbells, mine and another one. The other one was bigger, newer and was painted white on the ends. I picked up the bright, new, shiny dumbbell and brought it back to her. She was not happy.

She threw my dumbbell again. I waited anxiously for the command. "Take it," she exclaimed, and I headed straight out. Just then she started to say something to me. I turned to go back to find out what she wanted, and all of a sudden she pinched my ear! Next time I guess I just won't listen to what she says; it gets me into trouble.

***

He threw the dumbbell. I trotted out to get it, my tail waving high. I picked it up and spotted the High Jump. Wanting to please, I jumped the High Jump on my way back to him. All of a sudden there was a blood-curdling scream, "No!" That's funny, I thought; the last time I jumped the jump, he had really been pleased with me.

***

Her hand went up and I dropped to the ground. "Good," she commented. Then her other hand made some funny motion that I have never seen before. I stayed down, not knowing what else to do. She walked back to me with an angry scowl and snapped me up, insisting, "sit." Was I supposed to know that?

***

He commanded "come," and I briskly trotted toward him. When I got there, I sat, and he kicked me! "Straight," he kept repeating. Finally he gave up, and he set me up to do it again. He called me and I came, but not too close for I didn't know if his foot might be ready to kick. "No," he exclaimed. I guess he really didn't want me to come. He set me up a third time. This time he called me and I stayed put. He came at me with an angry look, and I was frightened. I headed in the other direction, and he got even louder. "Come over here," were the words he used, but I had never heard that as a command before, so I kept going. I think he will get over it. He gets like this every now and then. Maybe he just had a bad day?

***

Do we give enough thought to how our dogs perceive our corrections? I think not.
    You cannot correct a dog for something he doesn't understand. You must first teach him!

54

What May Have Caused This Problem?

Research indicates that no action by a dog is uncaused. When we relate this to training, it means that if your dog consistently gives you undesired behavior, it is likely a reaction to something you are doing. Sometimes, more important than correcting the behavior is to eliminate the cause of it.

Below is a list of common obedience problems that are more often than not "handler caused."

1. **Every time you halt, the dog leans on your left leg. What may have caused the problem?**

   Dogs develop the habit of leaning on a handler's leg when the handler praises the dog by petting the dog's head into his leg. To avoid this leaning problem, pet the dog on the chest for a good straight sit at heel. Lack of confidence on the part of the dog might also cause him to hug your leg for security.

2. **When the dog is excited, he continues to circle the handler before calming down enough to sit at heel. What may have caused this circling behavior?**

   Handlers sometimes get into a habit of heeling the dog in a circle (usually to the right if the handler is right-handed) to position the dog for an exercise. The circling problem can be avoided if the handler will vary circling to the right with circling to the left and eventually teach the dog to back up, move sideways, and make other minor adjustments into position.

3. **In beginners class, the dog is forging. By the time he gets to Novice, he is lagging. What may have caused the problem?**

   Lagging is often the result of giving praise at the wrong time and improper lead corrections. Too often handlers, in an attempt to encourage their dogs up into heel position, in effect praise them for lagging. Many problems are created when the handler snaps instead of tight-leading in an attempt to get the dog to move up into heel position. Snapping up clips the dogs with the snap of the leash under the chin, and he tends to lag even farther behind. The best rule is not to give a dog enough leash to lag in early training.

4. **A dog frequently sits at heel with his head next to his handler's left leg and his rear out away from the handler. What may have caused this crooked sit?**

    This is usually caused by petting the dog into your leg or by snapping the lead across your body instead of straight up over the dog's head to get him to sit. The snap across your body pulls the dog's head into your side, forcing his hind end out away from you. It is also caused by the handler making direct eye contact with the dog after every halt. The dog thinks he's supposed to look at the handler's face and the dog can do this more easily by turning toward the handler.

5. **A dog sits just out of reach after doing a Recall. What may have caused this?**

    This is usually a result of a handler who reached out for his dog when first teaching the Recall. Always let the dog *touch you first!* Keep your hands to yourself! With some dogs (often small ones), it is because the handler drops his eyes to look at the dog as the dog comes in to a front. The dog learns that it's easier to make eye contact with his handler by sitting farther away. Stop looking at the dog and he will come in closer!

6. **A dog consistently forges on sits. What may have caused it?**

    This is usually caused when a handler stops positioning the dog into perfect heel position in early training too soon or cues the dog by pulling up on the leash before every halt. The dog does not really understand where heel position is and is not catching the cue to stop. Some handlers stop too abruptly, making it impossible for the dog to anticipate a halt. A dog who is not paying attention will miss the cue to stop. In this case, don't worry about the sit; fix the attention. Cue the halt with your body, not the leash. By the way, backing the dog up once he has sat forged doesn't teach him anything. He must learn to sit in the correct position while going forward.

7. **A dog runs past his handler on Recall. What may have caused this?**

    The dog never made the decision to stop at the handler when the Recall was first taught on leash. The handler probably restrained the dog with the leash and did not allow him to run past and find out what happens. Go back on leash and allow the dog to run past. When he does, snap him again back toward you. Make sure the leash is loose after the snap. It must be the dog's decision to stop by you; to restrain him only teaches him that he is on leash.

8. **A dog does not change pace with the handler. What may have caused this?**

The dog probably does not understand the change of pace. This happens when the handler does not exaggerate the slow and the fast enough in training. Often the handler does not maintain the different paces for a long enough period of time. To teach the slow, go very slowly for a considerable distance. To teach the fast, jog with your dog! Maintain a steady rhythm at all paces. Remember that the dog must lower his head to go faster and raise his head to go slower.

9. **A dog does not respond on the first command to down. What may have caused this?**

The handler probably commanded the dog more than once instead of enforcing the first command. Now the dog waits to see which command will be enforced.

10. **A dog sits when the handler returns on the Stand for Examination. What may have caused this?**

This can be caused by sitting the dog directly after a stand. The dog anticipates the end of the exercise and sits. It is better to move the dog out of a stand after you praise for the stand. If the sit is submissive, it is usually because the handler has overcorrected the dog on the stand. If the handler attempted to correct the stand with the use of the leash, he may have pulled up, and the dog's interpretation of the upward motion by the leash is to sit.

11. **A dog is nervous and spooky on Long Sits and downs. What may have caused this?**

Some dogs, because of their breed or lines within the breed, are born with a tendency to be nervous and spooky. These dogs need lots of socialization when they are young to build their confidence in the world. More often than not, shaky sits and downs are a result of training where the handlers gained distance too quickly when first teaching the exercises. A better approach would have been to stay in close and proof the dog for steadiness around distractions. The handler who overlooks minor movement in stays is asking for trouble later on!

Some dogs suffer from separation anxiety. This can be helped with training and anti-anxiety medications. If you suspect that your dog can't deal with being away from you on sits and downs because he gets upset anytime you leave him, he may be suffering from separation anxiety. Talk to your veterinarian about medications that may help the problem.

55
The Relationship

For centuries man and dog have experienced a special relationship. Dog has worked for man and with man continuously. Whether it is sheepherding, hunting, tracking, protection, guiding the blind, assisting the impaired or merely performing circus tricks or obedience, the capabilities of dog as man's friend and employee appear endless.

Knowing how devoted, trusting and hardworking a dog can be, it seems tragically simplistic for people to think that the only way to get a dog to perform simple obedience tasks is to either bribe him with food or repeatedly force him with corrections. What has happened to the relationship with "man's best friend" in obedience training? Do dogs no longer wish to please?

I believe the problem stems from the trainers who do not take the time to build a relationship with their dogs before and throughout training. It takes less time and very little thought to correct a dog whenever he does not perform. Understanding a dog, reading a dog, and *teaching* a dog in a step-by-step process takes time and thought. Trainers need to be encouraged to give more time to *thinking* about how they train.

A sound working relationship is built on trust, honesty and mutual respect. The dog over time learns to totally trust his trainer. He knows that the trainer will not put him in an unsafe situation nor ask him to do something dangerous. For example, the dog trusts that if told to stay, it is safe to do so. If told to jump (for example, over a strange jump in a new location), the dog trusts that he will not encounter any "dragons" living on the other side. The dog trusts that if sent to retrieve, there is in fact something to be retrieved. The dog must know that the trainer will not arbitrarily correct him, nor correct him for what he has not yet learned. When a confused dog is corrected, he learns to fear instead of trust.

If you hand your dog over to someone else to work, or even worse, to correct, you destroy trust. Suppose your spouse or sibling handed you over to a stranger and said, "She won't listen to me. Here, see what you can do with her!"

Chapter 4, Honesty—The Best Policy, explains the importance of honesty in a training relationship. Telling a dog that he is correct when he is wrong confuses him. Correcting a dog automatically, before he has made a mistake, is dishonest and unfair. Threatening to correct, as in squeezing his ear just before you send him to retrieve, is equally unfair.

There are many dishonest training methods in use today. It is my belief that while such dishonest methods may temporarily solve a training problem, they often cause more serious problems later on since they destroy the training relationship.

Trainers talk a lot about how important it is for a dog to respect his master. This is true. It is equally important for the trainer to respect his dog!

Not long ago it came to my attention that I cannot earn an obedience title without the dog, and he cannot earn one without me. This makes us equally important. Viewing the dog as an equal partner sheds new light on the training picture. It suggests that the dog has rights.

While it may be my right to issue a command to the dog, it is the dog's right to say he doesn't understand, and it then becomes my obligation to listen to my partner. As a partner with rights, what the dog says is just as important to our relationship as what I say. Since dogs do not speak English, however, it is easy to tune them out. This would be very detrimental to the training relationship. If a friend of yours never listened to what you had to say, would you choose to continue to work with this person? Dogs talk with body language. The good trainer learns to read and speak "dog" fluently.

There are certain things that I don't do to my dog, and certain things my dog does not do to me. This understanding works as follows: For example, I do not command my dog to perform a Sit-Stay exercise in the bright sun when the temperature is over 90 degrees. In return, when I do command my dog to do a Sit-Stay, he does it.

It is your responsibility as a partner to protect your dog from unbearable and unsafe show conditions. If an obedience ring does not have adequate matting for safe jumping, you are better off pulling your entry than running the risk of injuring the dog and breaking the bond of trust you have worked so hard to build.

When you respect your dog, you believe in him. You give him credit for having the intelligence to perform obedience and exercises and you allow him the right to make the mistakes necessary for learning. The dog allows you to make mistakes in teaching, so why not afford him the same consideration?

Building the relationship I speak of requires putting your feelings of superiority and your ego on a shelf and working *with* the dog as a partner. If you are busy proving to the dog that you know how to do the exercise correctly and he doesn't, you are "barking up the wrong tree." Satisfying your need to feel superior by repeatedly telling the dog he is wrong does not encourage him to want to work with you. The essence of obedience is not who can force whom to do what, but rather how can we work together to learn obedience so that in the end we will develop into a smooth, stylish, happy team in the ring.

People train dogs for different reasons. Some dogs get trained because they are very talented and will probably bring home many awards. There are people who need to collect prizes. It makes them feel important. Some dogs are trained because there are people who need to control and dog training may provide the only sense of control they have in their lives. Some dogs are trained so that you can live with them! Perhaps the best reason to train dogs is that a trained dog can come closer to reaching his potential greatness. If you love your dog, then you need to educate him and communicate with him. A dog kindly trained achieves a higher level of awareness than a dog who is cared for but ignored.

This book is a combination of philosophy and technique. I suggest to you that the most expert training techniques available are of little value if there is no spirit of cooperation to begin with.

To build a special relationship with your dog, start with honesty, trust and respect. To this add patience, thought, and room for error. Do not hesitate to be demanding, but do so fairly and with kindness. When you have completed this recipe for love, add a touch of technique, and mail in your entry!

Diane Bauman and (left to right) Ch. Vandy's Q Leincha, UD; MACH Mysin's Alacazam, UD, TD; Am/Can OTCH Vandy's Faun, TD; and Vandy's Rikki, CD. Building that special relationship requires honesty, trust and respect.

Index

About the Author

Diane Bauman is an internationally known obedience instructor and has given obedience clinics all over the United States and Canada. Her articles have appeared in *Off-Lead* magazine and *Front and Finish: The Dog Trainers' News*. Her obedience demonstrations have been televised in New York and California. Diane is owner/trainer of the famous Golden Retriever OTCH Meadowpond Fem de Fortune, WC, winner of the Gaines Superdog title three times. The author's record includes 16 perfect 200 scores earned on four different dog breeds.